Dave Barr has had a penchant for trouble since day one: born in the back of a car; shooting by the time he was five; riding a motorbike at seven …

Dave regularly got into fights at school – and the only reading he would do growing up involved motorbikes, shooting, Westerns and the military. After reading *Battle Cry* by Leon Uris aged 12, he knew he wanted to be a Marine. Following a series of menial jobs – including working at a barbers and in service stations – at 17 he joined the Marines before shipping out to Vietnam. This was his dream come true – flying as a helicopter gunner – and he ended the war with an impressive 57 Air Medals.

After leaving the Marines, like many veterans Dave found it hard to hold down a good job and stay out of trouble. It was then that he read about Israel. Always looking for a rush, Dave learnt to skydive before deciding to take his chances – emigrating illegally to Israel. He was inducted into the Israeli Army and then the Paratroopers, where the training was difficult – involving long tough marches, as well as learning Hebrew. After serving his time, he left Israel – and back in the USA, Dave was stuck in a rut and ready for his next adventure ...

This is the first volume in the gripping and action-packed memoirs of Dave Barr – providing a rich and colorful account of one man's odyssey as a professional soldier: seeing war at the 'sharp end'.

I0892900

Dave Barr was born in Los Angeles California, April 12, 1952 and raised in West Covina California where he attended school; his high school was Edgewood High.

He entered the US Marine Corps on June 30, 1969; the Israeli Parachute Brigade from May 1975 to May 1977; the Rhodesian Army, Rhodesian Light Infantry, January 1980 to December 1980; and the South African Army, 44 Parachute Brigade, Pathfinder Company, from January 1981 to January 1983.

Dave now lives in Bodfish California, in the mountains and his hobbies include sky diving (from June 1973 to May 2011), pistol shooting and motorcycling.

He wrote *Riding The Edge*, the chronicles of a journey around the world on his 1972 Harley Davidson (self-published); *Riding The Ice*, his Guinness Record ride across Northern Europe, Russia, and Siberia in the winter of 1996–1997, on his 1996 Harley Davidson Sportster (self-published) and also made a documentary of his *Southern Cross Adventure*, another Guinness Record ride to the four extreme compass points of the Australian continent on a 2002 Harley Davidson Sportster.

Dave has two children, Luke and Jillian Barr.

FOUR FLAGS

THE ODYSSEY OF A PROFESSIONAL SOLDIER

Volume 1: US Marine Corps Vietnam 1969-72, Israeli Defense Force 1975-77

Dave Barr

Helion & Company

Helion & Company Limited
26 Willow Road
Solihull
West Midlands
B91 1UE
England
Tel. 0121 705 3393
Fax 0121 711 4075
Email: info@helion.co.uk
Website: www.helion.co.uk
Twitter: @helionbooks
Visit our blog http://blog.helion.co.uk/

Published by Helion & Company 2015
Designed and typeset by Farr out Publications, Wokingham, Berkshire
Cover designed by Euan Carter, Leicester (www.euancarter.com)
Printed by Lightning Source, Milton Keynes, Buckinghamshire

ISBN 978-1-909982-70-3

British Library Cataloguing-in-Publication Data.
A catalogue record for this book is available from the British Library.

For details of other military history titles published by Helion & Company Limited contact the above address, or visit our website: http://www.helion.co.uk

We always welcome receiving book proposals from prospective authors.

This book is dedicated to Colonel Breytenbach, but for whose bravery that fateful day on August 29, 1981 this story would not be told.

To Luke Coztze who was always there to listen.

To all the Marines and Israeli soldiers that I served with, thank you for the time we served together.

Lastly to my mother and father, Lucille and Preston Barr, for always understanding and standing by me.

Contents

List of photographs

Insert 1

Insert 2

Glossary

Bamahane	*In the Base Camp* (a Hebrew-language weekly newspaper published by the Israeli Defense Force)
Ben zona	son of a whore
Betzim	eggs (and slang for balls)
Ehad al ehad	one-on-one (fireman's carry)
En mesihin beshat aa'ruha	No talking at dinner while eating
Esh	shoot
Gashosh	Bedouin tracker
Goozenik	a tin can cut open and filled with dirt and diesel. Set alight, it could be used as a marker
Gosh	go now fast
Hamor	mule
Hayal cravie	operational soldier
Heder ochel	cafeteria
Hermoneat	hilltop command post
Hon	demolition group
Horrah	circle dance
Jabal	hill
Kaskeshan	someone that runs their mouth off all the time
Leahleaf	change positions
Maal	camp of tents where we lived in the deserts
Madoss	exercise
Magod	Battalion Commander
Mainikim	May intake of personnel (also *maynik, mau mau*)
Masa	force march (can be up to 80 km)
Masaw pacal	force march of 50 km with full ammunition and weapon load
mekapelet	a girl soldier that folds parachutes
Memcaf (plural: *Memcafim*)	squad leader
Mem-mem	Platoon LT
Mempay	Company Commander

Mesocco	of GOC
Metumtam	stupid
Mifcada	administration personnel
Mishav	privately-owned farms
Mizdar conenut	readiness inspection to go to war
Mutsav	fortified hilltop position
Ovlef	change
Paza-tztot	jumping to prone position from a run
Pikeyda plugatee	troop secretary
Pluga	Company
Pluga rabotim	Company of corporals
Princip	Principal
Rabat	Corporal
Rasap	Company 1st Sergeant
Ratz	run
Sade	open field fighting
Samal	Sergeant
Sararote	sin
Shefania	'rabbit house' (a little hole cut in the side of a trench)
Sirret Sheced	parachute demolitions
Targile seder	military parade
Tel Hara	'Hill of Shit'
Teronim	recruits
Treeg	a tall steep slope (in the case of Sanure the training base it was 700 meters)
Zion	slang for the dick

Acknowledgements

Thank you, to Colonel Joe Yannessa for the time and trouble to edit the Vietnam section so professionally, and for being a great Gunship pilot.

Thank you, to Jose Levich for all the very hard work to edit the Israel section – the sorting out of the names of places, and many other corrections was a big task.

1
Childhood

My name is David Scott Barr. I was born on April 12, 1952. My birth was not like that of most children, for my mother was carrying an illegitimate child. She was obviously a very brave woman, because in 1952 it was taboo to be pregnant and without a husband. I appreciate the fact that she did not get an abortion, because if she had I would not be here to tell the story of my life. I was put on the back seat of a car in a parking lot. That was the last time I ever had contact with my biological mother. To this very day I do not know who she is. I don't know who my real father is, either. There really was no way for me to find out, yet it never bothered me at all.

The owner of the car obviously came back and found a baby on the back seat, and probably thought that the stork had made a wrong delivery. He called the police and I was duly taken to Los Angeles General Hospital. I'm not sure how long I stayed there, but at some point I was farmed out to a foster home and remained there until I was nine months old. At that time I was adopted and taken to the home of my new parents, Guy and Lucille Barr. These two people provided me with a secure and loving environment. They were the epitome of their generation – kids who had grown up during the Depression era. I believe they, and others like them, were amongst the finest generation of Americans this country has ever known. They were people who gave their word and then stood by it. They could fix a car, build a house, run a company – all with little formal education to draw on. Everything they accomplished was through hard work and hands-on experience. My parents were all this and more, and as far as I'm concerned they were my true parents.

My father had gone into the navy in 1941, when he was 17 years old. He had not been able to choose to finish high school. He was at Kaneohe Bay, Hawaii where all the PBY seaplanes were based, when Pearl Harbor was bombed. He spent the whole of the war in the Pacific, only coming home once to do a course and then return immediately to the theater of operations, still in PBYs. It was during that instruction course that mom and dad met.

My mother Lucille came from Michigan, but during the Depression her family moved to Burbank, California. Grandma and Grandpa had a rabbit farm, so every day was a workday, slaughtering and skinning rabbits for market – not much of a childhood by today's standards. When the war came she was one of the multitudes of women who worked in the aircraft industry. She was a Rosie the Riveter.

I grew up in Southern California, and spent my early years in the Pico Rivera area. One of my earliest memories is of being at Sunday school on a rainy morning. I remember that I felt like leaving, so I just took off and ran home through the rain instead of waiting for my mom to pick me up. I was only about four years old and there I was, running through the streets all on my own. When I got home I was soaking wet, and understandably my mother was both shocked and furious to see me standing on the front step. Needless to say my dad immediately gave me a smack across my backside. Throughout my childhood I can remember receiving well-intentioned, but for the most part ineffective, whippings from my old man, and even more from my mother. I was one of those kids who was always in trouble for one thing or another. Looking back on it all now, I think I was just high-spirited. Dad just used to call me a "little fart".

From about the time I could walk, I remember I loved anything to do with cowboys – cowboy hats, cowboy guns and of course cowboy boots. I used to walk around looking like a miniature Tex Ritter most of the time. I guess all those movies my mom took me to on Saturdays kind of rubbed off on me!

One of the more traumatic memories of my younger years comes from my first real exposure to modern medicine. My folks decided that because the family doctor suggested that I have my tonsils taken out, they might as well just have me circumcised at the same time. Ouch! I can still remember the pain I felt – from both ends. My parents' reasoning was, "Well, if he's going to be in a little pain, what's a little bit more!"

I recall going to school for the very first time. It was just down the street from our house and my mom walked me there. She took me to the school gate, gave me a motherly hug and sent me on in. As she turned to leave I can remember feeling totally abandoned and very lonely. That lasted about two whole seconds until I saw the other kids and realized that I was in kindergarten now. That meant that I was pretty much all grown up, so I stuck my chin up and headed off into the crowd of screaming tots. Sometime during that year or the next, I remember being asked to stand in front of the class and share something about my family with the class. I told them all about my dad, who had been in the navy and who'd flown in big airplanes over the ocean. This was really big stuff to me, because my dad was a hero as far as I was concerned.

One of my more amusing recollections from that time involves coming home and proudly telling my mom what I'd learned in school that day. The teacher had taught us to spell the word "but," but one of my more advanced classmates had taught me an alternative spelling – "butt." Needless to say, my mother was less than impressed by her little boy's accomplishments in spelling.

I recall the big moment when I was given my first bicycle. Times were pretty tough and we were living in a twenty-foot trailer behind my aunt's house. Back then, my dad was working as a mechanic. He found a beat-up old bike somewhere and I remember him fixing it up and painting it so it was almost like new. I kept asking him who it was for and he kept saying that it was for someone else. When my fifth birthday finally came, there it was – my very own bicycle. I was so proud of that bike that I quickly learned how to ride it up and down the street. Because I was still so young, my parents set strict limits on how far I could ride on my own. Of course, like any other hyperactive kid I disregarded those same limits almost immediately. I can remember sneaking off and riding further and further away from my house. That was until my dad came looking for me one day, and finally tracked me over a mile away from home. According to my recollections of a rather sore backside, neither he nor my mom was very impressed with my roving ways.

I can still recall the intoxicating feeling of freedom, of being out in the world all on my own. Evidently my craving for travel and adventure kicked in pretty early, and it was something that was to stick with me throughout my life. Unlike the rest of the kids in the area I preferred to ride on my own. It wasn't that I didn't have friends; I did, but I just knew that I could go faster and cover more ground if someone else wasn't tagging along. Oddly enough, I have to admit that I still feel more or less the same way even today.

I've often wondered about the way my parents used to discipline me, and later on, my younger sister too. We were both frequently on the receiving end of what was known in our house as the "board of education". Quite literally it was a board of wood my Mom would use to remind us of the consequences of our various infractions. The number of times we were paddled would depend not only on the severity of the crime, but more importantly on our ability to squirm out of its stinging path. Don't get me wrong; our parents weren't really any harsher than those of our friends. That was just the normal method of parenting back then. Funnily enough, when I see my friends' and relatives' kids and how they behave, I can't help but think their homes might be better off if they had a "board of education" hanging off the backs of their kitchen doors. When I compare how we acted as kids and how the youngsters act today, I have to wonder if they aren't being shortchanged. We were always outside, running around playing all kinds of games and getting into all sorts of mischief. By today's standards, we probably would have seemed a little wild, but there's no doubt in my mind that we had more fun and had what you could call a "real" childhood. Kids today are either playing one organized sport after another, being chauffeured to their never-ending lessons or obsessing over the latest hi-tech computer game. When do they ever have time to be kids, to use their imagination, to get out there and – God forbid – even get into some good old-fashioned mischief? Maybe that's the whole idea behind it all. They don't.

Some of the best times of my childhood were spent with my mom's parents, Harry and Mary Carter. I loved them both dearly and spent quite a bit of time with them. My grandfather used to call me "Sewer Rat," or "Egg Plant." They had a rather primitive cabin up in the Yucca Valley area and every now and then I would get to go up there for a weekend. The very first time I went up there for a visit, it was love at first sight. The desert was the most amazing thing I'd ever seen. The barren terrain seemed to go on forever and was overwhelming at first, but I soon got over any fear and couldn't wait to get out there and explore my new surroundings. In no time I was out back of the cabin running all over the nearby hills. I soon became familiar with all of the wild creatures that called the desert their home; lizards, snakes and rabbits, and had the time of my young life chasing all them.

My Grandpa Carter had an old .22 single shot rifle and he let my dad use it to teach me how to shoot. I thought this was just the greatest thing ever. That old rifle made a loud noise and had a pretty good kick to it. It was the stuff that every little cowboy like myself dreamed of. From then on, I was always pestering one or the other to take me out shooting. More often than not, my unending requests to go "shoot the gun" would result in a clipped "Leave me alone!" and a smack across the head. Undaunted, I'd just do an about face and scoot off to the hills to terrify some poor unsuspecting creature. I was never the type of kid to go off and sulk if I didn't get my way. I'd simply get sidetracked by something else.

As a kid I never minded being on my own and when it came to the desert, my loner personality served me well. My parents quickly realized that they couldn't keep their rather hyperactive son and the Mojave apart and in all likelihood were probably thrilled to get me out of their hair for a while. I seemed to be impervious to the more common dangers of the desert and would take parental warnings to watch out for rattlesnakes as the official go-ahead to try and seek them out.

Getting back to life in the city, about that time my dad was holding down two jobs. He spent his days building a house in La Crescenta, which was to house his soon-to-be-expanding family. At night he would come home for a quick dinner with us and then rush off to his night job as a swing shift mechanic for California Truck Rental. Ultimately he did finish the house, but as he'd spared so little expense during its construction we could only afford to live in it for a short time and then it had to go on the market. Not long ago I happened to be in the area and drove by to have a look at the place. The old man obviously did one heck of a job, because it still looked great after more than forty years.

As I mentioned, the Barr family was growing and the new addition took the form of my new baby sister, Mary Ellen. Like myself she too was adopted, only at a younger age. I can still remember the three of us driving over to the hospital to get her in my dad's 1955 black Ford station wagon. On the ride back home my sister's hood came off and I couldn't believe my eyes. She was bald! I hollered something to that effect at my folks and then informed them that only old men like my grandpa were supposed to be bald. From my viewpoint there was obviously something wrong with her, and it wouldn't be a bad idea to take her back and get another one – this time one with hair. Needless to say, my parents weren't of the same opinion and we did keep her. Her bald head, however, did prove to be an ongoing source of amusement for me over the next few months.

Unlike myself, there was a record of Mary Ellen's biological parents. To this day, though, she has never expressed any interest in locating them. If that had been the case with me, I probably would have looked them up, at least my mother anyway. I would've liked to thank her for carrying me to full term and allowing me to be adopted into a good family. I have to hand it to my folks, though, they never had any qualms about telling us that we were adopted and even offered to help us find our other parents.

I remember living in the house that my dad built until about the time my sister started to crawl. Looking back on it now, I realize that as far as brothers went, Mary Ellen couldn't have done much worse. I used to torment her incessantly, much to her and my parents' dismay. To a certain extent I think the endless misery I subjected her to affected our relationship even into adulthood.

Our next move took us to West Covina, where my parents bought the house that they remained in for the next twenty-five years. When my parents finally decided to sell and move after my dad retired, the house was bought by my cousin and her husband, so it's still in the family, so to speak. It's really something to be able to drop by and see my old room and the big backyard where I played out my childhood. It was when we first moved there that I met a bunch of rough and tumble kids just like myself. Our group consisted of myself, the three Smith brothers; Randy, Greg and Mike, Blair Bushing and Cress and Jim Lorenzo. We were all pretty rambunctious back then and the numerous pranks we got up to cemented our friendship, which have lasted a lifetime despite the different twists and turns our lives have taken.

It was with Greg Smith that I probably got into the most trouble. I clearly remember the first time we decided to be tough guys and smoke. We were probably about eight years old at the time, and somehow Greg managed to get hold of a full pack of his dad's L&M cigarettes. I can remember naively saying, "Cool! Candy cigarettes," to which Greg replied, "Don't be a moron! They're real." We took off on our bicycles and pedaled over to a nearby wash. He pulled out some matches and we lit 'em up like the two tough hombres we thought we were. We'd brought some toy guns along and started to run all over the wash shooting it up, with the burning cigarettes clenched between our teeth the whole time. We pretended we were Al Capone and Elliot Ness and had a great old time, despite turning a sickly shade of green. Unlike most kids who smoked a cigarette, got sick and never did it again, we kept at it until we got it right.

I remember one of the more colorful scrapes that I got into, this time with Cress Lorenzo. There was a get-together going on at one of the neighbors'. Somehow seeing all those shiny cars parked in adjoining driveways and on the curb was just too tempting for us. The next thing we knew the two of us were hacking off the cars' seat belts, as back then it was common for them to hang out the door, if one did not make sure to put them back in the car. We then hung them in a tree growing in the middle of the front yard. Needless to say, we caught major shit that day, and were forced to apologize to everyone involved. I worked off the cost of the seat belts by mowing lawns. The fact was, we were made responsible.

Some of our favorite pastimes generally entailed making life difficult for the unsuspecting citizens of our neighborhood. We'd collect all the dog and cat turds we could find and then dump them in some poor unsuspecting fool's mailbox. We'd stick a couple of firecrackers into the pile as well. We'd light the fuses, slam the lid shut and take off running, falling all over ourselves with our hysterical laughter. One of us would sneak back and close the box. With the hot and humid summer days, it wouldn't take long for what was left in the box to ferment into something truly disgusting, so there would be a nice surprise waiting for whoever opened it up next. Using our brains obviously didn't come into play that often because we'd usually target one of the houses close to home – the result being the all too frequent phone calls from irate neighbors threatening some action or another.

We had a variation of this prank, and it involved nabbing some poor cat unlucky enough to have crossed our path. This time the unhappy recipient was the local mailman. It would take a combined effort to shove the terrified kitty into someone's mailbox. With the lid securely latched down it was only a matter of time until the cat was in a fever-pitched frenzy. When the unsuspecting mailman came sauntering down the street, finally reached the box and opened the door, the cat saw the light of day and exited with the force of a rocket and a roar just as loud.

My dad had built me a tree fort that was something else. It was actually higher up than the roof of our house, and thereby provided my cohorts and me with a dangerous amount of privacy. My dad had closed off the roof and walls of the fort with canvas, which made it all the more tempting for us to get up to no good. I used to climb up a rope to gain access to my private domain and would then haul the rope up after me, thereby ensuring total seclusion. I remember being up there with my buddy Greg one day after school. He'd brought a pack of his dad's L&M smokes with him, as it was his turn to steal them that week. We'd developed what we thought was a foolproof system for supplying our habit. One week I'd sneak a pack of Salem cigarettes from my mom, and the next week it was Greg's turn to get them from his old man. We figured that we were two pretty slick characters and never dreamed they'd catch on. Little did we know that our game was up as we sat up there that day, puffing away in contentment. Evidently mom's inner radar had picked up on some serious vibes, which likely translated into, "All right, where is the little turd?" The next thing we knew, my mother's face was staring right at us. Without giving it a second thought, we each dropped our smokes and dived out the back of the fort, only to land with a thud some twelve feet below. Greg was up on his feet in a flash and without even looking back he was over the neighbor's fence. I, on the other hand, was not so lucky. In a panic I started to scramble like some cornered rat, while my mother somehow managed to get back down the ladder she had brought and start after me. Before I knew it she had a death grip on the scruff of my neck and was hauling my ass in through the back door. I knew it was only moments before I was face to face with the "board of education". I could never figure out what was worse, the noise which sounded like artillery fire or the sting which felt like lightening striking. In the past I'd put my hands across my butt in attempts to protect it, but soon discovered that hurt even more. I remember wandering around in a miserable sulk for quite some time after that episode. Needless to say, no sympathy came my way.

Another one of our favorite activities with respect to tree houses was called "King of the Fort". A whole bunch of us would climb up into the Smith boys' fort and then we'd take turns trying to shove each other out. We all thought it was absolutely hilarious when one of us would tumble out. We'd just hoot and holler and look down at the one groaning and rolling around on the ground. When I look back on it now, I'm amazed that none of us so much as broke a bone. We must have been pretty tough kids.

I can still clearly recall Christmas that same year. I always looked forward to the holidays because my grandma and grandpa would always bring me my very own pumpkin pie. Now you have to understand the significance of this. As an eight-year-old if anyone had told me I could only have one food for the rest of my life without a doubt, I would have chosen pumpkin pie. Every year I got to pig out on the stuff and didn't have to share it with anyone, not even my sister. Well, that year I was in for an even bigger treat. A whole bunch of our family and friends had come over to celebrate. Us kids were busy working our way through what seemed to me, anyway, a mountain of gifts. The grown-ups meanwhile were growing more and more festive with each additional glass of Christmas cheer. I spied an unusual-looking package and could see that it had my name on it. I started getting excited even before I picked it up. It was long and flat and to me that meant only one thing. A gun! I could barely manage to rip the paper off, I was so wired. When I finally had it unwrapped I was absolutely thrilled. It was a 177-caliber pellet gun, with a box of pellets to go along with it. It was all shiny and new, and even more importantly, it was mine. That present basically ruined any enthusiasm I might have had for my remaining presents. I think I managed some rather perfunctory "thank yous" but that was about it. Inside I was just dying to get outside and start shooting up the neighborhood. As soon as my parents let me, I made my escape out into the backyard. With the warnings of "Be careful!" still ringing in my ears I joyfully embarked on a bird-killing spree, which in all honesty was to continue for the next few years. I guess my military tendencies started making themselves known pretty early on. Over the next few months, both my dad and grandpa instilled in me a good sense of weapon safety. My dad especially taught me about the right way to shoot the gun in and around our house. This consisted of things like: never shoot up into the trees, leave the neighbors' cats alone, don't shoot your sister – that sort of thing. I of course always reassured him that there was no need for worry, and in fact when it came to firearms my normal mischievous nature took a back seat.

It wasn't long before my buddy Cress was also given a pellet gun. From that point on, there was no doubt about it: the birds of the neighborhood didn't stand a chance. Oddly enough, the neighbors didn't seem to be in the least bit fazed when one or the other of us two snot-nosed little kids would clamber over their fences in search of our winged adversaries. Things certainly couldn't be more different now, as my sister pointed out to me in a recent conversation. Not long ago a friend of her twelve-year-old son had brought his unloaded pellet gun out on to his front yard to show it off to his buddies. A neighbor across the street saw the kid with a gun and immediately called the cops. It only took moments for LA's uniformed army to arrive and have the youngster surrounded and in handcuffs. As he was driven off to the police station his parents could only look on in disbelief.

Besides terrorizing the neighborhood birds, Cress and I had another use for our trusty pellet guns. Next to our house lived the Vias, a very nice and very large Mexican family. They had eleven kids. They would get one kite per child per season, flying their kites out in the street in front of their house. Cress and I would lay in wait in a little hole we'd dug out in the ground in an empty lot down the street. We'd wait until they had them well up into the air and then we'd take aim. Eventually we'd actually hit them and slowly but surely we'd put hole after hole into their flimsy little kites. At first the things would put up a valiant struggle, oscillating this way and that, but inevitably they'd start their slow descent down to the ground. We'd be nearly killing ourselves with laughing so hard while the poor Via kids would be staring down on the ground at their kites, now riddled with little holes. Despite all their hollering and carrying on, I don't think they ever figured out what happened.

One of the best places in the area to scope out birds was in the fruit trees in the yard of our neighbor, George Carns. He was a fascinating old character and I loved to spend time over there. He'd see me coming and would shout in his gruff voice, "Come on over here, Scotty. You can shoot all the birds you want." He'd sit on the porch and watch my attempts, and then when I'd tired of shooting he'd regale me with tales of his younger days as a government bounty hunter. His brother Fred, who lived with him, would tell me stories about George's incredible exploits with guns. They'd been orphaned early on and supported themselves as teenagers by trapping animals in the more remote parts of Kansas. I remember feeling real honored that these two old-timers would even give me the time of day – and even better yet, share all their stories with me.

About the time I turned nine, I developed an interest in money, and set about earning some in as many ways as possible. My first entrepreneurial efforts involved mowing lawns for several of our neighbors. George Carns was one of my first paying customers. He would let me use his big old King-O-Lawn mower and I headed over to George's every Saturday morning. I'd start the machine and let it warm up and then hit the drive button. I had to really watch it because that thing had a tendency to take off. Every now and then the drive button would get stuck and I wouldn't be able to get it to shut off. More than once the mower started tearing around the yard at full bore, dragging me behind it the whole while. I'd be running into things, and branches from the trees would be whipping my face. George would just sit there on his porch, his craggy weather-beaten face breaking into laughter. Every now and then he'd shout over at me: "Better be careful with that thing, young fella!" I've no doubt that it was a pretty amusing sight but the fact that he was about half tanked by then didn't hurt either.

By the time the job was finished I'd be all hot and sweaty, but good old George knew just the thing to remedy the situation. He'd slip me a quart bottle of Schlitz beer. I had a feeling my mom wouldn't approve of me drinking at such a tender age, but George didn't seem to think there was anything wrong with it. If I ever got called on it, I just figured I could use the excuse, "You always told me to respect my elders, didn't you?" George was definitely older and I certainly didn't think it was right for me to turn down his hospitality. One time my folks did catch me with beer on my breath, but I never told them where I got it. It didn't seem right to rat on my old buddy George. Years later when I was grown up, I recollect having a conversation with my parents. I don't remember how the topic came up, but they told me that they'd known all along about that extra little payment George used give me.

Despite all the childhood fun I was having in my spare time, the other areas of my life weren't so great. I couldn't stand school, and thought that most of my teachers were pretty lame. The fact that I was really hyper and had a problem concentrating on anything didn't help much with the scholastic efforts. Only recently did I come across an article on different learning disorders, ADD in particular. When I read about the typical characteristics that these kids have, I seemed to remember being almost identical in my behavior.

When it came to schoolwork, I had a real problem with reading. In fact, until I was eight I really couldn't read at all. That was when my mom decided I needed some help, and hired a tutor for me. The extra attention paid off, and I ended up catching on pretty quick. Within just a few months I was able to manage well enough that my folks bought me a whole set of Zane Gray's Western novels. From that point on, I was hooked. I quickly developed a love of reading and the whole world that it opened up for me. More often than not I'd hide out in my room and read some story while the rest of the family watched television. To me, there was nothing better than really getting into a story, and thinking about what an adventure life was like back in the old days. That love of reading has stayed with me right through my life, and even now I'll generally read for an hour every night.

Although my reading skills improved, my attitude towards school certainly did not. I still thought my teachers were more or less stupid. The fact that I refused to do any homework didn't make me too popular with them, either. I was giving them my time during the day and as far as I was concerned that was more than enough. When I look back on it, the only things that I did like about school were recess and spit wads. As for the latter, could there be anything more disgusting and delightful than to nail some unsuspecting classmate with one of those gooey little wads of paper? Some of our class spit-wad wars were so spectacular that I can still picture the floor strewn with them, and the face of the clock almost obliterated by our revolting ammunition.

As for recess, when it came to getting along with the other kids I can't say that I did too well in that area. I just had a feeling that I was different from them, and it probably came across in my attitude. I had no interest in conforming and being a good little student, like most of the other kids. I had a quick temper back then and it sure didn't take much to set me off. Fights happened regularly out in the schoolyard and more often than not I'd find myself right in the thick of it. When I think about it now it was all rather comical. All it would take would be for some kid to look at me the wrong way and I'd be on him like a terrier with a rat. My quarrelsome nature lessened only somewhat by the time I reached high school. I still wouldn't back down from a fight, but I like to think that I didn't go looking for them quite as much.

Like most kids, I lived for summer vacation. For the Barr family that always meant our annual two-week camping trip up at Lake Isabella. The lake was actually a man-made body of water, the result of Kern County flooding part of a valley in 1959. It was about a 180-mile drive up from the LA area. The drive itself was always exciting, because my dad and his best friend (Uncle Bruce to us) would race each other up to the lake every single year. Now to understand why I thought this was so much fun, you've got to imagine the following: two grown men racing up the winding – and I mean serious corkscrew winding – Kern River Canyon road in their respective family station wagons. Each car would be towing a 14-foot boat complete with an outboard motor. Now add a carload of toys, pets, a complaining wife and a couple of screaming, carsick kids – you get the idea. Occasionally neighbors down in LA would also be dying to get rid of their kids and my folks would happily bring them along as well.

I will never forget coming back into camp one morning with a live rattlesnake, and running proudly up to my father as this thing was whipping around and rattling loudly, while I held its head in a death grip. I shoved it proudly in my Dad's face and his eyes looked likely to pop out of his head! I won't repeat word for word what he said, but it was to the effect of: "Get that thing out of here, and don't ever bring one back into camp alive!" anyway. Ah, how some of my great moments of glory were dashed!

Looking back, I now realize how much freedom I really had as a child. When I was 11, I had a job shining shoes at a barbershop in a bowling alley, and worked at that until I was 13, then when I went to high school I worked in service stations, full time when I wasn't in school. The deal was that if I failed a grade, that was it – no more working. So I really applied myself and got average grades. I liked being independent, and having my own money. Maybe it was the only way my folks could get me to do any studying at all. By the time I was 16 I was working 50 hours or more a week, as well as school. I had bought my first motorcycle, a Honda 55cc, then my first car, a Volkswagen Beetle. I also rolled it a week or so after I bought it. Dad and I banged it out, then primered it up and that was how I drove it from then on.

Sometime in January 1969, my father and mother sat me down and said that that they thought that I was wasting my time in high school, which was true. They said that if I were willing to apply myself in school and get all "B" grades, then they would be willing to sign my papers to go into the marines. This was too good to be true, as I'd admired the marines since reading Leon Uris's *Battle Cry* when I was 12.

I asked my dad why I had to get "B" grades. My father looked at me with his intelligent, humorous black eyes, furrowed his brow, and said, "I want the rest of the family to know that you are not as stupid as they think you are."

The stage was set. I worked hard at getting those grades. The dream I had had was now within my grasp. Thinking back on it, the decision to allow me to go into the marines must have been a big one indeed. In 1969, the Vietnam War was in full swing. My father was no stranger to war. I asked years later why they had let me go with the war on. My father said that they knew that between what the Marine Corps was going to give me in training, and knowing me, they had little worry that I would come back like a bad smell. I am not sure that I could make a decision such as that for my child. Maybe they saw in me what I couldn't see in myself.

It was about this time that love started to bloom. There was a girl in my English class named Kristine Prause. She had shiny brown hair, brown eyes, olive skin – and to say the least she became the apple of my eye. None of the girls paid much attention to me as I was so outspoken about the Vietnam War. All the others were against it. I felt that they didn't know what they were talking about. None of them had been there. My country, right or wrong. That was what I felt.

There was also the fact that I always had grease under my fingernails. Working full time in a service station doesn't leave much time for socializing. Not that I would have anyway. I was more or less a social outcast. I did have friends, but when it came to sports I was the one that no one wanted to have on their team. I couldn't hit, kick or catch a ball worth a damn. This was also a big disappointment to my dad.

So with these things working against me it was a wonder that someone as lovely as Kris paid me any mind at all. We had the occasional date, but always the big time of my day was when I would go to pick her up at her house, and take her to school.

As the months passed on that last semester, I was in my own dreamland. I was going to go into the marines! This put me heads above the other kids, who were only going to finish high school. Then there was Kris. She really made me feel like I was someone special. A real man.

But the clock was ticking, and my life was about to start changing.

2

Marine Boot Camp

On my seventeenth birthday, I went down to the recruiting station in La Puenta, California. There I met Gunnery Sergeant Chivers and Staff Sergeant Jess Pachiko, the recruiters for the area we lived in. We sat down and started talking. They wanted me to enlist for four years and I agreed, but if they had said 10 years I probably would have enlisted for 10 years. We filled out the papers and then they told me that I would have take various tests when I got to the Los Angeles Induction Center.

I would have to take an examination, I thought to myself. Oh! Oh! – something to do with school again. I have to know something, and I never learned anything in school! I asked them whether there was anything I could do to prepare for the test, and they gave me some books to read. I can remember reading these books and saying to myself, "You have got to be a genius to get in the Marine Corps". Little did I know that you did not have to be a genius to get in the United States Marine Corps. You just had to have a hard ass. I reported to the Los Angeles Induction Center and took a whole lot of written examinations, which I found mentally challenging. Then I had to wait about a week for the results.

Once the results came, and they were positive – I was cleared to enlist – I was elated! I could have levitated! I walked as if I was a big man – a big shit. I was going into the marines! My father saw the progress that I was making and he signed the papers – but we were still going to keep our agreement. I had to get all "B" grades or he would take his blessing away.

That was all right. He did not have to worry about it because the one thing he had instilled in me was that if I gave my word to do something, then I would do it and that would be that – or don't give your word that you will do something. That was one of my dad's big philosophies and it has stuck with me to this very day.

We did my proper enlistment. My dad said I was only to go for three years, not four. If I wanted to re-enlist, that was my decision but he would only let me go for three years. I thought to myself, "Three years is better than nothing," so I went ahead. Both Staff Sergeant Pachiko and Gunnery Sergeant Chivers were infantrymen. They were both Vietnam veterans and Gunnery Sergeant Chivers was a Korean veteran as well. They were tough marines and I could look up to these guys. These were real people, to be admired at the time and that was what I wanted. I wanted to be in the infantry. If I went to Vietnam I wanted to fight, I wanted to know what it was all about; I wanted to be a marine. It was the first time I had heard the saying but I was to hear it many more times in the near future. Staff Sergeant Pachiko would say," Dave, when you become a marine, it is the day you were shot at and you killed the son of a bitch that shot at you. That is when you will really be a marine. In the meantime you are just going into the Marine Corps to be a recruit."

This time of my life was very special; I was continually on a high and also now had Kris at my side. We were at the stage of our relationship where we still had not kissed yet but she cared about me, or I thought she did. I picked her up at her house every morning (she lived on the other side of West Covina), dropped her off at school and then parked my car.

This was a big time of my day because I was working and she had a full day of classes. We saw each other at least once a day, and we also went to the odd movie on a Saturday night, if I was off. It was great for me to have a girl, and an attractive girl as well.

I remember that the biggest thing in my life that year was passing into the Marine Corps. The date for my induction into the corps had now been set: it was to be on June 30,1969. I was a big wheel around the school with all the other kids. There was no one else going into the Marine Corps at the time. No one was stupid enough. The marines were mostly voluntary and other kids that were going to graduate were either going to college or to some bullshit course where they could not be drafted into the United States Army. So there I was, the odd man out as usual, in my closing year of high school.

I recall that the time seemed to drag – Monday to Friday, the weekends. There was nothing else in my life except the prospect of going into the marines at the end of June. This was everything I had dreamed of and I was as good as away.

Driving, well, Uncle Joe, one of my uncles, always said, "You will be hell on wheels when you start driving," and he was quite right. It was a wonder that I did not wreck the Volkswagen a dozen times over. I was a wild kid and everything was going great in my life because I was going into the Marine Corps.

Some time around this time I bought a gallon of red mountain wine and went out into the desert. I climbed to one of the highest peaks I could find in the Lucern area, and put the bottle in a little cranny I had found in the rocks. I then went down the mountain and continued with my hunting. I took no more rattlesnakes home. I left the wine up there for a good two months.

I had a buddy, Mitch Christie, who lived in the area. One day I suggested we go out to the desert and I told him about the gallon of wine I had buried up there. That Saturday afternoon we drove out to the desert. I climbed the mountain and managed to find the bottle of wine. We took it all the way down the rock face – it was a challenge, even to anybody who was a rock climber, but I was totally without fear. We got down to the bottom and made a little fire, as it was dark by then. We started to drink the wine and finished the whole gallon. It was called Red Mountain something or other and it was rotgut piss. We got drunker than skunks. This was the first booze binge I had ever been on and when we woke up the next morning the sleeping bags had been burnt, the wine bottle had been broken and our heads hurt from being hung over. We then tried to shoot a jackrabbit but did not have much motivation. That was my first real hangover, and that was the last time I went on a drinking binge until I went into the marines.

So through the closing days of high school I went, and then school was over. June 12, 1969 was my last day at Edgewood High School in West Covina. There was no graduation ceremony for me, only for the seniors who were graduating that year. I was really on top of things. I had already quit my job and I had money in my pocket.

Kris and I spent the next two weeks together and it was beautiful. We went to Disneyland and San Diego Zoo. We went on our own in my beat-up old Volkswagen. It was a time when we were becoming adults and we felt like adults. I would say I loved Kristine very much, if a kid of 17 knows what love is. We also went down to Huntingdon beach and drove along the Pacific coast until we came to a restaurant that overlooked the ocean. We had dinner around sunset and watched the sun go down over the ocean. For a pair of young kids it was romantic and beautiful. It felt very special to us and made us feel like adults. After dinner we took a walk down on to the beach and I had a packing blanket, which I spread on the beach so we could sit and watch the waves crashing on to the shore. There was no one in sight. We were alone, so I kissed Kristine for the first time. I was in seventh heaven because she was the greatest thing in my life at that moment. She was fantastic, and she really cared for me. I had not experienced anything like it in all the time I was in high school. I was too busy working and getting into other trouble to have time for girls. Maybe it would have been different if a girl had shown an interest, but none did, only Kris. So that kiss, there on the beach, sealed my love for her and to this day I still have a very soft spot for her in my heart.

I also spent time with Kristine's family. Her father and mother really liked me. They thought I was great. Her father, Bill Prause, was in the Los Angeles police force and it was during that time he invited me over for a barbecue. Then my mom and dad had Kristine over. We were in a new league now, and we were adults. Her father recognized me as something special because I was going into the marines, and he could identify with that because he had been with the LA police for many years.

Kris and I went to a party one night; we were drinking coke because the parties at that time were pretty clean. We would listen to rock and roll music. Suddenly everyone was in the room and the boys had to kiss a girl other than their partner. I did not want this to happen, as I felt very jealous, so I said to Kris, "Let's go," and she agreed. At about that time we heard a crash. We went outside and found that someone had driven into the back of my Volkswagen, giving it another dent (but nothing serious). I ran out there and beat the hell out of the guy who was driving the car. I was a big shit now and had to live up to my reputation as I was going into the Marine Corps. I duly whipped the guy and was happy that I did. I don't know what I would have done with myself had I lost that fight, especially in front of my girlfriend. Typical male pride!

By this time I was smoking regularly and in front of my parents. As far as drinking was concerned, I would occasionally have a beer with my dad if he gave me one but had not been on any booze-ups except the one I described previously. I was not a drinker at all, although I did smoke cigarettes – often they were my mother's. She would always say, "Oh! So you're back into the cigarettes again! You know you should start paying for these things around here now." I always paid my way. My dad made sure I paid $40 rent per month from the time I started working full time. He said to me, "Well, you are not going to be keeping up the yards around here any more. I now have to hire a gardening service, and you are going to pay for it. You want to work, you have to pay rent." So for the past three years I had been paying $40 per month rent. It was only fair, because there was grease everywhere. I was never really clean and I remember being a source of irritation to both my parents. My mom would say to me, "Wipe your shoes, take your shoes off before you come inside, wash your hands outside, do this, do that, I do not want your grease all over the walls." Well, she was a typical mom, I suppose, and I was a typical son.

Time was running out – June 30 was fast approaching. I was more excited than I could ever express. All the adventures I had ever read about were soon to start unfolding for me. On June 30, 1969, a lifetime of adventure and insecurity were about to begin. The next few days were spent with my girlfriend Kris. I remember feeling on top of the world. Things were changing, and they were changing fast.

June 29, I went to bed as a civilian. I did not sleep very much that night and I was up and about at 5.00 a.m. the next morning. A new world was about to start for me and I was very excited, full of energy. Mom and Dad got up and Mom made me a nice breakfast. I can still remember sitting there, looking at my parents. I don't know what Mom was thinking, she had a poker face. My dad had a nostalgic look on his face – it seemed as if he was looking back at his life. Later I realized that he was thinking back to when he was seventeen years old and going into the US Navy: many memories of his past were going through his mind.

At 4:00 a.m. my recruiter, Jess Pachiko, pulled up in front of the house. I kissed my mom and dad goodbye; it was the last time I would ever walk through that door, facing something big and major in my life, without a tear in my eye. This time I had a smile. I was a boy going off into a man's world: a totally different world and devoid of the realities I had known all my life, or would ever know again.

As Staff Sergeant Pachiko and I drove down the street, I was so elated I was as high as a kite – and it was great. Today I would be going into the United States Marine Corps and it was the biggest day of my life. We drove to the Los Angeles Induction Center where guys were inducted into all four branches of the service, army, navy, air force and marines. I had an interview with a master gunnery sergeant, who told me a few odds and ends and who also asked me a few questions. I told him point blank, as only a kid would do, that I was awed by all the stripes and ribbons on his chest, his tie and his sleeves. He was obviously a Second World War, a Korean, and Vietnam veteran. I looked at this man in awe and remember asking him, "Is the Marine Corps really going to make a man out of me?" He replied, " Don't worry, son, the Marine Corps will make something out of you, that is for sure."

I left his office and shortly after that I was sworn into the US Marine Corps. I cannot remember exactly what the oath said but I know I had to raise my right hand and swear to uphold the constitution of the United States of America and there was something else in it. I remember feeling so proud. This was all a dedication to the United States of America, though perhaps not so much to the United States but to the Marine Corps. I had listened to the stories that Gunnery Sergeant Chivers and Staff Sergeant Pachiko had told me at the recruiting station. I had been down there a lot before this day. The stories they told me always had to do with serving not only America, but also serving the Marine Corps.

From there we went and had our first meal in the military. We went to Korkies restaurant, where we ate some crummy fish sticks and some other garbage. This was to be our new diet.

They still had openings, 10 to be exact, for anyone willing to join the Marine Corps. Since the army apparently had no difficulty, the gunnery sergeant gave the marines a helping hand.

He stood in front of the men lined up on the opposite side of the hall and with a loud, rather harassing voice shouted, "DO any of you fellows want to volunteer to join the United States Marines?" You could have heard a pin drop. "All right, every one count off, 'one–two–three'." After everyone nervously counted out their number he bellowed out, "All the number threes step forward!" and in a soft and rather smug tone, he said, "Welcome to the United States Marine Corps." At that, a young man collapsed. The silence continued. Without a word nine men moved over to the left-hand side of the hallway. The tenth was dragged along the floor.

A new language was then apparent to me; "shitbird" being the first word I learned. It was very late in the afternoon when the sergeant major announced, "OK, the rest of you shitbirds move on down the stairs and prepare to meet the buses. You'll be taken to the Marine Corps Recruitment Depot in San Diego."

The bus was filled with nervous chatter. Some of the recruits tried to overcome the tension by telling jokes. It was a long journey, 125 miles to be exact. The coastline appeared as we came to Camp Pendleton, 25 miles long and the home of 40,000 marines. My thoughts came to an abrupt stop as we exited the freeway at last in San Diego. The bus stopped outside two enormous gates. A sign read "Marine Corps Recruitment Depot." The bus doors opened. A man in a uniform entered. He had on a Smokey Bear hat. The bus drove on to the base, across the parade field, and stopped outside a large Quonset hut. In a loud, authoritative voice, he shouted, "Right, you bunch of shit maggots, off the bus now." This was not for the fainthearted or the thin-skinned.

We were herded to some yellow footprints on the ground, where we stood for approximately one hour. We were instructed to shout out "Here!" when they called out our names, at which time the instructors became abusive to some of the recruits. They then instructed us to leave our belongings on the grinder, also known as the parade ground. In single file, we went into the first house of horrors for the ultimate haircut. As I sat in the barber's chair my thoughts rested on sheep, and an understanding of how they feel was never so real. Zip! Zip! Zip! My hair was gone in a matter of 30 seconds: the tears fell down my face. Above the mirror before me was a humorous sign that read, "Please do not tip the barber." My feelings were rather if I could, I'd shoot the barber. I could hear the gasps coming from behind me as I stood up. "Shut your fucking mouths, worms," the barber replied. Two hundred and eighty men passed through those barber's chairs in 30 minutes.

The second house of horrors was where the abuse, physical and verbal, really began. Their vocabulary and language left something to be desired. "You're a bunch of mother-fuckers, shit maggots, you're lower than the whale shit in the ocean. What excuse have you bunch of hogs got that makes you think you should be in the marines?" It was after eleven at night, the room was dark and spirits low. When was this going to stop? Another drill sergeant stood up. " All your belongings, clothes, rings, watches – anything you hold dear I want putting into the boxes in front of you. That includes all the clothes you have on. Everything you will require will be issued by the Marine Corps and not what your mother thinks you need." Slowly we began to strip. The humiliation was overwhelming. I stood there naked, wondering what the next house of horrors would hold. We were issued the basics: tennis shoes, socks, utility trousers, sweatshirt and a utility hat that was ill-fitting. One of the new recruits decided he was going to speak his mind and informed the drill sergeant that his hat was to small and his sweats didn't fit. Before he could finish the drill sergeant grabbed him by the shirt and pulled him towards his face. "Worm, this is the Marine Corps and everything fits, now fuck off and get out my sight." You could have heard a pin drop. As we walked to the grinder, the drill instructors continued with the yelling and verbal abuse. The rest of our belongings were put into the boxes. Was I having second thoughts? I am sure everyone else was. I was on top of the world 24 hours ago, now the terror I felt had me shaking. How much longer was this torture going to last? We were then instructed to put our addresses on the boxes. "You can send them to the whore you call mother or to the pimp you call father," was one instructor's command. The boxes were then stacked neatly in the corner. My box of belongings was delivered to my mother's house, so I actually did something right that day.

As I stood waiting for the rest of the recruits to finish, a drill sergeant came up to me and started to scream in my face. As I started to respond, he said, "Your mouth is a sewer. Don't open your sewer in front of me." As I started to say, "Yes Sir…," he stuck his finger in my eye and said, "That is an eye, that is an eye, you are a private and a private is scum, and he doesn't open his mouth to his superiors."

The smell of the uniforms was one I will never forget. It will always remind me of my first night in the house of horrors. But it wasn't over. We were ushered back out to the parade ground and they made us stand there for what seemed it eternity. It was 4:00 a.m. The only reason I knew that was because I could hear the reveille being blown. Another hour passed. The slightest movement from any of us brought a barrage of abuse and a smack.

The next command was one of relief. "Hippity ho, mob go!" I could barely feel my legs as I took a step forward. As we marched forward I continued to hear some unlucky soul being punished. Oh boy! I missed a step, and as my thoughts wandered I felt a blow to the back of my head. No explanation came with it – I only knew I wasn't going to miss another step. "Hippity ho, mob to the right! Hippty ho, mob to the left!" It finally came to an end as we marched to the mess hall entrance. The clatter of trays filled the room as the drill sergeants screamed, "Hurry, private, hurry."

They lined us up in two columns. "All right, you bunch of pigs, you have six minutes to get in there, eat your slop and get the fuck out, go." As we moved through the lines I grabbed a big metal tray. The only voice you could hear was the drill sergeant's "Hurry, private, hurry." The mess men standing behind the counters had their spatulas and spoons ready. There were no choices. The food was slapped on the tray, and all the time you could hear, "Hurry, private, hurry." At the end of the food counter we were pushed to the far end of the mess hall, obviously reserved for the lowest of the low (that would be us). I walked to the table, hands and tray shaking. One recruit, who obviously was oblivious to the instructions, asked the drill sergeant, "Hey, where do we eat?" The drill instructor knocked his tray out of his hand. The food flew through the air as the instructor said, "Over there." I sat down and ate my food with great speed. "This isn't too bad," I muttered to the guy next to me, thinking the last time I had eaten was at Korkies the day before.

As I lifted my head for air, I saw a milk carton flying my way. I ducked, but the guy next to me was too slow. The carton fragmented, and milk went everywhere. Pointing at me the sergeant said, " Shut your fucking sewer." So passed my first meal in the marines. "Get up, get out!" were the next set of instructions, then "Hurry, private, hurry," "Come on, you hogs, move it!" As I got up I realized that some people had only just sat down. Their trays were still full of food. We were tripping over each other as we made our way out the back door. The barrels outside the door had a purpose. The first was to scrape off the slops, the second was to clean the trays, the third to dip and rinse. Then the trays were put into a rack prior to entering the dishwasher. Again the sergeant started to shout, "Over here, maggots, over here!" We all stepped forward into some kind of formation. The roll call lasted an hour.

"Hippity ho, mob go!" When was this going to end? As we approached another building, I noticed a Navy Corps insignia. It could only mean one thing, the medical. We stood there for what seemed forever. My feet were killing me. I thought I heard music coming from one of the rooms – it reminded me of Kris, and tenderness. I then realized how much my life had changed in a matter of 24 hours.

The radio said it was 6:00 a.m. I was in a world that was totally alien to me.

I thought I'd been a tough kid but this was the Marine Corps, which meant I had to get tougher if I was going to survive. We stood in single file. It was like the mess hall, but instead of the spatulas and spoons they had needles and syringes in their hands. Oh my God! I felt faint. I had an aversion to needles. The recruit in front felt the same as me, and he hit the floor with a bang. There was no compassion as they continued to give him the shots. In the next building we were required to strip off, bend over and grab our buttocks with our hands. The next inspection involved our testes and penises for sexually transmitted diseases. "We've got a crud, we've got a crud!" As the rest of the medics approached the new recruit they started to hit him, shouting, "Look at this fucker, he's got green around his balls." Still hitting him, they dragged him off towards the showers.

Out on the parade ground where no one could see us we stood waiting. As I lifted one foot, then the other, I felt the smack at the back of my head. "How the Marine Corps recruited slime like you into my group is beyond me." "Sir, I wanted to kill communists." Wrong answer! The sting across my face was still burning five minutes later. "And why did they let a maggot like you, with a face that looks like a hat full of assholes, into my Marine Corps?" "Are you as stupid as you look?" There was no response. The instructor took a step forward, his face nearly touching the young man's next to me. "Why did you join the

Marine Corps? Why did they let you in?" "I was drafted, I actually wanted to join the army, Sir." The sound of the smack echoed around the parade ground. Over the next hour 20 people were asked the same question and again the answer resulted in verbal and physical abuse. There wasn't a right answer. No one dared to move. There was a drill sergeant wandering around and you didn't know he was behind you until you felt the smack.

Roll call started again. Someone new had come on the scene, an older-looking staff sergeant. Tall, a bit over six feet, with thick glasses, crooked front teeth, a bit paunchy. He introduced himself as Staff Sergeant Platoon Commander Ross of the United States Marine Corps. "You are the sorriest-looking bunch of mother-fuckers I have ever seen in my life. How they ever let you into the Marine Corps I will never know. You take your orders from me and when I say jump you ask how high. I'm your mother, your father and your girlfriend. I am everything that will make any difference to you, you sorry bunch of mother-fuckers, when you get to Vietnam and the day you have the audacity to call yourselves marines."

We were on our feet the rest of the morning. Our next meal in the mess hall was lunch. They continued to knock us about and the slapping on the back of the head was a regular occurrence. During the march, to stop us they would shout, "Whoa, whoa, hippity hop, mob stop. Let's try it again. On the left foot, hippity ho, mob go." Someone always got it wrong. "Left right left, your left your right your left." It looked like a circus act. "Caterpillar whoa, hippity hop, mob stop." Smack – someone got it wrong. There was one command that I would hear over and over again. "Whoa, whoa, hippity hop, mob stop, get down on your mother-fucking knuckles, that means everyone." The parade grinder was hot. It was July 1. We were poised in the push-up position, our knuckles burning from the hot ground. If our bottoms were too high the sergeant would stomp on our backsides if our bodies were too low to the ground he would kick us in the side and scream. "Get your ass up. Get your ass down."

We finally arrived at the mess hall. We formed two lines as the drill sergeant shouted, "Gangway down the middle. OK you mother-fuckers, all the fat pigs repeat after me 'oink, oink, pigs to the rear'." Anyone who was overweight moved to the back of the lines. There was a motive to this madness, and that was they would have less time to eat. We hit the mess hall at the same pace as we did for breakfast. "Hurry, private, hurry." "This way, mother-fucker, this way," they shouted. The acoustics were like an echo chamber, as the mess halls were very old. We stood at the table until it was full, then we had to wait for the next. When the whole platoon was ready to be seated the drill sergeant gave his command. "Right, pukes, sit, eat." I have never eaten as fast as I did in those two days. The next command, "Up, get the fuck out of the mess hall." "Hurry, private, hurry." We went through the same routine as at breakfast, scrape the trays, wash, dip and rinse and stack them in the rack.

Next we were marched over to another building. Like all the others, it was large and dismal. We were ordered to sit, what a relief! My feet were killing me. After about 10 minutes a big sergeant major entered the room. His name never stayed with me but his first sentence stuck. "Some of you fucking idiots will be getting out of the Marine Corps within 30 days and some of you will be with the Marine Corps for the next 30 years." Thirty years kept going through my mind, 30 years. My mind began to wander. I picked up on the rest of his introduction as he informed us that during the next two weeks we were to have indoctrination into the Marine Corps. The real basic training would begin after those two weeks. "If you fail one aspect of the training you'll be put back, and you'll join the platoon that comes in behind you."

After the speech they marched us, if you want to call it that, off to some tents. We had not had anything to eat or drink except the two meals described and no water in between. If we had to go to the toilet, well, bad luck, we just had to hold it. When we got back to the tent area, they said, "Right! Five minutes for head call." We had to go and shit, piss and whatever else we wanted to do. We all went into a big communal toilet, where we sat on the toilets crapping, pissing and whispering to each other nervously. The jokes were over and there was no more nervous laughter either. Then we heard the drill instructor's voice: "All right, you sorry bunch of maggots, get back out on the road." There was everybody rushing, squeezing it off, pulling up pants and back on to the so-called road.

We were then marched over to our tents. I remember my first night sleeping in a tent in the marines. I was to do exactly the same in another three armies. We were in a sandy area – it was like beach sand, and the tents were located very deep in it. There were aisles in between the tents. They were about 15 feet wide, and this was the road. This was July 1, the middle of summer and it was hotter than hell in San Diego. The drill instructors were getting us into squads according to height, big guys up front and then down to the shortest fellows at the back. During this there was the usual confusion because by now our brains were numb. Then the drill instructor said, "All right, you fucking bunch of assholes, get down in the sand, everybody down in the sand, hit the deck." Then he said "All right, you ladies, on your bellies, on your backs, get up, stand up, on your bellies, on your backs, get up, stand up, down, up, down, up." We were moving as fast we could and at close quarters. There were 80 of us and we were running into each other, bouncing down and crashing into each other. "All right," he said, "throw sand. I do not want to see one of your sorry fucking knobs sticking out of the sand." We all started throwing sand at each other; it must have looked like a big brown cloud of miserable sand, with 80 miserable souls in it. Then he said, " All right, pukes, stop with the sand and stand up." Everybody had been perspiring before this and now we had a fine layer of sand over our faces and bodies. "All right squad one, face squad two. Squad three, face squad four." We now made a poor attempt to turn in military fashion, which we did not possess at the time.

Then he said, "I am going to explain to you sorry bunch of pukes what a hand salute is. Ladies, I will demonstrate." He brought his hand up in a salute, thumb along the forefinger, hand flat to the head and to the edge of the cover (meaning hat). "Drop salute and you sharply cut your salute down. Right now, you try it. Salute each other and say 'Good morning, Sir.'" We all started saluting each other and sand was flying off everybody's hands, where it had coagulated from the perspiration. Everybody was standing there gray-faced, covered in sand. We had sand in our breeches, sand in our tennis shoes, sand down our shorts, sand down the cracks of our asses and we were standing saluting each other, saying "Good morning, Sir." The drill instructor would shout, " I do not like what I see. On your bellies, on your backs, throw sand." And this is how it went on all afternoon, saluting each other. Of course, we never saluted properly, so it was, "On your bellies, on your backs."

Finally he said, " All right, everybody into your tents." So everybody scrambled for a tent, there was no order. If there were no beds in the tent, we would scramble for another tent until we finally found a tent with a bed. I remember the guys in my tent picking me out and saying, "Go and ask the drill instructor for some water." Everybody was very thirsty, as you can well imagine. I thought, "Well, all right." And went up to the drill instructor's tent. It had a big sign on the side which said, " Knock and request permission to speak to the drill instructor." I hit this thing three times, kind of meekly and I heard, "I can't hear you," so I hit a little harder and again heard, " I can't hear you." Finally after I had hit again, harder, a drill instructor stuck his head out of the tent flap, looked at me, his face right in mine so I could smell the onions on his breath. "What do you want, maggot?" I said, "Sir, I …" and that was as far as I got because a thumb came around, was stuck in my eye and he said, "That is an eye, you are a private, a private is a maggot, you are low, you are scum, you are puke, you are puke that dogs puke. Now start over again." By this time I was shaking and said, " Sir, the private would like to speak to the DI about …" This time a fist came out and hit me on the jaw so I flew off the little steps into the sand. I was lying there on my back, with the drill instructor standing over me saying, " What do think this is, a Jack Webb movie or something? Who are you calling a DI, do I look like Jack Webb? Who in the fuck are you to call me a DI? What is on your little pea brain, maggot? You are a bitch, a four-eyed bitch." He was obviously referring to my glasses. I had now picked up a nickname and to this very day I am self-conscious about wearing my glasses. He continued: "You four-eyed bitch, how dare you call me a DI? I am your drill Instructor, my name is Staff Sergeant Abels, Drill Instructor Staff Sergeant Abels." This was all in a Texas drawl. He stood back and told me to get on my feet. I was on my feet like a spring. He said, " Right, what do you want?" I said " Sir, Private Barr requests permission to speak to the drill instructor." " What do you want, miserable?" he asked, to which I replied " Sir, the privates have asked Private Barr to ask the drill instructor …" He grabbed me by the shirt, screaming " Hurry up!" This was when I started to stutter "for water". "Water?" he said, "water, come into my tent, I want you to meet the other drill instructors and I want you to ask them for some water." I went into the tent meekly, behind the drill instructor. He said, "Speak to Staff Sergeant Platoon Commander Ross." I stood in front of him and said, "Sir, Private Barr," and that is as far as I got when I was hit in the stomach and asked, "What do you want, maggot?" I was trying to straighten when he hit me again and said, "Maggot, speak beak and don't fuck it up or I will fuck you up." I was standing there, stuttering and tried again, "Sir, the privates have requested water, Sir," to which he replied, "Don't ever ask me for anything again, fuck off." and he smacked me. I bolted out of the tent and fell down in the sand. So went my first interview with Staff Sergeant Platoon Commander Ross. Once back in the tent everybody looked at me. They had seen and heard what happened and did not ask me questions. They knew in their hearts that no one was ever to ask for anything.

We were then called on to the road. "Platoon 1123 on the road!" Everybody then came running out and they informed us from that moment on, until we were told differently, everything a drill instructor told us fucking animals to do we were to repeat the command. When they said, "Platoon 1123 on the road," we all had to say, "Sir, platoon 1123 on the road."

Something else we were fast learning: every command had a time to it. When it was, "Platoon 1123 on the road!" we had 10 seconds to be on the road. At this early stage it took us longer than 10 seconds and this caused misery for everyone. At this particular instance it was, "Down on your bellies, on your backs, throw sand at each other." By this time it was late afternoon and time for dinner.

Once again we heard the command, "Hippity ho, mob go!" and everybody attempting to step off on their left foot. Obviously there were guys who were out of tune. I was one of them, and to this day I am out of tune. I never did learn to march properly and I paid dearly for that in the next 10 weeks. Once we arrived at the mess hall, the command was: "Oink, oink, pigs to the rear." Everybody in unison said, "Oink, oink, pigs to the rear." And all the fat boys ran to the rear. "Into the mess hall, gangway up the middle." Then once again we were running through the line with other screaming privates (mess men) slapping food on to our trays and over to the eating area we would go, double time. We would sit down and start to eat.

We looked around and saw other privates who looked far more military than we did, when we could see them. There were even some that had their top buttons unbuttoned. This meant they were in their last stages of basic training, nearly ready to graduate. That was a real privilege. Then there were other privates who wore a full green utility uniform but the legs of their pants were not bloused over their boots. They were a step ahead of us as well. Undoubtedly with our pink shaved heads, ill-fitting caps, (covers), dirty sweatshirts, green utility pants, and tennis shoes, nothing seemed to fit. We looked like what we were being called, maggots.

After dinner we cleaned the trays, got into formation and moved back to our living area. Once again they had us down and rolling in the sand and then it was time for a shower – no shit, let's go and have a shower now, with our issued soap and shaving gear (everything was issued, we had nothing that belonged to us). One guy in the platoon had a watch and he was called Private Watch. Into the showers we went. We were given five minutes to shit, shower and shave. We raced in, tried to get the sand out of our clothes and just got under the water to wash the sand off. Once done, quick towel off, back into our clothes and we were late. OK, they marched us back to the living area, and told us to roll around in the sand again, on our bellies, on our backs and we also had to throw sand at each other. By this time it was quite late, about 9:00 p.m. They put us into our tents and that was it, the end of our very first whole day in the Marine Corps.

I remember becoming one of the humorists of the platoon. I told a joke that I tell to this day, about the little class that had letter representation. This one little girl had her hand up and the teacher asked her, "What is A?" to which the little girl replied, "A is for apple, teacher." "Very good, Sally," the teacher said. Then she said "B". Little Jack had his hand up and she said " OK, Jackie," and he said, "B is for boy," and this went on through the alphabet. They got down to the letter "R" and the teacher finally called on little Johnny. He had had his hand up every time and what could he say about "R" that would be bad anyway? She said, "Right, Johnny, what is R?" and he said, "R is for rats, big mother-fucking rats, with dicks this long." That was the first joke I told in the United States Marine Corps.

We did not have any sheets on our racks (not beds, they were known as racks), so we just curled up in a blanket, sandy, dirty, miserable and very, very tired. That is how we closed our first day in the marines.

The next two weeks were absolute misery. We had now started to learn things about the Marine Corps. Our living area was right next door to the San Diego airport and every time a jet came in or out (which put a damper on the instruction being given to us by the drill instructor), the drill instructor would say, "Fucking civilians," and everybody would holler in unison: "Fucking civilians." If we were marching and he was going "left right left, left right" everybody would repeat the same after him. If he said, "Column left," we would do the same. They were building automatons and I can remember that it did not help me much, because I was never right. Drill Instructor Abels was the smallest of the three drill instructors, about 5' 9", with beady light-colored eyes, long nose and dimpled square jaw – in fact his head was square under the Smokey Bear hat. One day Drill Instructor Abels came up to me, and leering into my face, said, "What in the fuck is wrong with you? You are the most stupid, dumbest, four-eyed bitch I have ever seen in my life." I stood there looking at him, quaking with fear as he was screaming in my face and suddenly he kicked me on my left shin. Needless to say I hollered, so he kicked me again and I hollered again. "Now," he said, "Dippy, the one that hurts is the one you go with. When I say forward march, put your left foot forward first, think of the pain and you will know which one to go forward on." "Yes Sir," I replied. "Can't hear you, maggot," he said. " Yes Sir," I said again. "You are a four-eyed bitch," to which I replied, "Yes Sir, the private is a four-eyed bitch, Sir."

We also took a battery of tests that took us about two days to complete. These were general intelligence tests and in the end I found that I passed with something like 110. I don't know how they rated it but that was average intelligence, which suprised me. Usually, about halfway through any of these I would just start marking. I did not look at the questions. I did not see any point in them because I thought I was good enough to be an infantryman and that is all I wanted to be. The three drill instructors, Platoon Commander Ross, Staff Sergeant Abels and Staff Sergeant Lewis, were all infantryman and had served and been wounded in Vietnam. These were real marines. We looked up to them and wanted to be just like them. They always pointed out to us that the infantrymen were the backbone of the marines.

A little about being a four-eyed bitch wearing glasses. Anybody wearing glasses was automatically a four-eyed bitch.

Now, a little about the people we were with. There were guys who had volunteered for the draft. Now you might say, "What is a volunteer for the draft?" Well, that is where they volunteer to go into the marines for two years, when they received their draft notice for the US Army. They figured they had a better chance of survival in Vietnam with the Marine Corps than they did with the army and I daresay they were quite right. The discipline and the training the marines received were on a much higher level to that of the army, as was our leadership. It was basically called "volunteering for the draft itself." I am sure that many in the US Army might dispute this claim, but that is their right. In the end, we all did our duty and did it well.

The names of things were changing all the time. First of all the floor was known as a deck, a bed was a rack, pants were trousers and a hat was a cover. Our boots were also known as black Cadillacs. The wall was a bulkhead and a toilet was a head. These were all Navy terms, because the Marine Corps was a branch of the navy and it was steeped in tradition. The Marine Corps had been on the go since 1775, and apparently the marines were part of the US armed forces earlier than the navy was. This is also open to dispute. Marines were on board ships of the navy, and were the ones who jumped aboard hostile ships with the sailors and did battle with the enemy, when wars were fought that way. Over the years it progressed to different types of warfare. The marines had a tradition that went back a long way and we were very proud of that tradition, or should I say, we were made to be proud of our tradition.

Finally, after the two weeks of indoctrination, which had been pure hell, we started the actual basic training. A day was known as "T1" or "T2," meaning training day. Sundays were also training days. We were moved out of the tents and into billet areas. Our billet area housed 20 men per billet and there were 80 men in a platoon. The billet areas dated back to before the Second World War. They were 20-man Quonset huts. The showers, toilet and sink buildings had corrugated tin sides and roofs. Every morning we had to rake the grass. Raking the grass meant raking the sand between the walkways in between the billets. Quite obviously we were not allowed to walk on the grass.

The heads were about 150 yards down the road. If you needed to go to the toilet, you were told to go. For example, after a meal they would say, "Right, head call, five minutes," then if you had to have an emergency head call, and we were out on the parade grinder or somewhere having instruction, you would have to raise your hand if you could no longer hold it, and the drill instructor would say, "What do you want, maggot?" "Sir, the private requests permission to go and make an emergency head call." The drill instructor would usually make you repeat it a few times, until he could hear you properly. Then he would come over and grab your ear lobe, pull it and then you would start sounding off like a siren: "Whirhhhh". Back in 1969, sirens had to be wound up properly. "Whirhhhh" till you were gone, then he would slap you on the side of the head and say "Right, go maggot, run." Your hand would be going like a crank, as if you were winding a siren and you would be going "Whirhhhhh" all the way to the toilet area where you would wind down. The toilet area could be up to half a mile away and you would have to run all the way there. Having done whatever you wanted to do, you turned around, went out and wound up again: "Whirhhhh". You would then run all the way to where your platoon was. Once back there you could not jump straight into your space, you stood there going "Whirhhhh" until the instructor decided to walk over and pull your ear lobe. When he did this you could wind your siren down and then had to say, " Sir, the private requests permission to rejoin platoon 1123." "Right, maggot, join the platoon," he would say. So went an emergency head call.

We used to run anywhere from three to five miles a day, depending on what we were doing and which instructor we had. I remember that Drill Instructor Staff Sergeant Abels was a runner. Staff Sergeant Lewis liked to exercise our asses off and we did rope climbs or ran an obstacle course: there were all kinds of things. We were also learning about the Marine Corps traditions, and the history of the Marine Corps. We had classes all day. The average training day would start at 4:00 a.m. in the morning with reveille and everybody would fly out of their beds. We had five minutes to make our beds, get dressed and sweep out the billet. Once that was done, we had five minutes to rake the sand in the area and get all the dirt off the actual walkway. Then we had five minutes to run to the toilet area, to shave, clean ourselves and do our thing in the morning. We then had to run back and be in formation. From there we would go out for a run of about a mile, then we would do exercises, push-ups and that type of thing.

Then, before we went to breakfast, we would stop in front of the chinning bars and everybody had to do at least 10 pull-ups. We would form up again and march to the mess hall: there we would have the magic chant, "Gangway up the middle for the drill instructors, form up into two lines. Oink, oink, pigs to the rear." Then we would go in and get our breakfast. By this time we were starting to settle down and think about what we were doing. We were starting to learn to be military men, albeit poor excuses at this time, but we were learning. When we came out of the mess hall we cleaned our mess trays.

At the time we were learning things like "10 general orders". That was quite a bit of memory work. To learn those 10 general orders, I would practice them while standing waiting for the rest of the guys to come out of the mess hall. My first general order was to walk to my post in a military manner. I cannot remember the rest of them today.

We were then marched off and had to do 10 pull-ups again, or as many as we could do. Then we were marched to our first class of the morning. We were now learning about M14 rifles and they would always start off with nomenclature. The M14 rifle is a semi-automatic air-cooled, gas operated, magazine fed, 7.62mm rifle. They were also trying to impress on us all the time that our rifle was our best friend. The rifle was everything because it would be used to kill the enemy and save our lives, as well as that of our fellow marines.

The other classes covered Marine Corps traditions. They taught us how to march and drill, all disciplinary training. When we made mistakes, we heard those chanted words, "Whoa, whoa, hippity hop, mob stop". The reason they would do that was because we were messing up on something. Somebody was bobbing up or the platoon was out of step or we went column left instead of column right or left flank instead of right flank. When we heard the chant we knew we were in trouble. We didn't have rifles yet so it was: "Down on your knuckles, push-up position, ready, one two, up down, up down, get your ass down." The instructor would stomp on your pelvis to push your backside down or if it was too low you would be kicked in the ribs to bring it up. In the meantime your knuckles were being chafed raw on the parade grinder. Then when that was over, we would hear, " Right up, into platoon formation," and "Hippity ho, mob go." That was it. We were a mob, and off we would march until we started to get it right. Every time we started to make mistakes, it would have a domino effect, one after the other.

The parade grinder was about half a mile long. It was surrounded by structures of two or three stories, all in tan color, and in Spanish design. I used to have a problem with bobbing; my head would be bobbing up and down if I did not watch it. Suddenly I would feel a smack against the back of the head. This happened to everyone that bobbed.

The guys would stand there and were supposed look straight ahead. Our eyes were not supposed to move. If they did move, it was known as "Eye fucking the area," and that would get the whole platoon into trouble.

The other thing we had trouble with was the platoon opening or closing up too far on itself, because we were not keeping our distance. Life consisted of marching, then classes, but in the middle of the day, before lunch, we would have calisthenics. We would run three miles, then go through the obstacle course. We climbed ropes that were 30 feet high and were not allowed to use our feet on them at all; we had to climb hand over hand. At one point I was able to climb that rope in eight seconds. I was in better physical condition than I had ever been in my life.

Smoking was the greatest treat of our life. To have a cigarette was the height of luxury. If we were doing well during the day, we would have a cigarette after breakfast and again after lunch: we would also probably have a cigarette after dinner. Then there would be more classes and training; dinner was about 5:00 p.m. in the afternoon. We would carry on until about 9:00 p.m. in the evening and then we would hear the chanted words, " Platoon 1123, smokers on the road," which we repeated. This was the greatest; it marked the end of the day. We would go out and the instructors would say, " Right, smokers, burn one." And all the smokers would say, " Smokers burn one." We had our cigarettes in a little waterproof box from which we would take them out and light up. That was the greatest cigarette of the day, to be sure. This was our only relaxation. At the time there were many people who actually started smoking, as it was our only reward.

One thing the drill instructor told us never to do was to ask for a cigarette. Some wiseass asked for a cigarette one day. The drill instructor said, "Right!

You want a cigarette? Sure, come on, maggot. 1123 smokers on the road. Give this man four cigarettes." We gave him four cigarettes, lit them and then put a bucket over his head. Everybody then took out the bayonets that they had been issued with and as the guy walked between the billets on the pathway, they started hitting the bucket with their bayonets. All this time he was smoking the cigarettes. That cured us of ever asking for a cigarette again. That was taboo. If we did not do well during the day we would not get a cigarette after a meal. What was possibly four cigarettes per day could be as little as one. I will admit, though, I do remember a whole day without a cigarette!

Fitness! We were becoming fitter by the day. Then came the day, about two weeks into basic training, when we were issued with rifles. I remember drawing an M14, a rifle weighing nine and a half pounds. It was a beautiful piece of equipment in the way it was made and in its serviceability. These rifles' working mechanisms dated back to the Second World War. This was a very proud moment, because it was another step toward being a marine, a marine who has a rifle and who must learn to use it. The drill instructor told us that we must eat, sleep, breathe and live with our M14s. A song we sang while running was: " I don't want some teenage queen, all I want is my M14." We now also started to drill with the rifle, when we were troop and stomp – marching – we carried it at port arms, right shoulder and left shoulder. We were also starting to operate as a team. The words "gung ho" were heard a lot, and they meant "together." It was originally a Chinese word that came from just after the Boxer Rebellion in China, where the Marines did so well.

They issued us something besides sweatshirts, tennis shoes, a pair of trousers and a utility cover. They now issued us our full utility uniform. It was buttoned from the top down and the blouse on our boots was not done up, that meant that the pants leg cuff went all the way to the bottom. It was another step in the right direction, although we were stilled called maggots because we were maggots. The pink heads were now burning to a brown and we were given a haircut once a week. Every time we went in to get a haircut, Lord knows what they were taking off, because we had no hair on our heads at all, but they found something, obviously. So once a week we were shorn and it was a time of pure and utter misery. I always remember looking up and seeing the sign "Don't tip the barber." Fuck the barber!

We were becoming used to our daily life. Each and every one of us found our lives had changed drastically but we were becoming accustomed to it. We now had our rifles and we got up in the morning for our morning routine:

"1123 on the road," followed by breakfast, then classroom work, drill in the afternoon, then back to the classroom.

We had also started another part of our drill, which was to carry on from that time to the end of our training – we had to go to the pugel stick range. At the pugel stick range we learned close combat – how to engage your enemy at close range and beat the hell out of him with your M14 rifle. Our instructor was a big staff sergeant. He would say to me: "Come up here worm, you, four eyes" – he was obviously picking me out. I ran up, stood in front of him and said, " Sir, Private Barr reporting as ordered, Sir." He said to me: "All right, maggot, here is a knife. Come at me." I did not want to do this because I knew he was going to hurt me. I took the knife and went at him, the next thing I knew I was on my back in the sand, the knife was out of my hand, and my wrist was extremely painful. Nothing was done without pain.

They were also teaching us how to use the rifle with the bayonet on it, and the different types of strokes. Horizontal butt stroke was to hit the enemy in the jaw with the rifle butt. Then there were the slash stroke, the jab stroke, the vertical butt stroke – all these different maneuvers with the rifle. Then at the end of all this, after an hour out there in the sand and the heat knocking around, we put on football helmets, with one platoon lined up against the other platoon. Two guys would then go into the ring with a pugel stick. This weighed the same as the M14 rifle and it also had rubber tips on each end. The two maggots would then do battle and everybody else would be chanting: "Kill, kill, kill," in unison. The two guys would go in there and just beat the hell out of each other – in the end, when one went down, the other one would get a free hit and everybody would have their thumbs pointing down, chanting: " Kill, kill, kill." I inevitably had my ass beat and ended upon the ground with the other guy getting a free stroke. I was not very big and I also was the second youngest in my platoon. The football helmets left something to be desired – there was no padding inside, so if you were clobbered on the side of the head you could be knocked out cold. I saw more than one guy being knocked colder than a turkey and the other guy would still get his free hit. We were learning close combat, a skill where we got rid of our aggression but which also made us aggressive – which we needed to be. I personally dreaded it, and I am sure everybody else in his own private way did as well, but it was something we had to do.

Now we were starting to march properly. We had also moved to a stage where we did not have to repeat everything the drill instructor was saying. He would say, "Sound off," and we would go: "1 2 sound off, 3 4 sound off, 1 2 3 4 United States Marine Corps, kill, kill, kill." Another saying we had was: "War is our business and business is good." It made us want to go to war. It made us think that this was what it was all about.

We did hear the questions come up. "Why would all this drill help us in Vietnam?" And the drill instructor would say, "We have got to make you disciplined soldiers before we start teaching you infantry tactics and how to kill as a team. Right now, we are teaching you to kill as an individual, with the pugel sticks."

Now the time came for mail call. At the end of every day, before "1123, smokers on the road," we would have mail call. The drill instructors would always have some comment. "Here's a cute one from your girl – it smells like a French whore," and he would throw the letter at you. "Here's this from so and so," and then, " Oh, look what we have here, Private Preston has got a package from home. Mother has sent him some goodies. Private Preston, come up here." Private Preston would stand in front of the drill instructor and say, "Private Preston reporting as ordered, Sir." The instructor would then say, "All right, maggot. Open the box, let's eat." Maggot would open the box and there would be all types of cakes and goodies. "Start eating," the drill instructor said. "No, don't take them out of the wrapping, you eat the wrapping as well, eat it all, right now." This gave me a pretty good idea.

There was a guy from Louisiana in my squad named Disatel. I managed to get hold of his girlfriend's address and wrote to her, saying that Disatel was too self-conscious and proud to ask her himself, but he would like a stick of gum per day. I told her that he would really appreciate it because he really liked gum. I told her that everything was regulated and that just one stick per day would suffice. I know he would have to eat everything at once, wrapper and all. Anyway, within a week a stick of gum arrived. "What is this, Private Disatel? Come here, maggot". Private Disatel was standing there and he was told to eat the stick of gum. It was wrapped up in tinfoil and we could see he was in agony, his fillings were giving him trouble but he ate the gum. He sat there chewing it for five minutes before the drill instructor took it away from him and threw it out.

At mail call at the end of our exercises next day, Private Disatel received another stick of gum, and this went on all week. He was eating gum every night, including the tinfoil. He wrote to his girlfriend asking her to stop sending the gum, while I was writing my own letter, telling her to continue sending it. I told her he was too self-conscious. Finally after about two weeks of this, Private Disatel finally realized what was happening; at least he had a good sense of humor. I agreed to write a letter to his girlfriend saying that he didn't want any more gum. He was tired of the gum.

I was very hot tempered and at times I did not hesitate to lay into somebody. I would sometimes be knocked around as well because I was not very big; I also came short a few times: more times than I'd like to admit. I was in there slogging away: I was a marine recruit and a marine recruit had to fight. I remember one particular afternoon we were doing something and this black fellow was spouting off. His name was Miller. I can't remember what happened, but he told me to shut up. Anyway we ended up really going for each other and I whipped his ass. This was the first time I had got into fisticuffs with a black. He never bothered me after that, or I him. To be sure, he got in a few good ones.

Everything was timed. Thirty seconds to fetch your notebook, 30 seconds to do this, t30 seconds to change into running gear, 30 seconds to do that. So everybody would put their locks on the last digit and all they had to do was go in and pull it open. We had combination locks on our footlockers. One day, when we came back into our living area, we walked down the little path in between the huts and the drill instructor said, "Platoon halt. Eyes right." He continued, "Over here we have a pile of locks and they are all locked together. Now you maggots who want to hurry things up, women of experience, now everyone into the billet, and whoever doesn't have a lock on their footlocker will then present themselves out on the road in thirty seconds, with the footlocker held in front of them. All right – form up." So we formed up. "First man, go and find your lock." The first man put his footlocker down and tried to find his lock. Now the footlocker weighs about 35 pounds. He was in there messing around with all these locks, trying to find his to open it and get it out. When he was done the next guy had to go. After about 15 minutes we were sweating blood, and this just carried on. After 20 minutes things were not so good in our lives. We were in pain; the guys were groaning. Then the drill instructor said, "All right, all you turds who want to move around, everybody into one billet, now, 30 seconds." So there were 40 guys, with big footlockers in front of them, all trying to get through a little door in 30 seconds. We were running into the door, bouncing off, pushing each other in the back with the footlockers. Once in the billet the instructor said, "Sorry, too slow, get back outside and do it again." We did this for about half an hour, running around with footlockers in front of us. I have had pain in my arms from physical stress many times in my life, but I look back at that incident and still feel how difficult it was to carry that footlocker in front of me and do this little exercise.

One of the drill instructors' favorite punishments was to choke a private who had goofed up on something. They would sometimes choke you with a straight arm and push you against a wall, or with both hands until your eyes were popping out, while your feet were dancing around.

Another time when we had really been goofing out on the drill field they got us back into our living area and said, "Right, everybody into one billet, move. Ass hole to belly button, let's get going." Everybody went into one billet and once inside, they said, "Right, squat thrusts forever." Everybody was down in the squat thrust position, up down, up down. Now this was a twenty-man billet and there were eighty guys in it. It was hot there in San Diego, about 100 degrees Fahrenheit. We were doing squat thrusts inside this tiny billet. The guys were coming down, kicking their legs out behind themselves, on to other people's hands. People were hollering at each other and the drill instructor was just standing there shouting: "Squat thrusts, up 1-2-3-4, down 1-2-3-4," on and on. That was another favorite little punishment. Another one was to have us hold the M14 straight out in front, palms down, until we were sweating blood and our faces contorting.

Air raid drill was another favorite punishment. We would be walking into the living area and all of a sudden they would shout, "Air raid!" Everyone had to dive into the sand, also known as the grass, then we would have to roll over in the sand and try to hide ourselves. Then they would say, " Right, maggots, back on the road! Let's go."

Emergency head calls at night. Sirens were heard all the time. To give you a typical example, if you had to have piss in the middle of the night, you would have to go to the drill instructor's billet. You had to leave your billet in a military fashion and march over to his billet. There was a spot on the wall where people had been banging for 50 years. You had to bang three times, bang, bang, bang, and you would hear, "What is it?" to which you would reply, "Sir, Private Barr, platoon1123, squad number four, position number four, requests permission to make an emergency head call, Sir". He would always reply, "Try again, maggot, can't hear you," and you would repeat the whole procedure. This would sometimes go on for five minutes or longer. Finally the drill instructor would come out and say, "What do you want, four eyes?" I would say "Sir, Private Barr, platoon 1123, squad four, position number four, requests permission to make an emergency head call, Sir." He would then pull your earlobe and say "Right, go, move!" And he would slap the side of your head. You would then wind up your siren, go "Whirhhhh" and off you would run to the head. You would hear sirens going off periodically all night. Now, once at the head, you would wind your siren down, do whatever you wanted to do and then go back to the drill instructor, still going "whirhhh". He might let you stand for 10 minutes, all the time hollering at the top of your voice. Then he would finally come out, and in his benevolence, would pull your ear so you could wind down your siren. Then he would smack you on the head and say, "Get out of my sight, maggot, you make me sick". You would then run off to your billet and crawl into your rack.

There were three men at that stage of my life who made me quake in fear. They were Platoon Commander Staff Sergeant Ross, Drill instructor Staff Sergeant Abels and Drill Instructor Staff Sergeant Lewis. Abels was a small Texan, Lewis was from Louisiana – a big guy, 6' 4" and a little heavy in the middle. He was the one that was the best in rifle drill instruction, and had been on the Marine Corps drill team. Ross – I don't know where the hell he came from. He was just big and mean. He also had big, ugly, Marine Corps glasses. By this time we had been issued with Marine Corps regulation glasses. When you were wearing them, they made you look more like a bug than a human being. These men impressed teamwork on us in everything we did. "Gung ho."

At the end of the day, we had our last cigarette if we had been good. We had taps just after 9:00 p.m., and we would recite something that went: "We are United States Marines recruits. Goodnight Chesty Puller, who was the greatest marine officer who ever lived." After goodnight we would say, "Gung ho, gung ho, gung ho." That would end the training day.

We received no news from the outside world. There were no radios, we ate no candy bars, there were no Cokes or Pepsis – nothing like that. You drank water or coffee or milk when in the mess hall and that was all. We had none of the luxuries of normal life. We were in the Marine Corps and what we ate, drank and wore was issued by the Marine Corps, even our razor blades – everything except our cigarettes. We could choose the brand we wanted when we went to the PX, and we were allowed to go once a week to buy Kiwi black shoe polish, the only type allowed. We were also allowed to buy one type of brush. Everybody's brush was the same, so that no one had any more than anyone else. Everybody was the same, everything was the same, even our way of thinking.

I remember picking up the lessons very nicely. I found out that my memory was working, far better than some that were not quite as intelligent as I was. There were a few young ones like myself and Baton, there were also some other 17-year-olds, but the majority were between 19 and 25 years of age.

One of my weak points was running. I was not a great runner, and a good way to find the drill instructor's boot in your ass was to fall out of a run. I do not recollect ever falling out of a run, but I remember sometimes falling behind. I would then have the drill instructor come up behind me and kick me in the ass to get me back in with the other guys. There was once a guy who fell out of the run altogether. The drill instructor said, "Right, mother-fucker, wait till we're on our way back." It was a three-mile run along the camp perimeter and we could look at the jets coming in and going out of San Diego airport. I remember the drill instructor calling cadence: we were singing, "Fucking civilians on the left," and then we would come around a corner, and we could see all the navy recruits hanging over by their fence, so we would holler at them, "They are squids," and other derogatory remarks. We never saw those guys running or doing any exercises. We sang songs like: "I know a girl up on the hill, if she won't blow you her sister will," or "I don't want a teenage queen, all I want is my M14."

Once back, he told the guy who had fallen out to dig a hole in the sand, which he duly did. The rest of us had to bend him over, hold his feet up in the air, and then we covered his head with the sand. "That will teach you to fall out of a run, you are a little girl." That was the mentality and funnily enough, it worked.

As far as being fit was concerned, I was fitter than I had ever been in my life. We did a lot of arm exercises and I could do 18 pull-ups, climb a rope in 30 seconds and do 60 push-ups. I had gained more confidence in myself.

We then had two weeks at Camp Pendleton. One morning we were shipped up there in cattle cars, with our rifles and gear. We were taken to the rifle range. During the next two weeks we would be snapping in and qualifying as riflemen. The emphasis put on this was very heavy. Every marine was a basic rifleman and every marine had to qualify as a rifleman or he would be sent back. Those were the worst, most horrifying words one could ever wish to hear, to be sent back.

The first day we learned all about setting the rifle sights, snapping in, how to squeeze a trigger, how to breathe and squeeze a trigger. There was a thing called "BRASS" in the Marine Corps – "Breath, Relax, Aim, Slack (take it up on the trigger) and Squeeze," and the shot would be a surprise it was supposed to be so gentle. They would say, "Don't jerk the trigger, Dippy, squeeze it. What do you do with your girlfriend's tits, do you jerk on them or do you squeeze them? Now, just treat it like a tit." A rifle was never called a gun. If a private did this, the drill instructor would tell him to take out his cock and repeat: "This is my rifle, this is my gun, this is for shooting, this is for fun." That got people over calling a rifle a gun.

For punishment there at the rifle range what did they do? We were living in big three-storey barracks and of course we were all the way to the top. They would tell us to go to the top and come down, go up to the top and come down. We would run up and down with the buckets – everybody had a bucket as well as their rifles. Everything we did now was with the rifle. Once on top there were anywhere between 50 and 60 racks in the squad bay, double racks. They would say, "Let's play fuck around the girls". "Fuck around" meant we had to jump over the top of one of the racks, then we had to get down on the floor and go under the next one. We did this regularly after lunch, almost every day until we went through the whole squad bay. If you can imagine what it is like to go over and under sixty racks, you will understand that you are stuffed at the end of it.

Once down, we would sit down and clean our rifles. We would do this sitting on our buckets. Keeping the toilet area clean was my responsibility. Everything had brass fittings, so all the fittings had to be shined and everything had to be spotless. The floor was cement, but it had been waxed smooth by brooms covered with T-shirts and Pledge, which meant we could slide through quite easily when we played fuck around and went over and under. It was well worth our while to ensure that the floor was smooth.

In the second week of training, we had to start shooting. We put dope on the rifle, setting the M14 sights. 'Dope' was clicking on the rear sights to zero in on the target. How we set them was by having a mechanical zero where the rifle was zeroed in and then at 100m you might have to be two clicks to the right and one click up. At 300m you have to be four clicks to the right and two clicks up. Then we also had a shooting book, once the rifle was properly sighted in. We would look at the book and see that at 400m you had to set the sites at two clicks to the right and two clicks up, or what was specifically right for your rifle. You had to then set it up to that and then sit down and start shooting. If you did not qualify on a particular day, that afternoon it was run around. You would have to run up and down the stairwell and it was three stories high. Once on top, you would have to go over and under the racks. "That's it, girls, let's fuck around." Over and under, over and under we went. Imagine if you can what it must have looked like with half a platoon of recruits going over and under the racks, running into each other, jumping down on each other – it was like a bloody circus. Then of course there would be another platoon also sharing the stairwell on the other side of the squad bay. They might be going up or coming down and we were doing one or the other, which meant everybody was crashing into each other. Quite often some pretty mean fistfights ensued. That was the non-quals, or people that didn't qualify on the range that day. If it was general punishment, it was also up and over the racks and it was quite something to see a whole platoon of 80 guys doing this. I would have liked to see it on videotape; it would have looked funny, but to us it was a very miserable, painful and nerve-racking experience, I can assure you.

By this time they were building us up mentally, because one day we would have the title of marine. They never called us anything like that. They never called us men: we were girls, ladies, maggots or any other derogatory name they could think of. We were still lower than whale shit in the ocean, but the bottom line was that slowly but surely the days were slipping by, and we were progressing ahead. Our marching and running was in unison, it was in tune. We were what they referred to in the Marine Corps, as the "Green Machine". We made up that machine; our platoon was operating like a machine now whenever we marched. There were still mistakes and there was still punishment, but looking back at the guys who were just starting, they really looked like maggots. We then knew how far we had come.

We had yet to unbutton our top button or blouse our boots, but the day was coming. Things like that made a great impact. They were building pride in us; they were making us proud to be in the Marine Corps, yet at that stage we dare not say we were marines. I remember the day before qualification on the rifle range. I did not qualify and a lot of other guys did not qualify either. So we had to play fuck around all afternoon. We ran up and down the stairwell and over and under the racks until we were red in the face. Some guys actually passed out in the heat. That night they took us out and made us run at port arms for about five miles, carrying that nine-pound rifle, and that was fairly common. We were calling cadence, "One, two, three, four, United States Marine Corps, kill, kill, kill, kill." Everything had kill on the end of it when we were running or marching.

The next day came. We had to qualify; nobody had slept the previous night.

This was the biggest moment so far of our time in the marines. If you did not qualify, you were sent back. I was worried. I had performed fairly well right up to the previous day, but then I began to feel more nervous than usual. We went out to the shooting range and had to start freehand at 100m, then back to 200m, 300m, 400m and 500m. We were shooting with open iron sights, peep sights if you like – we did not have telescopic sights. In the end I qualified, which gave me a marksman shooting badge (it was affectionately referred to in the Marine Corps as a toilet seat). It looked like a toilet seat. The next grade up was sharpshooter and then rifle expert. I was pleased that I had qualified and would not be sent back. A few guys in the platoon did not qualify and were sent back to the incoming platoon. So, with light hearts and feeling happy, we went out to the back of the squad bay so we could look out on to the Pacific ocean – it was that close. We sat there cleaning our rifles and prepared to be deployed back to the Marine Corps Recruit Depot in San Diego.

It was at this time when they called us down in the evening for "the smokers to burn one" that they called the whole platoon down. The instructor said; "Right maggots, you can blouse your trousers now." That was a big moment. We stuck our chests out and were filled with pride because we had accomplished something. We had qualified as riflemen in the Marine Corps and we were now allowed to blouse our boots.

When we arrived back at the recruit depot in San Diego, the shit started again. In the next two weeks we were issued with our greens, our full issue of uniforms. We started having "junk on the bunk" inspections. We had to lay everything out nicely on our bunks. The drill instructor would come in, find something wrong and throw it all on the floor then we would have to start over again. I'm afraid my stuff was on the ground most of the time. I never could get it right.

My military bearing left something to be desired. The drill instructor would see my cover on the back of my head, with the bill sticking up. He would grab the cover, pull it down and smack me on the side of the head and say, "You have got as much military bearing as a sack of shit." There was always something wrong with me at an inspection; I just never seemed to make the grade like the rest of the recruits. I would always have a wrinkle or a piece of thread hanging out somewhere. My boots always sparkled. Nobody in that platoon could shine a pair of boots like I could. The other thing that really upset the drill instructor was when he looked at my bunk in the morning. He would take a quarter, throw it on the bunk and it was supposed to flip over.

I'm afraid the quarter would just lie there on my bunk, as I hadn't pulled the coverings taut enough. I would find my bunk and everything on it flying through the air.

We had to mark everything with our names. They had given us these rubber stamps some time before to mark the few meager possessions that the Marine Corps had issued us. I remember Drill Instructor Abels saying, "All right, you bunch of Idiots, don't put the letters in the stamp back to front." There was even a little inkpad that came with it. So, naturally I got mine on backwards and we were not to check our own. He took the stamp and put it in the ink, put it on a piece of paper and there it was: D S Barr backwards. He put in the ink again and said, "Step over here." I did just that and he hit me square on, stamping my name on my forehead backwards. I found myself lying on my back in the sand. I was then told to wear that for the rest of the week. I got the letters into the stamp properly after that. I was not the only one that got that treatment: there were a few of us running around with our names stamped backwards on our foreheads. It was one of the only times that I remember our hats had to be on the back of our heads, so that everyone could see what a bunch of idiots we were.

Then of course there was footlocker inspection. They would look in our footlockers to make sure that everything was laid out the way it should be. Of course there would be something wrong with mine and everything would go flying out the door. I would then have to gather everything up from the so-called grass. I was always in trouble.

We were back to having the shit pounded out of us once a day on the pugel stick range. I do not think I ever won a pugel stick match, although I tried very hard. When we were marched back, we felt different; we were exhilarated with the position we now held in the marines. We would look at new recruits coming in – they looked like maggots and we felt like marine recruits. At the end of the day, when we said, "Goodnight Chesty Puller, gung ho, gung ho, gung ho," they would now let us say, "and we are almost United States Marines" – this was big time for us.

We were hungry all the time. We were on the go from early in the morning to late at night. There was adequate food, but it never seemed enough because we were always hungry. When we went to eat, there were always packets of saltine crackers on the table. So when we sat down to eat, everybody would help themselves to a few packets of crackers and put them in their pockets. Clean the tray at the end of the meal, stand in formation and get ready to be marched off to wherever. Once in the rack that night, we would start munching on our crackers – it sounded like a bunch of chipmunks. One night the door flew open, the light was put on and there were about half a dozen recruits in my squad with crackers in their mouths.

The drill instructor said: " OK, maggots, get up and out on the road, get your dicks in the dirt." There we were, rolling in the dirt, and everybody had to have crackers in their hands as well. The next day he said, "Everybody take crackers, we want each of you to have at least four packets when you go to bed tonight." Everybody stocked up on crackers and we went back to the billets. Of course we did not get a cigarette that night. We got into bed and the drill instructor made us open all our packets of crackers, crush them in our hands, and then sprinkle them on our beds. We then had to sleep in them. If somebody farted it looked like a dust storm coming out from under the blankets. That ended the luxury of munching on crackers after hours.

I've been asked, "How many recruits did you lose out of your platoon?" Well, there was once a guy who tried to kill himself, so we beat the hell out of him because he was not going to leave the platoon. Then there were guys with low motivation, so on Sunday when everybody was supposed to be taking it easy – the day was only going to be 16 hours long – they went to the motivation platoon. We could hear this platoon hollering in the middle of the night with the things they would do. I don't know what happened there, but the privates that had a day in it were motivated afterwards. If they slowed up, the drill instructor commanding the motivation platoon (they were all transients, in and out of different companies) would kick their asses to the point where they found the will to carry on. Usually when a private came back from motivation platoon, the stories he told after 24 hours in it scared the rest of the guys enough to ensure they did not go there. If you were not a motivated private – be sure that you were on your way to the motivation platoon. As it was, our series of four platoons was fast on its way to being an honor series. We were excelling at everything.

I never had the urge to throw in the towel, I was tired, fatigued, in pain sometimes, had the shit smacked out of me regularly, but my motivation never flagged for a moment. The biggest thing in my life was to be a US Marine – I wanted to measure up to those three men who were our drill instructors. They were the greatest men in uniform I had known up to that time and they represented something to me. They represented honor, straightforwardness, moral principles and the backbone of the US Marine Corps.

One guy tried to jump Drill Instructor Staff Sergeant Abels. To say the least, he came off very short. He was sent to Correctional Custody Platoon, and we never saw him again. There they really give it to the guys – we could hear them hollering off in the distance even at night. They kept those guys off in a separate compound. Who knows what happens?

The Marine Corps had ways to motivate you – those ways are long gone: none of them exist today, just as the pugel stick range no longer exists. The Marine Corps now train recruits with more patience and understanding. The drill instructor was a mean son-of-a-bitch in our day: he was a man you feared and respected at the same time. If you didn't, you would be flattened. They were not there to be our friends; they were there to build marines. There was a saying at the time: "The Marine Corps builds men," and I daresay that is quite right. They were preparing you to go to the other side of the planet to fight a war that was not our own, to do it successfully, and hopefully return in one piece.

Another question I'm asked is what we were paid during our luxury tour of the Marine Corps. We were being paid as privates in the US Marine Corps – $91 per month. That was not a lot of money for what we were doing, but we were certainly earning every penny of it. It was a dedication to the Marine Corps and all it stood for – it was not the money we were after. We wanted to do our job and do it well for many reasons. One was that we did not want to be sent back and another reason that we wanted to avoid the motivation platoon, a third reason was that if we kept on in this direction, sooner or later we would get out of the Marine Corps Recruitment Depot.

Time was going by and we were in our final week of basic training. We were now allowed to open the top buttons of our utility uniforms. It was a week of inspections. There was junk on the bunk – I was up all night getting ready for that one. There was someone who helped me, though; that guy got my bunk ready and I shined his shoes – or it would have been curtains for Private Barr. Then we had our final inspection in what we called "our peanut butter suits" – our tans. I remember an officer coming up to the guy next to me – Harlan Jeffers. He said, "Private, you don't look happy with things. What is the problem, what is wrong with you?" "Oh Sir," he said, "I fucked up in the last inspection." Now never say fuck in front of an officer. The drill instructor's face turned red. The private was doomed. He said, "Well, private, you have just failed this one as well," and they went on down the line. I was so pleased that when they got to me they did not ask me a thing. The officer looked at me with a disgusted look on his face. I know what he must have been thinking: "Well, it won't do us any good to throw him out and it won't do us any good to put him back – there is not much hope for this clown. We will just leave him alone and hopefully he will able to do his job for the Marine Corps." That was fine with me. I passed inspection, though I do not know how. The drill instructor leaned over as the officer went by and whispered in my ear, "Private Barr, you look like a sack of shit tied in the middle." This inspection took about one and half hours and we just stood there looking stupid. We had to keep our eyes glued straight forward and stand properly. We heard a thump in the back – one of the guys had passed out. He had locked his knees too long, which resulted in him fainting.

When the inspection was over and the officers had left, we heard the command: "Hippity ho, mob go," and we knew there were going to be problems – there was fear in our hearts. They marched us back to our billet area and shouted, "Air raid drill." Everybody had to jump in the dirt – still dressed in our dress uniform. "Right, roll around, on your faces, on your bellies, on your backs."

At this time there was no more "Oink, oink, pigs to the rear," because the fellows that had been going to the rear had been working as hard as the rest of us. They were hard muscle and bone by now. They looked 100 percent better than the flabby, fat boys they were when they had come in. "Oink, Oink, pigs to the rear," had been deleted from our mealtime rituals. Harlan Jeffers just happened to be one as well – he also stuttered, but he could also knock the shit out of you if he was upset about something. The alternative to "Oink, oink, pigs to the rear" (they were eating less because they had less time), was the Physical Correction Platoon. All they did, all day long, was exercise. They kept the hogs going, until they could be put into a platoon at a fairly high physical fitness level, so they could carry on with the rest of the men. We did not have problems with fat men in our platoon – the fat men in our platoon got their act together, lost weight and toughened up.

A few days before we graduated we found out that we were an honor series. A series is a company of four platoons and our platoon, 1123, was an honor platoon, same as 1122, 1121, and 1124 – so we were an honor series. This was a big achievement, and something to be proud of.

Two days before we were supposed to graduate, we were in the shower and everybody was hollering, grab-assing and carrying on, shooting shaving cream in each other's faces. We were on top of the world – in another two days we would be out of this and on our way to an infantry training, as marines. Some drill instructors walked by and heard all the noise coming from the showers and one of them stuck his head in and shouted, "Shut the fuck up in there." Somebody hollered back at him "fuck off." There was a deathly silence, except for the water running in the showers, and everybody had a worried look on their faces, wondering who had done that. The drill instructor's face left. He had gone and it was quiet – everybody was trying to get his clothes and just get out of there. The doors flew open and there stood Staff Sergeant Abel and Staff Sergeant Lewis, and they said, "All right, you bunch of septic old whores, get out. You want to play fuck around, we will fuck around. You think you are marines now, we will show you what you really are – you are still a bunch of shit maggots, you are still lower than whale shit in the ocean, you are not marines' asses. Get out." Everybody was about half dressed by this time and out we went. It was, "On your bellies, on your backs, down, up, down. Throw sand at each other." Sand was thrown in every direction and in the end he said: "Into formation and those who are not completely dressed, get dressed. You got 30 seconds." That little job taken care of, we went on to the parade grinder and marched around. The drill instructor then sat us down and said, "All right, platoon 1123 smokers, burn one." So dirty and grimy though we were, out came the cigarettes – it was always a pleasure to have an extra cigarette. Both the drill instructors were standing there and they said, "You ladies, don't ever get the idea in your silly stupid heads that you are marines. When the day comes that an enemy stands in front of you and tries to kill you and you kill him, that is the day you will truly be United States Marines."

Our days of basic training were over. We had another day and then it would be time to graduate. I remember the day before graduation we went to church on Sunday morning as usual. Now church on a Sunday morning was a place to go and sleep. We would listen to a dreary chaplain giving a sermon; in the meantime we were sleeping. It was the only peace we had at any time during the whole week – that hour in church. Even the atheists looked forward to going to church. When we heard the last "Amen," we knew the shit was about ready to start again.

If your family had come to the MCRD to see you graduate, you were able to have four hours with them the day before the ceremony. My mom and dad were there, my sister Mary Ellen, my cousin Mindy and most important of all to me, Kristine, my girlfriend. We had written to each other almost every single day of boot camp. I guess that is where I got the skills of keeping a daily account of what I was doing. Kristine was everything to me, and I was so proud that I was in the Marine Corps uniform. She was in her senior year of high school – she was younger than I was, although I would have been a senior in high school if I'd stayed. It was a very proud time to say the least. We were able to smoke cigarettes for the first time without being regulated and our parents also brought goodies and things like that – so we were just pigging out. I invited a few of my buddies from the platoon over for some cakes and things that my mom had brought. We were not allowed out on the parade grinder and we did not have base liberty either – we were confined to one small grassy area (real grass!) with our families.

At the end of all this I went back to the billets with the rest of my buddies. There some guy named Kirby said something derogatory about Kristine. I took offence at his comments so I hit him. He hit me and then we were in a fully-fledged fight, knocking the hell out of each other, over the footlockers and everything else. I came off short in all of this – I had a black eye and it was very swollen. In the end I had to find a way to do something about this eye. I could not graduate with a black eye the next day – my whole family would be there. So I lay down on the rack and tried to get some rest and hoped the swelling would go down. The afternoon passed and we had liberty amongst the billets. We could stay in our billeted area and we could smoke cigarettes as we pleased. It was a pleasant interlude, only in my case it had been ruined by the fact that I had been in a fight and I had not come out top. It would have been another thing if I had beaten the hell out of him, but I hadn't.

Anyway, the next day came – September 6,1969 – and we were to graduate. We put our peanut butter suits on; tan uniforms or summer dress and were marched out to the theater where they also had church services. All the families were there – sitting at the back, listening to a speech about how we had been pushed beyond what we thought was our normal endurance. They had taught us, built us up, torn us down and now we were to bear the title of United States Marine from this day forward. They also said something that I had heard throughout my boyhood and I was in fact to hear for the rest of my life. The base commander said, "Once a marine, always a marine. There is no such thing as an ex-marine. You people will share the title of United States Marine for the rest of your life." We were then formed up and they said, "Dismissed to base liberty of four hours." Everybody then threw their hats up into the air and that was it; we were now marines, as the base commander had just told us.

I could not have been higher, or more proud, black eye or not. I remember when I met up with my family; my dad asked, "What happened to your eye?" I said we had been playing basketball after we had split up the previous day and the ball had hit me right in the eye, and then I fell down and hit my head as well. There was my mom and Kris, my cousin and my sister, all looking and fussing about the eye. My dad just looked at me as if to say, "Bullshit, you got into a fight and were whipped."

Two days previously we had turned our rifles in and we definitely had that naked feeling of being so-called marines without a rifle. We had been married to that thing for the past six weeks. We were looking forward, not only to getting off MCRD San Diego, but also getting on with the job of learning how to be a combat infantry marine.

The four hours passed in bliss with Kris and my family. Some of my buddies came around – we were allowed base liberty, i.e. to go around the base, on the parade grinder, but not near any other area where the base personnel worked. At the end of the day I said goodbye to everyone, my mom and dad, Kris, Mindy and Mary-Ellen, and we went back to our living area in the billets. We removed our dress uniforms and the drill instructor called us for final mail call.

At the end of the final mail call he said, "All right, listen up, ladies. I have your MOSs" – MOS being military occupational status: what we were going to do in the Marine Corps for the rest of our enlistment. "Jones, 0311" – meaning infantry. "Jackson, 6114" – meaning helicopter mechanic. "James, 0321" – mortars. This is how it continued. Then he got to me and said, "Barr, 3516," meaning motor transport mechanic. It was a blow to me – I wanted to go and hide. It was an incredible disappointment; I was going to be a grease monkey, working on trucks, just the way I did at the service station. It felt as if I had been hit by a ton of bricks, I hurt so badly. It was the most disappointing news a person could possibly have – I was not going to be part of the backbone of the US Marine Corps. We will see about that.

The next day, after breakfast, we bade farewell to our drill instructors and were loaded on to trucks. I was never to see Drill Instructor Abels and Platoon Commander Ross again (though I did see Staff Sergeant Lewis at Da Nang airport when I was being shipped out of Vietnam about two years later). We were on our way to the infantry training regiment at Camp Pendleton, San Honofray. We arrived there a couple of hours later and the shit started again. We had our seabags on our shoulders and they started running us a mile or so to our living area – more billets, and they dated back to the Second World War. Generation of marines had passed through here, preparing for the art of war and conflict in other parts of the world. As we were running along, one of the first things that struck home was what happened when one of the guys goofed up or dropped out with a seabag on his back. The instructor would say, "Hurry, marine, hurry." They said it in such a way that it was humiliating – it would have been better if they had called us maggots again – we understood that. Now they were calling us marines, not to make us feel proud of what we were – they were humiliating us. In their eyes we were not marines. We had not stood up to the supreme test.

I was put into Mike Company,2nd Infantry Training Regiment (ITR). We spent the rest of the day cleaning out our billets, which were already clean. Then we were assigned our different jobs. I was to become a "hootch commander" in one of the billets. I was responsible for assigning jobs to people and they had to clean up in the morning. Our day started at 4:00 a.m. once again – we had to clean the billets and then clean out the big shithouse and shower down below. There were about two hundred marines in our training company.

The next day we were briefed on what we were to be learning and experiencing while at Camp Pendleton. We were then marched off and drew 782 gear – combat gear, everything from a canteen to a rifle and bayonet. Here, too, we were issued the fabled M16 A1 rifle – it was a lightweight rifle and it felt like a piece of junk after handling the M14 in basic training. I still feel that the M14 was one of the best military rifles ever manufactured.

Then it was time to clean everything, so we spent the rest of the afternoon cleaning up and that evening it was time to go out for exercise, a three-mile run. When that was done we were released to clean out the billets and settle in for the night, which we duly did. The next day our infantry training was due to start.

One of our troop leaders, a sergeant, was a pineapple, meaning Hawaiian – he was also a Vietnam veteran, and a nasty piece of work. Every one of our troop handlers were Vietnam veterans and the company sergeant gunnery was a Korean veteran as well. So the level of the people training us was actually quite high – they all had war experience.

The next morning we went to breakfast and the food was terrible, but at least we were not hearing, "Hurry, private, hurry, private." Things were generally changing. We were starting to hear terms like, "When you are finished with your training and you go out into the real Marine Corps, you will reflect back on what we are saying and I hope you do well." "In the real Marine Corps" was a sentence that we were to hear a lot for the rest of our training – anywhere and any time.

We were taught infantry tactics, running, shooting, using the M16, doing jungle lanes. I cannot remember in which sequence, but we were learning jungle warfare.

One of the more serious parts of our training in the ITR was live fire training. We were using our M16s in different exercises. One particular obstacle course we had was about 100m long – we had to crawl under barbed wire and there were explosives planted in different places. They would detonate and blow dirt and pieces of junk all over us. In the meantime there was firing over our heads – they wanted us to get used to the sound of the crack of a rifle bullet moving at supersonic speeds over our heads so we would have some understanding of what it was like to be shoot at. This was the reality of war, and preparation was very important.

Our days were also very long. During basic training our day had started at 4:00 a.m. and lasted until 9:00 p.m. – it was a full go day, but at the end of the day we were able to rest from 9:00 p.m. to 4:00 a.m. Whatever we did in the morning we would do again in the afternoon and again at night – we ran from thing to thing. We had meal breaks in between, morning inspection of rifles and so on. We would also learn different things in the classroom and then we trained – sometimes even at night until 11:00 p.m., 12:00 p.m. or even 1:00 a.m. the next morning. We would then have a final formation, have a cigarette and then it was time for "taps." Once again, we were up at 4:00 a.m., cleaning the billets, the showers, the toilets and then off to breakfast. After breakfast it was morning inspection of our living area, our persons and our rifle. Marines always have a clean rifle and a clean body. "Clean body, clean mind, twisted laces, twisted mind," was an old saying.

Whenever they called us anything, it was always "marine," but it was always with that snide, nasty look. We would of course answer to the name marine, never with any particular pride because of the way our troop leaders would say the word. They said it in a degrading way, as if to say, "Hey, worm, come here." In their eyes we were not yet marines. That was yet to come. Of the guys there with me, 80 percent would be going to Vietnam.

We started to feel cockier once in the 2nd ITR. If we got demerits, it meant we could not get a weekend pass. Weekend pass meant Saturday afternoon to Sunday afternoon, 24 hours. We were due for this pass after two weeks of very intense training. We trained for six days per week and on Sunday we had a bit of rest. We would shine shoes, do normal PT, have general harassment and then we would go and relax (if you could call it that).

Finally, our first liberty was to be granted and I remember preparing for this on Friday evening. I was spit-shining shoes. When you went on this liberty, you went in uniform and you had to get yourself cleaned up. We had inspection on Saturday afternoon, and if you did not pass inspection you did not go on liberty. I think I never looked better than when those inspections came around, but I still didn't look as good as the rest of the troops. I wanted to go on liberty, I wanted to go home and see Kris.

Anyway, we got ourselves all spiffed up and had inspection. Then they said, "Right, the following names have demerits." Needless to say the looks on some of the guys' faces were of utter disappointment. They had been under the impression right along that they would be going home as well. My only disappointment in the Marine Corps right now was the fact that I was to be motor transport mechanic and not an infantryman. I was learning infantry training and loving every minute of it: to me it was great.

Now I was going home to Kristine, in my uniform. I was so proud that I was in the marines, and according to her letters she felt the same way. Her father loved it as well. They sounded liberty and then I caught a cab (a big Cadillac taxi) that used to ferry marines from Camp Pendleton right up to Anaheim, where they had Disneyland, if the guys wanted to go there, or other points further north of Los Angeles. A bunch of us from Mike company and Charlie company got together. We all lived in the San Gabriel valley. There were eight of us and that was enough to fill a cab, which meant that we all got a ride out to San Gabriel valley, a good 120 miles from Camp Pendleton. Once there, I got out the cab in great spirits, I said goodbye to the driver, himself a former marine (over 20 years ago, and a Second World War veteran). I got off at the Arco service station where I had worked before I went into the service and started walking. Little did I know that years later I would be walking home right past that service station and I would be coming home from another army, or that I would be walking in a far different way.

When I got home I threw my arms around my mom and dad. We all rejoiced and it was great fun to be home again. I was so proud. I know my dad was proud of me too. I was not home for fifteen minutes and already I wanted to borrow the car. I wanted to see Kris. This of course disappointed my mother, because I knew she wanted me to be around the home. Anyway I got the keys to the car and I was off like a light.

Once over at Kris's home I remember going up to the door and knocking, tidying my uniform a little. She opened the door and her mouth just dropped open because she had not been expecting to see me. I stood there and had a big hug and a kiss from my girlfriend. That was a hero's welcome, as far as I was concerned. I was in seventh heaven. Then her father was there, beaming. He even shut off the football game. The Rams were playing somebody and probably losing. He came over and gave me a big handshake, welcoming me home. It really made me feel good. I was somebody now – I was no longer the high school kid. All my friends were doing their senior year and I was in the marines. I was learning the art of modern warfare, I was doing something with my life other than being tied to my mother's apron strings. To me this was the high point of my life. It was an accomplishment, something I had never felt in my life before. I was doing a man's job in something that was renowned throughout the world as one of the better military organizations. They told us this while doing our training but we already *knew* it was one of the world's best military organizations. Any of us would have argued that point right to the death.

Anyway, I had a blissful Saturday evening with Kris. I was her hero and I felt like one. I guess I did not spend as much time with my mom and dad as I should have done. Something else I was not used to – I was smoking cigarettes like a steam engine. When I got home that afternoon, Kris was with me. One of the first things my dad did – and I remember this plainly because he had never done it before –was to go to the icebox and got himself a beer and opened it. Then he got me a beer and opened it and then he set it down on the table. We sat down and drank a beer together like equals. My father and I never spent time together. I would like to have spent more time with him as a kid growing up, but he had odd working hours and then I started to work, so the time was never right.

Sunday afternoon, Mom and Dad said, "Right, we will run you down to the base." I put my uniform on again, said goodbye to Kris, my love, went back home, got into the family car and we drove to Camp Pendleton. My folks got clearance to go in and they took me to the San Onofre area and dropped me off. I was on time, went in, put on my utility uniform and then checked in with the duty NCO. Liberty was over. I relaxed for the rest of the evening – the guys who had been out talked about their time away from base. It had been four and a half months before we had any time off from the Marine Corps. It had been a very welcome reprieve. Some of the guys had gone out and had themselves tattooed over the weekend, with the "Devil Dog," a bulldog's face, with USMC under it, or a Marine Corps emblem.

On Monday morning, training started once again at 4:00 a.m. The training day consisted of live fire exercises, jungle lanes, and familiarization with the M16. The rifle was with us all day, all evening and when we went to bed at night, it was kept locked to our racks. The rifle was our friend, it was our wife, it was everything. It was the only thing that would save our lives in combat. Our instructors were instilling this into us every single day in ITR training. It was still hot and dusty in Camp Pendleton.

I remember there was a march that happened almost on a weekly basis. It was called Mount Motherfucker. I cannot remember how high this Mount was, but it was high enough. There would be many more in my life in the years to come. Whenever we climbed it, we had to put all our gear on, take our rifles, load our magazines with bullets, go down to the hill and up the mount in company formation. You just hoped that you were in the front platoon. If you were in the back platoon you ran up all the way. It was straight up, and showed the wear and tear of many generations of marines that had climbed it.

Once on top, the view was stupendous but they did not give us much time to look at it. They would run us right down again. When in training, if the instructors felt that way inclined, they would run us straight up the mountain again.

As far as getting into trouble was concerned, I was in trouble quite a bit of the time. I was still a worm, a 17-year-old kid, and I had more arrogant pride now than I did when I was in boot camp. My troop handlers were all corporals or sergeants instead of staff sergeants. They did not wear Smokey Bear hats either. They wore shiny helmet liners with the Marine Corps emblem pasted on to the front. I now felt more equal to these people, and one day I was to find out that this attitude was a mistake.

We had one sergeant, the "pineapple," tall, lean and dark of complexion, with a flat nose, and black penetrating eyes. He asked me something. My reply was, "What did you say?" He ran over to me, very quick, grabbed me and started to choke me. That was a favorite thing in the marines, choking the guys. He said: "Do I look like a female goat to you, that you call me a ewe?" "No, no, Sir," I said, "the sergeant is not a ewe, the platoon sergeant is Sergeant Pineapple," and I said whatever his name was. I cannot remember it right now. He was nasty and mean looking. He had seen his share of shit in Vietnam – he was the epitome of a marine sergeant and I was the epitome of a worm. I remember that day clearly – it also happened during basic training. If we referred to anybody as "you," it meant you were referring to him as a female goat. That was a good way to get your ass kicked. With ITR nothing had changed.

The instructors were always good for choking someone during training. They would run at us and straight-arm choke us, shaking the shit out of us. Well, there I was being choked and saying: "No sir, no sir." I was ready to agree to anything because this guy was likely to kill me. Anyway I had a more healthy respect for his swiftness and strength after that, as well as the fact that as far as he was concerned; I was not a marine although he used the word marine all the time. I was a worm and I was being treated like one.

Marines have a funny way of relating to things and I should have known better. You never refer to yourself as "I." You are a private in the United States Marine Corps and that is all we were, besides other derogatory things we could be called.

One thing they never did was call us late for a meal. We were always on time. Punctuality for meals was of the utmost importance because of the quantity of men that had to be fed – and quickly – in the mess hall. Meals were still six minutes: in, eat and out. There was no problem with fat boys, because of the amount of work we were doing. We would eat whatever they put on our plates, relish it and still would not gain weight. Guys like Harlan Jeffers had been bubble men at the start of basic training. They were now hard, tough guys: not people you would go up to and start messing with.

Mentally I still felt very proud of what I was doing, even though we were treated like dogs. That was just part of the Marine Corps. Everything had to be hard, tough. As marines, we felt everything we did could not be done the easy way. There was a saying in the Marine Corps, "There is a right way, there is the wrong way and there is the Marine Corps way".

We were very proud that we were referred to as the "Green Machine," because a machine has many parts and all the parts work together to do a job. That is what we were doing. We would still chant when we ran and one of the ditties went like this: "I know a girl up on the hill, if she won't do it her sister will, one, two, three, four, United States Marine Corps." We still screamed: "Kill, kill, kill," at the end of it.

Motivation was fine. We were not beating the hell out of each other now with pugel sticks. Instead, we were going through some other types of training. Basically this consisted of jungle warfare, booby traps and warnings about getting venereal disease. They would say to us: "Stay away from those Vietnam whores. Not only are their teeth black and ugly, but their pussies are black and dirty."

Every time I thought: "What am I doing here?" I would think of all my friends. They were seniors in high school – and look what I was doing! I was preparing for Vietnam, and that as a United States Marine. To me this was uplifting. No matter what they threw at us, we handled it; it rolled off us like water off a duck's back. We were tough, and becoming tougher all the time. Though our training was adequate at the time, nothing would truly prepare us for Vietnam except being there, and learning on the job. To us, though, it meant advancing towards the fulfillment of the so-called prophecy of being a marine and how to be a marine.

I will not say that everybody was as gung ho as we were. As I said earlier, there were a lot of guys who had volunteered for the draft. That way they could conveniently get out of going into the US Army and then to Vietnam. Then there were guys who did not want to go to Vietnam – perhaps they were married or had other plans for themselves once their two years in the marines were completed. Then there were a fairly good number of guys, like myself, who had joined the marines to go to Vietnam, and if we had any say in the matter we would be going as soon as our training was finished.

I was billet commander, and I remember that I had trouble with one fella named Cook. We would get up at 4:00 a.m. in the morning and everybody would turn to – everybody down to the shower for shit, shower and shave, and then back to the billet. We would then start sweeping out the billet, clean up, doing our thing. I remember that we had more brooms and better brooms than the rest of the company. I would go around at night, when the other guys were sleeping and take their brooms if they were better than ours. If they had two brooms, they would only have one after I had paid them a visit, which meant each of us had a broom and our billet was clean and neat. Then we would detail one or two men to go down and be part of the group that cleaned out the showers and the toilet area. Sometimes the guys would even want to borrow brooms from our billet – tough shit, Jack, no way! We guarded our brooms at night.

This one lazy fella, who was an African American, did not want to do a thing. I would go to him and say: "Get out of bed, Cook," and he would say, "Fuck off!" – typical of his attitude. He was always on the top bunk – then one day the whole bunk went flying on to its side, and he was on the floor after he had bounced off a couple of footlockers. The fight was on. I had started to take a strong dislike to this guy and I got the best of him. Before I went to the Marine Corps I had no feeling about black people one way or another. In the Marine Corps I did not like what I was seeing as far as what a black could do and get away with, compared to what a white could do. The long and short of this is that Cook went down to the duty NCO and told him what happened, and I was then told to report to the duty NCO. I told the duty NCO that he was a lazy son of a bitch and would not get out of the rack in the morning. He turned to Cook and said: "You are not going anywhere on weekends for the rest of your time in 2nd ITR, and if there is any more trouble we will send you back to 1 Company." I did not have too much trouble from Private Cook after that during our time in 2nd ITR.

One of our exercises was an all-night bivouac out in the hills, setting up defensive positions and things like that. One of the great parts about this was that we were about have our first sea-ration meal of combat rations. On the box it said: "Meal Combat Individual One Each." There were different types of tinned food. There was "beany weany," which was the best of them all as far as we were concerned. It was a big tin of beans and franks. There were also crackers in the rations, as well as chocolate and other goodies. There were beans and meatballs, which also wasn't bad. There were ham and lima beans, a little bit of fruit and a little of this and that. With all these different meal combinations that the Marine Corps had come up with, they even included two cigarettes. You might get Chesterfield, you might get Salem, you might get Lucky Strike. The unwary smoker would light one of these up. That person was in for a big surprise. You would put the cigarette, which appeared normal although had been in the box for about twenty years, to your lips, light it and draw on it. Suddenly your cigarette would disappear. There would be smoke coming out of your ears and nose, and you would be coughing and gasping. The cigarette literally disappeared with the first good draw on it. It would go right back toward your face and smoke would come out of every orifice of your body. It basically satisfied any tobacco urge you might have had. It was probably a joke thought up by somebody in the planning office – more good Marine Corps deals. We had a saying, "Another good deal from the Marine Corps, bend over, we will drive you home."

I remember my first C-ration in the Marine Corps was a can of ham and lima beans. Now, what is ham and lima? It was something that makes you fart. There was generally no ham. There was a lot of congealed fat, mixed up with some lima beans in a big tin. If you were hungry enough, you would eat it. There were little crackers, and these things were enough to make you fart dust because they were so powdery. Then of course there was fruit. By the time you opened the tin the fruit was so old it had all stuck together. The taste had some resemblance to fruit and also to tin can. Yeah, this was the only way to live in the marines.

Anyway, our overnight bivouac once finished ended up being more of a boy scout outing, except that when we got back we had our asses chewed out for something we had done wrong the previous night. Somebody had smoked a cigarette and the whole company was punished. We went out on a three-mile run just because some clown had smoked a cigarette. That clown of course never owned up to having smoked a cigarette.

Then at the end of all this, there was the graduation from 2nd ITR. We had to write examinations and I managed to pass mine, as almost all of us did. I do not remember anybody having any real problems, unless they were very stupid or slow individuals. I cannot remember the exact date we were to graduate, but I do remember this. They had a list of names of people being promoted to PFC (private first class), and they were calling out the names. My name was on the list to be promoted. It was a very proud moment for us, and we now had to get stripes sewn on to our uniforms. On our utilities we had a little black metal chevron, turned down, that we wore on each side of our collar. This was a big time for us.

We graduated, and then we were sent to the headquarters of our different school battalions. I remember guys that were on a four-year enlistment going to aviation guarantee (a school for aircraft maintenance) and being sent back east, but before they went they had a 20-day leave. Infantry with 0311 related MOSs were all going to BITs battalion, which was basic infantry training. That meant another five weeks of intense infantry training for them. At this time it really started to dawn on me that I was not to be an infantryman in the marines. I was not to be part of that backbone that had been drilled into us when we were in boot camp and in 2nd ITR. I, along with a few others, was to go to motor transport and we had to report to "25" area, which was the motor transport headquarters. When we reported in there we were told that the next course was only due to start the following month, so we were told to go on leave for 20 days.

Although the other guys were exuberant about going on leave I was not so happy. I was parting with a section of the Marine Corps that had meant a lot to me: the part where I was training to be an infantryman.

Anyway, I went home and had a very pleasant 20 days. Obviously most of it was spent with Kris. I picked her up every afternoon after school. I had a little money in my pocket. We had been paid a whole $200, plus back pay and – Holy Mackerel – this was a fortune for a fellow my age. It was an incredible amount of money!

So I enjoyed my leave at home and I can remember that it was marred only by one Saturday night, while I was driving home after dropping Kris at her house. I came past a park and saw a car parked alongside it. The park was right across the road from Edgewood High School. One car door was open and a girl was trying to get away, while a guy was trying to pull her into the car. I pulled up behind the car and the guy jumped out of it. I jumped out of my little beat-up Volkswagen. The guy went for me and I ended up hitting him first. Now I was a lean, and tough, or thought I was, anyway. We ended up in fisticuffs and in the meantime there was another guy trying to grab the girl. By this time, though, I had created the necessary diversion and she got away. I never saw her again, and she never thanked me. By this time I was fighting with these two characters. I had one guy on the ground and I was pounding the hell out of him. The other one then kicked me in the ribs and when he did, I rolled off the first guy, got to my feet and went for him. By this time the first guy was up and I was now fighting the two of them. I was afraid I was not doing a very good job. About this time, things just seemed to slow up. They realized that the whole situation was useless and that was to my very great pleasure, because at this particular point I was no longer on top of everything. One guy just said, "Oh, forget it," and they both started walking toward their car. That was fine with me and I went back to my car and drove off. When I got home I went to bed; a chivalrous deed had been accomplished.

Once back at Camp Pendleton I checked into the "25" area and started doing guard duty. I did a week's worth of guarding at night, in preparation for the mechanics course that was to start the following week. There was a difference now. I drove myself to Camp Pendleton in my little beat-up Volkswagen Beetle – it still had a caved-in roof and a front end and roof filled with putty and primer from when I had rolled it. I produced proper documentation to get it on the base and drove it to the "25' area. This Beetle was to be of great value in my life.

We would walk on post in a military manner as our 10 General Orders told us to do. I also made enquiries as to how I could get out of motor transport. They said that once I had a MOS, the only way I could get out was to reenlist for six years and I could not do this until my existing enlistment time was up. "Fuck you, Jack, you are stuck in motor transport." The idea of being in motor transport still stuck in my craw. It was something that I would never settle for. Anyway, I was now stuck with it and would have to see it through.

Motor school was six weeks long and I remember that it started around the first part of November. In this time I had to learn about servicing trucks and general preventative maintenance. I learned my lessons like everybody else and I do not think anybody failed the course. Everybody had a general mechanical aptitude. I will not say it was good, I will not say it was bad, but some were definitely better than others. I was not in the upper part of the class and I would say this because I lacked motivation, as well as the ability to be a mechanic. I am definitely not a mechanic.

So work we did, but of course we always had some pranks. Our cover "hats" were starched real nice and neat, and so it was a big joke to take some graphite grease and smear it inside the brim. That meant that when a guy put it on after a practical application class where we would actually work on a truck, he would feel something gooey. When he took his hat off there would be a big smear of grease across his hairline. We had a set of work boots and a set of highly shined boots. These boots would come off and we would wear our work boots while in the workshop doing practical applications. The other fun thing to do was to take a grease gun, stick it down into the toe of the boot, shoot grease into it and then put it back. The owner would take the boots, put them on and of course they would fit. He would then walk along and as soon as the grease had warmed up a bit, he would feel the gooey graphite grease had permeated his socks. The grease was now around his toes and all over the inside of his boot. This was great fun.

Another thing was high-pressure grease fittings. We would be working on a truck, and there would be some clown working on another truck with a high-pressure fitting. He would shoot a big wad of grease, about 15 feet across, to another clown that was working on the truck. You would hear the air escaping and then the grease would fly through the air and hit clown number one, while clown number two pretended to carry on with his work.

Another great bit of fun was drinking after hours. I was now learning to drink. We did not just sit down and have a beer. Everybody sat down and got drunk. This was nothing new to the older guys. They would drink until quite late. I remember drinking three or four beers and I would be pretty drunk. One day I went wild and ran right through the billet. The door was closed at the far end, so I crashed right into it. The door sprang open and I landed out in the mud at the back. I was a mess, to say the least, and that put me in bad stead with the rest of the guys for a few days. I never did learn to handle my booze. I was always an exuberant type of drinker. I was never mean drunk, just a clown, and sometimes I paid the price: I would have a hangover the next morning. But this was big time: just being able to walk down to the pub, sit down and order a beer, like a real marine. This was something I could not do when outside Camp Pendleton, and it was actually illegal to do it inside the camp, although a blind eye was turned to it. As far as the Marine Corps was concerned, if you were old enough to serve you were old enough to drink, as long as you behaved in a proper manner, which we rarely did.

We used to have some pretty good fights in the so-called "EM" club (enlisted men's) club. It was just a Quonset hut that had a bar, with a cold box behind the counter and all they served was beer. There was no hard liquor or anything like that.

We had every weekend off because we were in school. They wanted us to be refreshed and ready to go at school on Monday. For many of the guys it was a matter of coming back with a hangover. For me it was a time to make a little money. I would load five guys into that little Volkswagen, at $5 per head. I would take them up to Anaheim and drop them at Disneyland. These guys would then go and do their thing. I would pick two up on the way back: one was Schneider and the other was Disatel. Schneider, Disatel and I had all been in platoon 1123 at boot camp, and the same at ITR, so we were pretty close buddies. They were both from Louisiana; one from Lafayette and the other from Mamu. Our relationship grew.

I was offered $25 a load, and in those days it went a long way. It did a lot for Kris and me because it would pay for my petrol to get home, and pay for Kris and me to go out and have a nice dinner somewhere on a Saturday evening.

On November 10 the Marine Corps birthday celebrations were to be held in the Hollywood Palladium, and I bought tickets for Kris and me to go. She dressed up in her nicest dress and I dressed up in my green dress uniform. We drove the beat-up old Volkswagen down there that Saturday evening. There were colonels, officers, a brigadier general there. It was a gala affair and I think I was probably the lowest-ranking marine in the whole place, being a PFC and also a 17-year-old shithead. We got a table up on the balcony and they served us beer and wine. We were two kids and we were both in our glory, being treated like this. We took part in the whole marine ceremony that they had down below. This was most incredible affair that the two of us had ever been to in our lives. I remember dancing with a colonel's wife and the colonel dancing with Kris. She was dazzled by all of this. He was wearing his dress blue uniform, covered in ribbons, buttons shining; it was just wonderful. I am not a good dancer. I do not think I had ever danced before that evening. I felt so much like a man, I was so proud of being part of the United States Marine Corps. I was part of something that had real meaning.

The evening passed in mystical magic. Kris and I really felt part of something incredible. We drove home as if on cloud nine.

Back at our school's battalion, as the time passed into December we learned the mechanics of different types of vehicles that the Marine Corps used. We were under no particular pressure where guard duty was concerned, no pressure where physical fitness was concerned. We ran a bit, exercised a bit, but the main theme was learning how to be a good motor transport mechanic. I was passing my tests and doing OK in my training, but my will and resolve to do it were not the greatest.

I remember that one of the best things about the whole training time was motor transport driver training. We had to get a military license, and that meant we had to learn to drive the different heavy vehicles, i.e. two-and-a-half-ton "six by" trucks, which all had six wheels driving the truck. Then we also had to learn to drive the turbo-charged five-ton trucks. These vehicles can go under water and will do quite a few things. They were amazing vehicles. We did not only drive on normal paved roads. A lot of driving was done on dirt roads, which were numerous at Camp Pendleton. Just before the qualification, we had to take a written test for our driver's license and then we had a practical test. We drove during the day in different situations, and then we did a night drive on what they called cat eye lights only. We would have to follow the next guy, just by a tiny light mounted on the back of his truck. This was all tactical convoy at night work. Driving the trucks was the highlight of the whole course. It was quite interesting and a lot of fun to us, unlike learning to work on the damn things. I was not interested in that. I felt I might just as well be back at the service station again, only in a different set of overalls.

Anyway the day came and we graduated from our course. This was just before the Christmas holidays and we were given time off to go home for Christmas and the New Year. We were also told to report to our different duty stations at the end of our time off. My duty station was to be Weirs 37 at El Toro Marine Air Station, which was about 60 miles north of Camp Pendleton, towards Los Angeles.

I had a lovely Christmas with my mom, dad, the family and Kris. On New Year's Eve, Kris and I got into the old Volkswagen and drove down to the Rose Parade in Pasadena. This is a very big New Year's Day parade. We found a place to park the car off the beaten track and we spent that night petting one another in very intimate ways we had never done before. I was in blissful love. Our relationship had now spread from high school through into the Marine Corps. To me at least. it looked like a serious relationship in the long term.

The next day we saw the Rose Parade. On January 2, I reported for duty at Weirs 37, El Toro Marine Air Station. I had to go through the normal rigmarole and bullshit getting shots, checked in all over the base, doing this and that. Once at the duty station it dawned on me that I was in the real Marine Corps now. I was no longer in training. Life did not now consist of school battalions, infantry training, boot camp or whatever. We were now earning a living and I would be giving back to the Marine Corps what it had given to me (or some of it, anyway). I did not know what the future held on that base, but my main job was not that of motor transport mechanic. I now drove trucks.

Every morning I would draw a two-and-a-half-ton truck and would drive heavy parts back and forth to the different support companies or squadrons there at El Toro. I also delivered to Marine Corps Air Station Helicopter up in Santa Ana, another 15 or so miles further north. I used to make as many as two and three trips a day, and that filled up the day. Once back, I would shut down the truck, fill out my trip ticket and maybe go to the EM club or just go to the barracks and read a book. Sometimes I would go into town with one of the guys who wanted me to run him into Santa Ana or Anaheim. He would have to pay me five dollars. I was making extra money with my little car. That Volkswagen was a gold mine.

About midway through January our motor transport gunnery sergeant said: "All right, we have a quota for 15 people for RVN." (Republic of Vietnam, and this was the first time that I can remember it being referred in such a manner.) My hand shot up immediately, as well as some other hands – guys that wanted to get away from Stateside duty, guys that had just come out off training – they were all itching to go to Vietnam. This is what it was all about. War!

The gunnery sergeant took the names of all the people who had their hands up and that filled the quota nicely. We were then sent to the motor transport office, where we filled out the papers. Then gunny said, "Now wait a minute,

Barr, you are only 17 years old. You can't go over there right now." I replied: "Gunny, just let me go. By the time I am done with staging battalion, which is five weeks, I will be almost 18, and if push comes to shove they can put me on mess duty for 30 days and that will take care of my age". He started thinking about it and said, "Well, all right. If you want to go to hell, here you go," and he signed at the bottom of the form with the orders that had to be processed. These orders were then sent to company headquarters, and from there forwarded to the authorities, who would cut a set of orders for the Republic of Vietnam, RVN.

The rest of January was spent driving trucks, which actually agreed with me. The weekends were spent with Kristine, if I did not have duty. Our relationship was growing far more familiar, and it was a very beautiful time in my life where she was concerned.

In the first few weeks of February orders came down from Marine Corps headquarters that the other guys and I had been put on quota for RVN. We had to report to Marine Corps base camp staging battalion at Camp Pendleton. Things were now starting to happen, and moved at quite a pace. I could see myself going to Vietnam, which – besides wanting to be a marine – for me was the whole basic reason that I had joined the marines in the first place.

We then packed our bags and checked out of El Toro. The next time I was to go to El Toro I was to check out of the Marine Corps altogether, but that was still some time in the future.

Once we had checked out, we reported to Camp Pendleton staging battalion and were then assigned billets. In between all this we had a week out for the guys to go and see their families. I, of course, spent as little time as possible with Mom and Dad and as much time as I could with Kristine. I picked her up from school, and I was a big shit around the school. All my buddies were still in high school and now I was on orders for Vietnam. Word got round, and of course I was walking 10 feet tall.

Once I reported back to Camp Pendleton I was assigned to mess duty because of my age. I had to do this for 30 days. I took care of the NCOs mess. Mess duty was a seven-day-a-week detail, and you are supposed to catch a month of it every year. I was lucky, because I only caught one month the entire time I was in the marines. My day started at about 3:30 a.m. and I worked until about 10:00 p.m. It was a long, hard day and there was a lot of bullshit involved in it. When we were done with the meal, we would have to clean, then there was inspection, and then we would get ready for the next meal. This would carry on for three meals per day and at the end of the day we would have a major cleanup. We would scrub the entire area down: the walls had to be washed, as they had to be meticulously clean. By that time it would be late and we would just go and crash into bed. There was no break in between, just work for 30 days.

I had been feeling very poorly right from the start of mess duty, and three weeks into it I came down with pneumonia. I was then shipped over to Camp Pendleton hospital, which was all navy. It was like walking into another world: the Marine Corps being off on one end of the scale for being hard on you. The navy on the other hand, was not only professional but also very kind and considerate, both to your feelings and you as a person, something the Marine Corps does not seem to understand.

Once at Camp Pendleton hospital I was assigned to a bed. Everything was done by numbers. Three times a day the navy nurse would come in and say: "Everybody on your stomachs, leaning over the bed". Our legs would dangle over one side of the bed and our heads would dangle over the other side, and then she would say: "Start coughing," and everybody would have to start coughing into their cup, because everybody had pneumonia. When that was finished we would throw the cup out.

Now the routine in the hospital was this: reveille at 4:00 a.m. Anyone with a temperature of over 103 degrees did not have to get out of bed. The rest of us had to wash out the toilet area, mop and polish the floor with a buffer. We had a general field day, which lasted two hours, every morning. Then at 6:00 a.m it was breakfast time. I must say the navy feeds well.

One fellow across the way from me had visitors on a Sunday afternoon. This really slick girl and some other guy drew up in a brand new Corvette Stingray. (This was 1970.) This guy had been handing magazines around the ward and a few of them were Vogue magazines. This girl, wow, as sick as we were, we had our eyes on her. She was a real living doll. They visited with this guy for a while and later I went up to him and said: "Hey! How come you know people like that, being a shitbird private in the Marine Corps?" He replied, "Well, have you ever watched Get Smart?" (A TV comedy series.) I told him I had watched it and he said that his father was Don Adams, the star of "Get Smart". I could not believe this, and the story got around real quick. We then realized who the girl was – she was a model and also his wife. When I asked him what motivated him to join the marines, he said that he was having problems with his marriage. So instead of running off to the Foreign Legion, he joined the marines. I wonder if they are still married today?

Anyway, a few days after I went into hospital I received the news that Kris's mother had committed suicide and I asked for compassionate leave from the navy doctor. He agreed, gave me a prescription, told me to cough twice a day and then I got into my Volkswagen and drove up to West Covina. Kris's mom had shot herself in the bathroom one morning while the rest of the family was in the house. It was a very sad and tragic affair. I spent the next week with Kris. My mom and dad had gone on vacation and that meant I had the house to myself. Kris was with me more or less the whole time. I will leave it to the reader's imagination as to what went on. I was able to console her and be with her during the most crucial time of her mother's passing and her grief. At the same time we had come to love each other very deeply and we expressed that love in everything that we did.

I saw the family through the funeral the following week and then reported back to hospital at Camp Pendleton, where I stayed the next few days until they felt that I had recuperated sufficiently, and returned me to my unit.

It was mid-March when I got back to my unit and to mess duty, where I worked for the next two weeks. My mess duty ended up being about 37 days. I remember some of the guys in the mess and maintenance detail – there were some pretty colorful characters going on to our next step, staging battalion. There was Tom Burkett, who was as mean as a rattlesnake, and there was a guy named Copaci, an Italian. He was a giant, and also very meritorious in everything he did. He was already a lance corporal and had not been in the Marine Corps any longer than I had. When he told you to do something, he was the type of guy for whom you did it. He had good leadership capabilities. Then there was a friend I had met there, still my friend to this day, Kenny Prewett. Kenny and I hit it off right from the very start as drinking buddies, and we saw each other through many adventures while still in the Marine Corps – there at the staging battalion, in Vietnam and afterwards as well.

When our mess and maintenance was up, we moved over to another barrack area, where we were to live while doing our staging training. That meant five weeks' Infantry training, prisoner of war indoctrination, venereal disease indoctrination – you name it, we were going to get it all. Something that still stands out in my mind is the amount of running we did. We ran everywhere. The camp we were on was as much as five miles from the different training areas.

We had drawn M16s and all our 782 gear and were detailed into platoons and squads. Kenny and I were in the same squad and in the same platoon, quite obviously. I had a very difficult time when it came to running. Not only was I smoking, but I had not fully recovered from the double pneumonia – my lungs really hurt with all of the running.

We trained at jungle lanes. With some of the training we would have to run through an obstacle course, shooting at different targets. The course could be as much as two miles long. It was very grueling and difficult. We did this in squad tactics as well, with targets popping up. We started using real grenades and then of course there was combat town.

This is where the Marine Corps differed from other places where I did training. We would put suppressors on the rifle muzzles and we would fire blanks. It was still good training, but it was not the real McCoy, and it did not have the feel of using live ammunition. It did not put us on edge. We then moved on to a more serious part of our training. We cleared houses, and this was done with imitation grenades. The training was good as well as interesting, though live fire training, which I was to receive later in military life, was by far superior. The Marine Corps had a different way of doing things. I am sure they were afraid of the liability if people were killed using live fire exercises. I would remind the reader that the Americas were very divided, for and against the Vietnam War, the training and anything that went with military life. They would get stuck in and make a big issue out of anything. As far as I and most other marines were concerned, if something like that happened, it was just plain bad luck. It was better to spend a penny now and save many a dollar later because of the training. Though it was OK, it was nothing like the training I was to receive in later life. But of course, anything to placate the American public, because of the media. It still happens today.

The anti-war feeling was at a crescendo in 1970, like no other time. Some readers might have been a part of the protests then. The Vietnamese had gambled largely with the Tet offensive. The Vietcong threw everything they had at the US armed forces – in a military sense, very unsuccessfully. At Hue they lost thousands of Vietcong soldiers, compared to the losses of the marines. The Marine Corps had just kicked their asses. The thing is, this gamble worked in the long run because by 1970 the Vietcong's forces were virtually depleted, and we were actually fighting the NVA, which was the North Vietnamese regular army.

The North Vietnamese gamble was that through the liberal media and all the misguided American feeling about the Vietnam War, our leaders would be forced into doing something that would be beneficial to the North Vietnamese, like pulling out of Vietnam – and in fact this gamble worked.

There were two big factors that contributed to why America lost the war in Vietnam. One – too much media cover about the doings of the military. The media created an anti-war mentality back home. The media made politicians act. It also created animosity towards the government and the military service with all the anti-Vietnam, anti-military articles, and the Marine Corps was right in the forefront of their attack. This was because the majority of the forces were volunteers. When the quotas came in, many actually volunteered to go to Vietnam. We just had a different way of doing and seeing things. We had been put in the field to do a specific job and we did it. Our leadership was good from my standpoint. I had no complaints.

The second reason was the fact that the government of South Vietnam never could govern its own people. The government was full of corruption. They were generally a bunch of incompetent officials and the people of South Vietnam as a whole, as far as I saw them, were not loyal to anything but themselves. Looking back, how could they be any different, with such leadership? One might ask how they would keep Communism at bay if the Americans weren't there? The feeling that we were winning something, even back home, was negative. The people did not want the war because of negative media coverage and the bottom line is, we backed the wrong horse. If the South Vietnamese had had half the dedication and motivation that the North Vietnamese had to their cause, we would have won hands down within a few years of our arrival, and we could have been out and gone. As it was, things were not working out that way. The Marine Corps had been in South Vietnam for five years, and the US Army had been there with forces of varying size for almost 10 years.

Our training carried on and I was still having problems with running and my lungs. I was never a good runner anyway. Anything I attempt I complete through sheer determination, be it running, climbing hills or whatever.

Tom Burkett was in the mess hall once when one of the black marines jumped up with a fork in his hand. Tom said to him: "You are going to have that thing shoved up your ass about one minute from now, sport." The fellow still went for him and Tom Burkett grabbed that fork and he beat the living daylights out of the clown. Then he took the fork and poked him in the ass a few times. Tom Burkett was not a man of great humor but he certainly showed a different side of himself while knocking the crap out of that fellow.

I could see racial tension in the Marine Corps, something we had never seen in training. This was something new. We were seeing a black mentality and a white mentality in the Corps. The Marine Corps was the "Green Machine," the colors, green, crimson and red were ours and not black and white, which we were all beginning to see. I did not know anyone who liked what they saw, and it was to get worse in later years.

We finished our staging battalion somewhere around April 13 or 14, the day after my birthday. I was now eighteen years old. I remember that I went home that weekend. Our company had been moved to another area in Camp Pendleton, to a big barracks. I drove home in my Volkswagen. A few people were jealous about that car, and I had had a lot of trouble with the guys in the company over the past five weeks. Whenever there was time off, I would go back home to see Kris and my folks, whereas the other guys would be stuck there on the base. Then, if they wanted me to take them anywhere, they had to pay five bucks each, just to get in the car. I was still making money out of that car and this created animosity, but it was something I shouldered and just carried on. I was the guy with the car – the only guy in the whole company with a car.

I drove home that weekend to say goodbye to my family. It was not a weekend of great joy. At one point I was elated about going to Vietnam. I was going to do what the Marine Corps had trained me to do. I was going to be working at being a real marine in war, and I did not know what to expect. My dad did know what to expect. Being a Pearl Harbor veteran he had been right through the Second World War in the Pacific Ocean. He knew all to well the realities of war. Life held no surprises for him. My mother of course was apprehensive and Kris – well our parting was to be very sad.

I remember that my folks took me back to Camp Pendleton on the Sunday afternoon for our 24-hour lock-up. The rest of the blokes had not been out that weekend at all. I had been out because I had wanted to return the car. Everybody had been locked up and on Monday we were to be shipped to El Toro, to be transported to Okinawa.

We loaded the old Oldsmobile and drove down to Camp Pendleton. I remember that that Sunday afternoon was one of the saddest of my life to that time. I actually broke down and started crying. To this day I will not let my mother or father take me to the airport. I always get a friend to take me. I broke down and cried and I guess my drill instructors would not have been very proud of me because there is certainly nothing admirable about a guy sitting there sniveling, tears running down his cheeks. I was not happy like the day I left home on June 30. To me this was not an adventure unfolding, I now had an idea of what war was, and people died in war. I was being separated from my mom and dad, and I wasn't coming back in a few months; I was going to Vietnam for a year. I was so miserable and depressed – I was leaving Kris behind and I could not stop myself from crying. I must have cried an hour on the way down. I think my dad understood and I knew my mom did her best to keep a stiff upper lip – I was the only one crying in the car.

Anyway, we arrived at Camp Pendleton, at the area where I was supposed to report in. I looked down the hill and could see the rest of the marines lounging around the barracks. I very tearfully hugged and kissed my mom and dad and my girlfriend. My dad handed me a small pocket Bible. There was an inscription in the back that said, "Preston Guy Barr, entered US Navy April,1941." It had been given to him by his mother. Just under the inscription was another, and it said, "David S. Barr entered US Marines, June 30.1969." They got in the car and drove off. I remember Kris looking back at me as I stood there forlornly, tears running down my cheeks I wonder what she thought. Did she think I was just a sniveling little rat? I don't know. The pain in my heart was deep and heavy. I was about to face the real adventure of a lifetime. I was going to come to the very grim reality of what war was all about. There would be no more bravado: at this moment that was all stripped away. I was now entering another world, devoid of women, and the social life was something that dealt with the situations of war at all times.

Once the car was out of sight, I sat down on a log and looked down at the guys lounging around the barracks. I cannot remember which area of the staging battalion barracks it was. I had a cigarette and kind of composed myself and when I stood up, I stood up as a marine again. I walked down to join my friends, and to get my gear ready for the following day when we would be shipped out to El Toro. The rest of the afternoon was spent doing exactly that. We then had dinner and the lights were out at 10:00 p.m. that night. A lot of the guys had managed to get some booze and they were off drinking in the corners. I did not want to join them. I still felt miserable inside, but I also experienced a hardening process coming over me, a process I was to feel many times in my life from that point on.

The next day we got up, had morning inspection and breakfast, and then the trucks came. Our gear was all stowed on to the trucks and then the buses arrived. We got on to the buses and were driven to El Toro. There we sat in a hangar, allowed to go nowhere but the toilets. We were not even allowed base liberty. Later that afternoon a jet landed. I cannot remember what type it was; it was not a 747 or anything like that. It was not a fancy jet. The company's gear was then loaded and I remember USO girls coming along with big tables loaded down with cookies, cakes, coffee and stuff like that. It was a kind of a send-off I suppose. There were no bands and no fanfare. Vietnam was an unpopular and miserable war as far as the American people were concerned, so we were just leaving the United States very quietly, almost as thieves in the night. Quite obviously the only kindness and concern shown was that of the USO itself. USO means United Services Organization. They are a charity organization and they give small comforts to military men in far-off places or living and serving in adverse situations, within the United States or other parts of the world. Shortly after our cake and tea, we loaded on to (I think) a 737, and took our seats. This was the first time I had ever flown in an airplane. Once settled in, the plane taxied to the runway and we took off. We were on our way to Vietnam.

Dave, aged two, with Taffy – the family's collie dog.

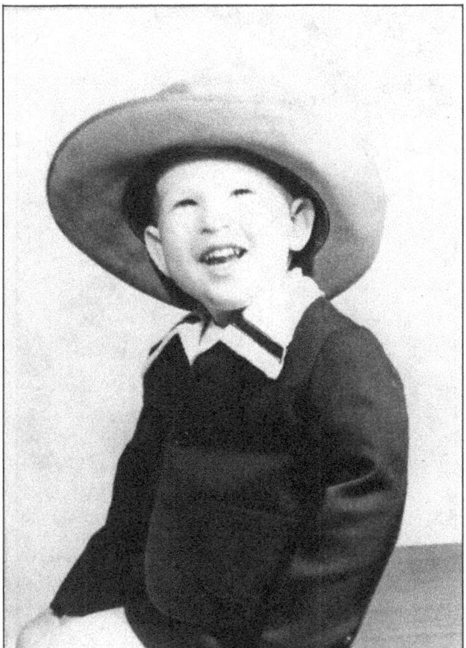

Dave, aged three, posing for a photo.

Dave, aged four, with his father, Preston; his mother, Lucille; and Taffy.

Dave, aged four, with a young neighbor in La Crescenta, CA.

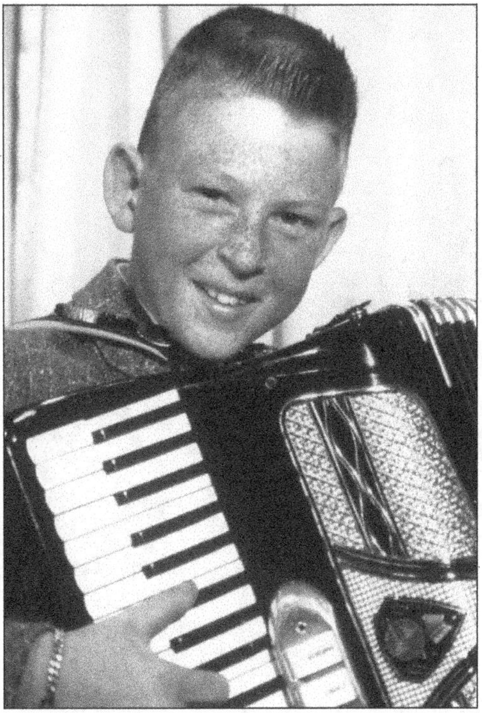

Dave, aged 10, playing the accordion – and not so well!

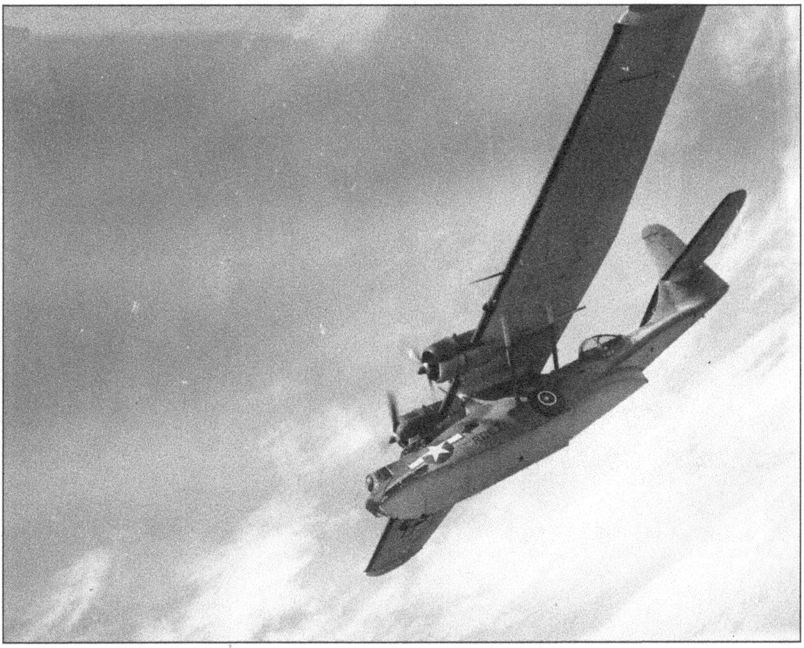

A PBY Catalina in dive somewhere over the Pacific Ocean between 1942 and 1945. This photo was presumably taken by Preston Barr from his aircraft.

Preston Guy Barr and his friend, Bill, standing in front of the PBY in the Pacific, 1943.

A crew posing in front of the PBY in the Pacific, 1944. Preston is in the middle of the front row.

Dave on Graduation Day at the MCRD in San Diego, CA, September 14, 1969.

Dave in his hooch after a brawl at Marble Mountain in Da Nang, Vietnam, 1970.

Graduation Day – September 14, 1969 at the MCRD in San Diego, CA. Standing from left to right: Cousin Mindy, Kristine Prause, Dave, Lucille Barr, Preston Barr and Mary Ellen (Dave's sister).

Dave and Kristine Prause going to the Marine Corps Birthday Ball at the Hollywood Palladium, CA, November 10, 1969.

Another photograph of Dave and Kristine going to the Marine Corps Birthday Ball.

Dave leaning on the external LMG of "The Greasy Rider" in Vietnam, December–January 1970–71.

Dave in front of the TV-13 "The Greasy Rider". This gunship had four external LMGs and two internal LMGs. The rocket pods could hold 18 2.75" 7 lb warhead rockets.

3
Vietnam

We stopped over in Hawaii to refuel and then our next stop was Okinawa, where we were put on to buses and transported up to Camp Hanson. At Camp Hanson we stowed all our gear away and the following day, started three days of indoctrination. We also received more shots for anything and everything you could think of. We had had these shots while still in the staging battalion and now we had them again in Okinawa – vaccinations and all kind of things for our upcoming excursion into Vietnam.

We were also getting prisoner of war indoctrination, plus highly focused VD classes. In one of the lessons I remember the instructor standing up in front of us and saying: "Gentlemen, you stay away from these Vietnamese whores. They are scum, they are dirt, and they are filthy. Their pussies are full of disease and misery. Some of them have got gonorrhea; some of them have syphilis. Some of them have gonorrhea and syphilis. Don't take a chance on these scumbags. Besides the fact they are ugly, most of them look like a hat full of burst assholes." I remember listening to all this and then he said: "Above all things, there is a disease you can get from these women. It is called 'the Black Syph'. 'The Black Syph' is a venereal disease and if you get it you will die from it. There is no cure for it because we don't know how to treat it."

Looking back over forty years to that time, I wonder what they knew about Aids then that we all now know today. The thought of it is actually staggering. "The Black Syph" had to be Aids by any other name, because if you had venereal disease at the time and had it treated it would not kill you. So it was quite an amazing revelation to hear this.

We had the rest of our lessons here and there, not thinking about this or that too much, only concentrating on the prisoner of war indoctrination. Fewer marines were taken prisoner of war than any other branch of the service – a minute number, and most of them were aircrew. The Marine Corps had a very good reputation for recovering its dead from the battlefield. There were far fewer MIAs (missing in action) than in the army. I think a lot of it had to do with the prisoner of war indoctrination we had received: how to act, how to escape and evade. I feel that the training, when it came to this particular area, was most efficient. The statistics certainly told their own story. For the amount of fighting the Marine Corps did, there were few prisoners of war or MIAs.

The reader might ask: "Were you still classified as a motor transport mechanic?" I just had another five weeks of infantry at the staging battalion. Every marine is a rifleman, every marine is an infantryman, and then he has his specialty. It is not uncommon to see a guy as typist in an office back in the United States. If when he got to Vietnam they did not need a typist, he slogged it out in the infantry in the jungles. They saw all types of combat action, just the same as everybody else. If they did not need cooks, you would draw a rifle like everybody else and you joined the Marine Division in the field.

I was still motor-transport bound and in the initial stages served in that MOS from the time I got to Vietnam. At the end of our three days' initiation, there was a lot of boozing and everything else, especially in the evening when they opened the EM club. We were dancing with Okinawan girls at the EM club. This was a great way to get into a big fight: guys trying to cut in on each other. Guys were falling in love with these Oriental girls immediately.

On April 20 1970 we boarded a C130 transport plane at Kadena Air Base. When the plane took off I was sitting next to the window and thinking I was flying for the second time in my life. This in itself was a great adventure for me. We flew down to Subic Bay in the Philippines, refueled and then continued across to Da Nang Air Base located in the Northern I Crops area of South Vietnam. We soon learned that the Da Nang Air Base was referred to as the "Freedom Hill" air base. It was freedom for some, because the guys that were going to fill that plane on its way out were going home and, conversely, it meant a one-year internment in the Republic of Vietnam for the rest of us who were getting off that plane. Once off the plane, we collected our gear and waited for what came next.

At Okinawa we had turned all our dress uniforms in and we drew jungle gear. All our utilities were for the jungle and we even had jungle boots issued – the whole nine yards. We looked quite different as marines now. For me, however, nothing would fit since I was still skinny as a rake. If it doesn't fit, it still fits the Marine Corps way!

I reported to the Induction Center located at Freedom Hill and was told that I would be assigned to Marine Air Group 16, Marine Air Base Squadron 16 (MAG-16/MABS 16) at Marble Mountain Air Facility. I was to report to the MABS motor pool there. I asked whether they had a lot of shooting out at Marble Mountain, and the guy looked at me in a funny way and said, "What the fuck do you care?" I was being stupid and replied, "Hey, I came over here to get into it," to which he replied, "Give it time, cheese dick, I am sure you'll get what you want."

The next morning a vehicle came from MAG16. It picked me up and took me to the motor pool, which was on a large asphalt lot with a tall corrugated tin building about 20 yards long. It was located on the west side of the runway, near the main gate. Once there I was given my normal check-in form and told to go all over the base: to the medical officer, to this place, to that place, draw a rifle and all the other things. That took care of the rest of the day.

Then I reported back to motor pool and was assigned to the C&I van – auto and electrical. I was to be working with a big fat marine, Sergeant Ski. I do not know his real name, but we called him Sergeant Ski. He was very knowledgeable when it came to his motor transport duties, a good mechanic and a hell of a humorist as well. His light-colored eyes always sparkled with mirth, looking out at you from a round, pale-skinned face. We used to joke and clown around quite a bit, but I always did my job for him and used to put in quite a lot of extra hours as well. I thought, "This is Vietnam, this is what it is all about." If I looked down the base beyond the south end of the runway, I could see Marble Mountain, quite a way in the distance. Everything around us on the base was covered by sand – MAG16 was right on the ocean. The Pacific Ocean was literally 100 yards away from the east side of the base. The base was flat and sandy, so if you wandered off the tar or cement you just waddled along in the sand. We lived in semi-bunker hooches, which had tin roofs with screens around the inside of the roof. Our bunks were against the actual bulkhead and the bulkhead consisted of sandbags down to the wooden floor. These places were lousy with cockroaches, the biggest, meanest cockroaches I had ever seen. They grew up to four inches long. These things would fly in squadrons at night and attack you. Waking up the next morning, we found cockroaches had bitten us. If you had a pack of cigarettes and had not shut them in a box, they would eat through the cellophane to get to the cigarettes. If you had a care package from home, you would open it up and cockroaches would come out of it like a Halloween movie. They would eat the food before you could get to it, especially if your mother sent you a cake.

I asked many questions of the guys around me in my hooch. One was a Mexican fellow named Jesus, another was named Mike and there were Joe and Bill. My first question was, "Do you guys have any action here? Are things happening?" We had drawn magazines, loaded them up, had our M16 rifles, and there was also a bunker dug into the ground right next to the hooch. They said they had not seen anything. Most of them had never been shot at. I asked whether they expected any big attacks, anything like that. All they said was "NO," and "Why don't you shut up, new guy." I was now a new guy, and a new guy is a cheese dick, a "pion" (pee on). I was still a PFC and did not have any particular rank. The rest of the guys around the hooch were lance corporals or corporals.

So I would work all day. I was trying to get into the war some way – this was a mixture of patriotism, a longing for adventure, and wanting to do as well as my father and uncles, who'd all been active in the Second World War. Whenever a convoy came up I would immediately put my name down to go, and Gunny would send me as an "A" driver. I would ride on an AvGas (Aviation Gasoline) truck in these convoys, with about 4,000 gallons of Avgas or JP-4 in the back. If we got into an ambush situation, our asses would have been grass, fried grass. It was pure adventure. We were out there driving through the countryside in Vietnam and could see the indigenous population out in the rice paddies, doing the daily labor they had been doing for centuries. There were burnt-out houses dating back to a grander era, built in French style. They were the ghosts of the past and I was to see things like this many times over in the future in my military service in different areas of the world. At the time it had unique meaning for me. It was an adventure, and around every corner I expected to be ambushed and get into a big firefight. At the time this was great, but by the time we got to An Hoa, where we dropped off the fuel and ammunition, we had not had a shot fired at us. An Hoa was one of the forward bases out on the edge of an area called the Arizona Territory, about 40 miles south-west of Da Nang. It was exciting going across the river with one of those underwater bridges that the Cee Bees (Construction Brigade) had built. We would be sitting in the truck and water would come up over our legs, up to our knees and the truck would just plough through it. The trucks had big snorkels, extended tubes going to the engine intakes so they could breathe, with fording valves. We would pull the fording valve and this would build up pressure in the engine and so keep the water out. Once through the water we would release the fording valve.

Out at An Hoa was a marine named Ron Justice, and I would help him with any vehicles that needed servicing there. Then late in the afternoon we would drive back to Da Nang and go back to the normal mundane routine.

Something I use to do: for 10 dollars I would drive the reactionary driver's slot. If the scheduled driver did not want to work that night (perhaps there was a poker game on, or whatever), I would take his duty. I would go out to the infantry company's hooches and ready a two-and-a-half-ton truck for a quick reaction out at the bottom of Marble Mountain, or elsewhere on the perimeter of the base. I remember that if we had a reaction, a bell would sound and everybody would rush out to the truck and climb in. By this time I would have the truck turning over and warmed up, I would hit the gears and as fast as we could, we would head for the main gate. The main gate would fly open and we would drive out on to the main road. We would drive one and a half miles or so out of Marble Mountain base and the grunts would deploy. I, being the driver, would then go into the bush with my M16 and wait for whatever was going to happen and nothing ever happened. I would drive out there 20 times in the next few months. I became very frustrated. We had listening devices all over the place. What we did not know –I only found out 20 years later – Marble Mountain was as hollow as an egg that had no yolk in it. We later learned that there was an entire enemy hospital and perhaps a battalion of North Vietnamese in the mountain, where they had lived for a number of years.

Marble Mountain helicopter base was unique. On the ocean side, or what we called the lower side, was the Marine Corps. Our living area left much to be desired especially our showers, which only worked sometimes. The hooches had tin roofs and were more or less open so, when the wind was blowing you froze your ass off when you tried to take a shower – hot water was a rarity much of the time. Conversely, the army was located on the other side of the runway. These guys had nice modern-looking helicopters and beautiful living areas with air conditioning in their hooches and other things like that. We could also see that their mess hall was better then ours, although it was quite a distance away. We also had a detachment of ROK (Republic of Korea) Marine Aviation as well as ROKMC (Republic of Korea Marine Corps). Their aircraft were mostly utilized for observation missions. Also, about five miles south of Marble Mountain, a regiment of ROK Marines were stationed right there on the beach.

I remember once being invited by a friend, a guy I had met in the EM club, to go on a CH-53 helicopter that was to go and drop a load of napalm the next day. The CH-53 is a massive helicopter. The blade span alone is 80 feet in diameter and the thing is higher and far longer than a two-storey house. It weighed over 43,000 pounds and could carry 38 fully-equipped combat troops, which should tell you how big it is. Anyway I wrote a letter to my mom and dad and Kris telling them all about this. I was off to war the next day; I was going to see big action and to pray for me and all that. The next day I was out on the flight line and got into this big CH-53. Their call sign was "Dimmer." We took off and flew to hover over the south end of the runway facing Marble Mountain, where we picked up a big load of napalm. There were about 20 55-gallon drums. The crew chief guided the helicopter over the load and, once the load was hooked up, "The Dimmer" took up the slack and lifted off as if it were only picking up a ping-pong ball. We then flew off into the wide blue yonder.

I do not know where we went or in which direction, but after we had been airborne for about 40 minutes we could see some Cobra gunships off in the distance. They were circling over something. They said they had found a big hospital complex. "The Dimmer" started picking up speed. By this time we were flying along at about 120 knots. We flew over the area where the Cobra gunships had been circling and pitched the load into the area. The napalm hit the ground but I did not see any great explosions. "What is this?" I asked, "it is not like television at all." It was then that I saw a Cobra gunship fly in behind us and fire a phosphorus rocket at the napalm. When the rocket hit, the napalm exploded into massive flames. Everything just went sky high. It was an amazing sight to see. We didn't take any fire, just turned around and flew back to Da Nang and that was the end of my great adventure in a helicopter – my first flight in a helicopter.

One of the first things I had done when I arrived there and started to work in the motor pool was to put my name on a list for a TAD (Temporary Additional Duty): gunner on a CH-46 helicopter. I was told I had to wait about eight months before my name would come up, to rotate to the 30 days of flight duty as a 50cal gunner. This was not good enough for me. I did not want to sit for eight months in that motor pool, farting around with trucks. The idea was the most depressing thing I could think of. I had to do something to change it. My staff NCOs in the motor pool were already taking notice of me and the fact that I would work longer hours. I was always out there taking over as reactionary driver because I wanted to get into a fight. Little did they know that I was also getting $10 a shot. I took over from the duty driver as well and sometimes ran officers through to Da Nang. We went through the civilian populated areas at night – this was quite risky. I would do anything because I wanted to get into the war.

I was creating quite a bit of animosity amongst the other guys there, and I was also drinking quite a bit in the EM club when I was not doing something at night. I can remember some of the guys bracing me at the club, saying I had better lay off trying get on to the TAD gunner because there were other people waiting. If not, they would do me a number. I of course told them to fuck off. A fight immediately ensued and I got my ass kicked up around my shoulders but good. This did not deter me at all. The next day I was at work with a big closed-up eye, skinned-up face and fat lip, and I worked as hard as ever. I was the reactionary driver again that night.

I wanted to be the marine that my drill instructor had told us about, not this rear echelon bullshit in the Marine Corps, working on trucks. I wanted to fight, I wanted to be in the infantry and if I could not get into the infantry, well, helicopters would do. Helicopters saw a lot of action. They were in it almost on a daily basis.

Our life was a bit better as we got more hot food and did not live in mud and muck, but it was also very tense in those machines. I still kept the pressure up on a daily basis and this was to go on for the next few months.

Finally, in July I was told that I had been put on quota for HMM-262, the Flying Tigers squadron, which was located right on the other side of the motor pool. I went into the CH-46 squadron as a 50cal gunner and was placed months ahead of other guys wanted to get there. I was highly elated, but there were also marines who were very pissed off at me as well. I was determined to do my best to serve actively in the war. I had been in Vietnam three months and hadn't had a shot fired at me. What type of war was this?

I still had silly ideas as well about why we were in Vietnam, and what we were doing. I still felt that it was a good and worthy cause. Actually, the ideology behind it was OK – the government we were serving was the problem.

Anyway, it was in July 1970 that I was told to report over to the squadron and that the TAD gunners were going to be taken out for gunnery training. We would be shown how to use the Browning 50 caliber machine gun. This is the weapon that the helicopter carried and there were two of them. We went up in the helicopter – this was now the second time for me. We flew out over the ocean, right there at our back door. Some pallets were thrown out the back of the helicopter. These pallets were floating around in the water with the helicopters circling the pallets. We were about 150 yards above the pallets and we started shooting at them. I remember that I did not do too well, and was very disappointed. I was greatly concerned because I knew they could cancel my orders and send me back to the motor pool ... I was heartbroken. When we got back on the ground after everybody had done their shooting, I knew most people had done better than I did. I was finally told to report on August 1 to Squadron HMM-262 as a TAD gunner. Needless to say, my relief was immense. Now I would get into the real war and see what the Vietnam experience was all about. The rest of July went by without incident and I reported in to HMM-262, as directed, on August 1. The night before I went, I slept in the C&I van. I was now doing this a lot instead of sleeping in the hooch as there were a lot less cockroaches, a lot less bullshit and a lot less drunks. Also, since the van was normally quiet and nice, I would even sleep there if I was drunk which, in all honesty, was more often than I care to remember.

I slept that night and next morning I reported over to the flight line for HMM-262, known as the Flying Tigers. I was then sent to the armory, where I drew a 50 caliber machine gun and was told to take it out to a particular helicopter. I lugged the 85-pound machine gun on my shoulder as it dug in deeper and deeper while I walked to the flight line, which must have been nearly half a mile away. Then I struggled for the next half hour, sweating like a whore on a payday, trying to get this massive gun on to the mount. It was about this time that another TAD gunner from another part of the Marine Airbase Support Group, a fellow named Macky, came strutting along. He was to be the gunner on the left of the helicopter. The best side was obviously the right side, because that is where the crew door is, and there was also a better field of vision than on the left side.

Anyway, Macky mounted his gun. He was a tall skinny fellow with a beak of a nose. We were to become friends and in the next 30 days we became inseparable from one another. We were a team – it was always Barr and Macky or Macky and Barr.

After that was done, a fellow named Mike McCravy came out. A short fellow of Irish background, he said he "was the helicopter crew chief and his name was Corporal McCravy." He said we had to do what he told us to do at all times, and this was only superseded by what the pilot said. We agreed to all these rules and he told us to help him open the helicopter cowling. By now it was 5:00 a.m. and we opened the cowling for pre-flight inspection. Once that was done we loaded everything up for Mike. He then ensured that we had done our job properly so that the cowling did not fly off in flight. The pilots came up and did their pre-flight checks and once that was done, everything was buttoned up. The pilots gave us a briefing as to what we were supposed to be doing during the course of the morning. We were to do resupply.

Every time we did a resupply or flew on any mission, it was done with four helicopters. There were always two CH-46s, and we were accompanied by two AH-1 Cobras, or Huey gunships, just in case we took fire along the route. Once we turned up the main rotors and had done all the pre-flights checks, we taxied out to the runway and flew off to Da Nang where we picked up a load of sea rations and ammunition. We then spent the rest of the morning going to Elephant Valley, Arizona Territory. There were little hilltop positions occupied by infantry as well as by many heavy mortars. Once there we would drop the load of food. Whenever we dropped it, all the little two-man tents would start flapping. Sometimes they would just fly off into the breeze – gone! The grunts had this mean, irritated look on their faces whenever the helicopters came in, bringing their resupply. They resented us, even though we were bringing them their food.

Once back at our base, and just after the helicopter had been shut down, McCravy told us to hold on. He had received another briefing: the helicopter was to go out on another mission. Eventually he said that we were to go and extract a recon team. "What is this?" "You just wait and see". That was our briefing.

Anyway, back we got into the helicopter and away we flew, as far as I know into some place around Elephant Valley. At the time I did not know the lie of the land, but this was all to change.

We flew out to this particular area and all of a sudden we could hear some shots being fired. The helicopter gunships were there already, blowing up the hillside. It had now become an emergency extraction. We had to get the recon team, which consisted of eight men, out. A ladder was dropped down from the back of the helicopter. The ladder was about six feet wide. It had steel rungs on steel rope. The recon guys climbed on to the ladder, the first man going up higher, then the next man and the next man. They would hold on to the ladder with one hand and hold on to their rifles with the other hand. We could actually hear them shooting from underneath us and suddenly there was McCravy slapping me on the back and saying; "Shoot, shoot, shoot, over there." For the life of me I could not see what I was supposed to be shooting at. He then pointed the gun and fired, all the time shouting: "Shoot there." I then started to press the butterfly on the big Browning machine gun, blowing away the hillside, all the time not knowing what I was supposed to be shooting at.

By this time the recon team was on the ladder and we could hear them screaming from underneath the helicopter; that recon "gung ho" kind of a growl they had. The helicopter turned away and I was still shooting with this big machine gun. McCravy walked up to me, hit me on the back and said, "Are you out of your mind? Why weren't you shooting?" I stood there looking at him and said I didn't see any targets. I looked at the area I had been shooting from and there were a few bullet holes above my head. I did not even know we had taken incoming rounds, let alone see where the enemy was. I do not know whether I shot anybody that day or not. I am sure I scared them with that big old machine gun, though.

We got the grunts back. They spent 15 minutes on that ladder in flight, all the way to the recon base in Da Nang. We landed, rolled the ladder up and as they were walking away, they turned around to give us a thumbs-up sign and their growl. These guys were the finest the Marine Corps had – the Marine Recons. They were tough, no doubt about it. They had a hell of a reputation as fighters.

Once the ladder was pulled up, we flew back to Da Nang and I remember feeling very downcast. I had done such a terrible job on my first day out in the helicopter. "Take fire, return fire." Well, I had done that, but if it had not been for McCravy, I would never have shot back at the guys that were shooting at us.

I spent the rest of the day cleaning the machine gun. There was sand everywhere, especially around the flight line as the helicopters churned it up all the time. Therefore it was important that the weapons be washed out and properly oiled.

I was not scheduled to fly any more that day, but later that afternoon I was ready and rearing to go. I wanted to rectify my mistake, being shot at and not even knowing it. I did not want to go back to my hooch, so I went to the C&I van where I had my sleeping bag rolled up. I rolled it down, lay down and tried to relax for the rest of the evening. I could not sleep very much.

The next morning was the start of something that was to become a flight record. The marines had just invaded Laos and Cambodia, and there was another massive invasion going on somewhere else as well. That morning, at 4:00 a.m. I reported to the flight line. I was told to draw a machine gun, and put it in the helicopter. Macky was right there with me. Then the crew chief came out, a fellow named Beech, and he did the pre-flight of the helicopter, and then the pilots did their pre-flight. We turned up and were on our way to pick up troops.

The CH-46 is a Helicopter Marine Medium, HMM. It has twin horizontal rotors that are synchronized and intermesh. It almost looks like a banana. There is a transmission in the front, and a main transmission in the back. It is powered by two turbine engines, mounted in the rear, and connected to the main transmission. They are marine green, and HMM-262 had a Tiger's head cowling on the tail that covered the engines and main transmission.

We then did an insertion of troops. It wasn't long and then the medevacs started. We flew the rest of the morning and on into the afternoon, just doing medevacs. During the day we took fire and returned fire. I was now in the war. I realized something I had not realized the previous day – I was actually in a war, a shooting war. It had not dawned on me with all the excitement of getting started, the noise and the flying in the helicopter, as well as the great disappointment at my own performance. *I was in the war.*

The next day we were in shooting scenes, off and on. We were inserting troops and then we did a resupply of food and ammunition. There were also medevacs. We were starting to pick up the wounded as well and that night we were told to move our guns over to another helicopter. We did night medevacs all night long. The medevac bunker was at the end of the 262 flight line.

We would sit there in the bunker, and our food was brought to us. Our turn was either all night or all day, 12 hours at a time – sometimes even a full 24 hours on alert. There was a bell in the bunker and if the bell rang, we would run for the helicopter and take the ties off the blades. In the meantime, the pilots would be getting their briefing. The crew chief would get the engines started and the main rotors turning. By this time the pilots would have had their briefing and been given the grid co-ordinates of where the medevac was. We would all get into the helicopter, taxi out to the runway and take off. We flew out over the I Corps River (this was our name for the River Han) and then off to wherever we were going.

Now, there were different types of medevacs. If the guy hit a booby trap then the site was not hot. There were medevacs where they had been taking incoming fire and that meant the zone was hot. They could have been mortared, machine-gunned, be under attack, you name it. We just wanted to get the wounded out. This was a pretty hairy night. The medevac bird flew at an altitude of between 2,000 and 2,500 feet, while the gunships flew between 1,000 and 1,500 feet above ground. We got out to this particular medevac, and there was fire coming into the zone. I am color-blind, so I could not tell which were red tracers and which were green tracers. (I should explain that I managed to hide my color-blindness. I could see camouflage when others couldn't. When it came to who was shooting at whom, I listened to the directions from the ground as to what direction the enemy fire was coming from.

They just said incoming fire from the north, so that when the helicopter went into the landing area and the wounded were being carried on board, I was pumping away on the 50cal. When we came out, whenever I saw a muzzle flash, I would pump about five rounds in that direction. Most of the time I would not see any more muzzle flashes after that. Now, I was definitely in the war.

If I were asked: "Were you not scared by now?" I'd say I was too stupid to recognize my fear. My greatest fear was not doing a good job and thereby letting the team down. That would always be my greatest fear as a solider.

The whole month of August was spent flying, mainly medevacs and insertion of troops. We did two more emergency extracts. We went in to pick up a recon team that was under fire. I do not know how many times I pressed the firing butterfly on that 50 caliber Browning, but it was plenty. I also do not know how many rounds came whistling through the helicopter, but I knew what they sounded like by now. They made a sickening crack. If you have not heard it before, you will not be able to identify what I am saying, but it put fear into your stomach like nothing else I had experienced in my life. By this time I was beginning to recognize what fear was, and how to suppress it. As the stories go, the main rotor blades of these helicopters mesh with each other when they crash. When this happens, the engine over-speeds, causing an explosion, and the entire helicopter goes up in a big ball of fire. Not one of the 46 people on board would survive. They were also known as Boeing body bags.

I remember one of our pilots was a man named Fred McCorkle, a captain. He was better known as "Crazy Fred McCorkle." He had dark hair, penetrating eyes, and radiated confidence. With that, one still felt that this was a man who would get a job done quick and in a professional manner. Look out for Crazy Fred. He had quite an illustrious flying record behind him as far as Vietnam was concerned. I remember that whenever we flew with this man he threw the helicopter all around the sky. You might be standing there holding on to the machine gun and suddenly you would be crushed against the wall of the helicopter if he had made a hard turn. He was an incredible pilot, to say the least, and whenever we were flying with him, we knew we would pick up gun time. As a footnote, Captain McCorkle went on to become a lieutenant general and was the senior aviator in the Marine Corps when he retired in the late 1990s.

The month of August had no particular daytime and no particular nighttime – it was just light and dark. Macky and I were beyond fatigue. Sometimes even my teeth ached, I was so tired, but I felt that by now I was a marine. I had taken fire, I had returned fire and snuffed it out. This was what I was supposed to be doing in Vietnam. This was what I was supposed to be doing as a marine – fighting the war, not working on trucks (or screwing them up as I worked on them) back in the motor pool. We are all made to do different things in life but mine in Vietnam was not to be a motor transport mechanic. I am not putting anyone down for this. These people were needed as much as any other part of the team. Here I was excelling: in the motor pool I was not doing well. I was not a good mechanic.

I later started thinking about this. My father had been a plane captain (crew chief), on a PBY seaplane. He had also been a gunner. I was doing what my dad did in the Second World War, only I was on a helicopter. Funny, like father, like son. I found this quite amazing. At the same time I was very proud of the fact that when the day came and I went home – if I went home, this was still undecided – I could say to my dad: "Yes, Dad, I have done my duty, same as you".

I remember that I had my father's Bible, which he had carried in World War II. I carried it in my upper left pocket. I looked once again at the inscription in the back: Preston Guy Barr, age 17, entered the United States Navy, April 1941." Underneath this it said: "David Scott Barr, age 17, entered the United States Marine Corps, June 1969". This brought a tear to my eye. There I was with the Bible that went through the war with my father, and now it was going through my war. I felt very proud being in the Marine Corps, doing my job as I was supposed to as a marine. Not for the cause of stopping Communism. That was a farce, because of the South Vietnamese government.

It had long been apparent to me, as well as to most other marines there, that we were not in Vietnam to help the Vietnamese people. We were serving the Marine Corps and our fellow marines. We were helping the medevacs, we were doing resupply, close air support for our own, so that they could do their job and one day return home to the United States and be reunited with their families. That was our duty. Our duty was to each other: our motivation was to each other and to the Marine Corps. As far as the United States government was concerned, we said, "To hell with the United States government". They were doing more to defeat our cause than anyone else because the politicians weren't leaving the generals alone to get on with the job.

We had only heard the cowardly people on television saying we should not be in Vietnam and not be doing what we were doing. We called them "Kennedy types" after Ted Kennedy – we loathed him! We had this little television in the medevac bunker and we used to see people running around protesting, saying: "Get out of Vietnam.". "Do this and do that." Who are these scumbags who have never been to Vietnam? I agree with them in one sense: that Vietnam was a lost cause because of the attitude of the government we served and of the news media, but who were they to tell us to get out? Who were they who had never been there? It was something that irritated me at the time. It also made most of us feel proud of what we were doing. We were not doing it for the Vietnamese people – we were doing it for the Marine Corps. Gung Ho Together, the old Chinese proverb. Our feeling of being marines was very solid, at least for me. I looked at it this way. My friends had graduated from high school two months ago and at that time I was in Vietnam. What were they doing and what was I doing? I was doing a military man's job while they were worried about getting a job, or going to college.

Time was moving on. The month of August was passing. Macky and I were flying all the time. We were fatigued, and it was hot and miserable. When we got to An Hoa the temperature would be between 108 and 112 degrees and the humidity would be tremendous. Macky's tall skinny frame was always bent over his weapon, with his sunken, beady, dark eyes constantly moving, looking out over the barrel. He never fouled up. At times it was as if we were competing with each other. He was very intense all the time. He said he didn't care if he lived beyond 40. I thought that this was strange, and we argued about it at length. He felt that most people were worthless after 40. Maybe there had been problems in his family with his elders after they had turned 40? I wonder what he is doing today.

The hotter it got, the more difficult it was for the helicopter to fly. The helicopters had turbine engines and the more outside heat there was the less efficiently they worked, as opposed to the opposite when it is cold and wet. We flew medevacs, and we flew permanent routines picking up bodies but that was low priority. We only did it as long as it was secure. I was told about one permanent routine in which the body actually exploded in the body bag in the helicopter. It had been left a couple of days before it could be safely removed. Once up to 2,000 feet, the difference in pressure caused the body bag to explode. Maggots and shit flew all over the helicopter and crew. The crew chief who told me this said it was quite awful.

Normally, once we picked up a medevac we got out of the drop zone quickly. It was then time to try and relax a little. Usually we were so high up by that time that our guns were ineffectual. Then, if possible, we would try and help the Navy Corpsmen with the wounded. I would lean over them and try and give them some encouragement: give them the thumbs-up sign and tell them we would get them to First Med in Da Nang. They would look with woeful eyes, full of pain and there would be blood all over the place, sometimes a foot, hand or arm missing. I remember trying to give them some kind of encouragement. Little did I know that 11 years later, on another continent in another war, I would be lying on the floor, looking up at a crew chief. He was trying to give me the same type of encouragement, and he would have the same look on his face as I once had.

August was one long month of insertions in different places in the I Corps area, and emergency extracts of recon teams. When everything settled down at night we would be on medevac duty. We would sit there in the medevac bunker, waiting for the bell to ring. When the bell did ring, the crew members ran out to the helicopter By that time the pilot would have had his briefing and would also know what we were flying into whether it was a hot LZ or a booby trap or whatever. LZ means landing zone. From there the pilots would throttle up and lift the collective, which varies the pitch of the blades. They would begin to whop, whop, whop, and we would lift off and fly out of Marble Mountain. Sometimes the pilot would lift the helicopter and move forward at the same time so fast that our knees literally buckled. It was everything we could do to hold ourselves in the standing position over the machine guns. We would fly out over the I Corps River and on to the designated area where the medevac was. This occurred every night.

The whole month was just one experience of flying, up and down, day in and day out. It just never seemed to end. Macky and I were extremely tired. We had been flying more than the other gunners. We did not know how many missions we had flown that month, but we knew we had earned our wings. To get a set of combat aircrew wings you needed three "take fire, return fire" situations and one air medal, which was twenty combat missions flown. On the combat missions we did not have to take or return fire, it just meant going into hostile territory. By the end of the month of August we were called by the commanding officer of HMM-262 and congratulated for setting a flight record. We had flown four hundred and twenty missions during the month, and it had never been done before. He gave each of us a letter of commendation to put in our service records and thanked us.

When we parted at the end of our month together, Macky said a very unemotional goodbye, and went back to his duty station. I believe that he soon rotated back to the US, "The World," as it was referred to.

In the meantime, I had asked my gunnery sergeant in the motor pool if there was any duty I could go on in one of the helicopter squadrons, because I did not want to return to the motor pool. I was doing a far better job as a gunner than a half-way motor pool mechanic. At the end of August, I took my letter of commendation, with the number of air medals that I had received, and went to see the motor transport gunnery sergeant. He was very impressed, to say the least, and said, "Well, Barr, you have done a very good job. You have earned the right to fly; you did a good job. You have lived up to everyone's expectations here as far as the staff NCOs are concerned." I thanked him and asked him if there was any chance of going over to HML-167 – HML meaning Helicopter Marine Light to work there as a driver, instead of in the motor pool. I reminded him that I was not much of a mechanic. I wanted to spend the rest of my time in Vietnam pushing it right to the edge. He asked me if my military license was up to date, which it was, then he said he would get everything cleared and have me sent over there as a driver. He said I could check out of the motor pool the following day, which I happily did. They were, from the angle of bad mechanics, only too happy to see my ass go through that door for the last time.

On September 1, I reported to HML-167, on the other side of the runway, for duty as their squadron driver. The first thing I did after checking into the squadron, and moving all my possessions over to one of the squadron hooches, was to see the flight line gunnery sergeant. I asked him how long it would be before I could go on flight skins. He did not think it would be too long, and then I produced my letter of commendation from the commanding officer of HMM-262. He was very impressed with what he saw, and said that it would be within about two weeks. I would go for my first training flight in a Huey gunship.

Later in the month after I settled in as a driver for HML-167, one of our helicopters was shot down outside Da Nang and we had to recover some of the wreckage. They sent Top Alfred (who was a master gunnery sergeant) two other crew chiefs and me from the flight line out to Da Nang to pick it up. We had to drive through Da Nang's difficult areas. There were a lot of tin shacks and gooners (Vietnamese) everywhere. I remember that we picked up the tail boom of the helicopter as well as some other pieces – all that was left of it, apparently – and drove back to base. I was driving way too fast with the tail boom just hanging over the edge of the pick-up truck, a Jeep Wagoneer. I was wrongly driving very aggressively. I was responsible for other people's lives, the lives of those travelling with me in the vehicle. I was weaving in and out of traffic, just going like hell and I remember passing a truck. The tail boom hit the truck and it was pulled out the back. It was just lucky that neither of the two mechanics were sitting on the tail boom. They were sitting on the other side of the pick-up truck, so they were not hurt. The tail boom and the tail rotor gearbox were smashed to pieces on the highway. Top Alfred gave me a real verbal lashing, as he had told me to slow down and drive properly. He told me to conduct myself in a proper manner and not like a hooligan while on the road. Who the hell did I think I was? I was acting like a shit maggot recruit. I just kept saying, "Yes sir, yes sir." To say the least, I was so relieved that PJ and Bob had not been hurt. They were both top-notch crew chiefs. I will never forget that experience, because it was one of the times when my stupidity nearly killed someone else.

Some might ask, "What is 'HML', Helicopter Marine Light?" In this case, the Huey helicopters are "slick" with no outside weaponry and no more than two internal guns. They frequently carried a higher-ranking officer who controlled and directed missions from the air. There were only about eight gunships in the whole squadron. I never saw more than six Huey gunships in the air at any one time. It was not a big squadron, and I cannot remember exactly how many aircraft we had. I think it was something like 15. The old UH-1E helicopter had been around a long time and these things were definitely battle-stressed to start with. The Huey gunships carried four external M60 machine guns, which fired 7.62mm rounds. They also carried two rocket pods that were capable of carrying seven or 18 shot, 2.75 inch rockets, with (I believe) seven-pound high explosive warheads, phosphorus rockets, flechette rockets or high explosive rockets – whatever was called for at the time of the flight that the ordinance people could supply. So that gave us the capability of up to 36 rockets and the two internal M60 machine guns – one for the crew chief who was on the right side of the helicopter and one for the gunner who was on the left side of the helicopter.

I remember the first time I went up in one of these helos. These were single engine helicopters without anywhere near the power that the CH-46 had. As I have already mentioned, a turbine engine has a lot less power on hot days than it does on a cold day. On a hot day we would be carrying seven-shot rocket pods and not the 18-shot pods. That was all the helicopter could handle with only its 1,100 horsepower engine. It still carried all the rockets, and 10,000 rounds of extra ammunition, over and above what was carried in the ammo cans, which was an additional 2,500 rounds per side. That meant another 5,000 rounds for the external guns. With that, the helicopter was fully loaded and then there was still the four-man crew. There was the pilot on the right and the copilot on the left in front, gunner on the left and crew chief on the right in the back. We lifted off the runway at Marble Mountain and got about four feet off the ground. They then dipped the nose of the helicopter down and flew down the runway just like a fixed-wing aircraft. It was quite amazing. Down the runway they would go and at the end of the runway there was a fence, and a scrap yard we would have to go over. About 100 yards further down we would go over the bank of the I Corps River. Once over the river we were safe if we had engine failure or dropped to the main rotor turns. We could at least dive into the drink right there in the river, and we would have a reasonable chance of survival. If that happened while coming off the end of the runway, it was curtains. Once over the I Corps River we were pretty much out of the dark, but at the same time we could start picking up enemy fire.

We flew out over the ocean, threw out some pallets and started shooting at them. To say the least I did a pretty good job this time. I was starting to understand what aerial gunnery was all about. It was totally different to what we had been taught on the ground. I shot up some pallets, and it was great fun seeing what my shooting ability was like. Of course there was a lot more to learn and there were things we had to watch out for. These were Aerial M60s. They had no sights and a short butt stock. It was all Kentucky windage shooting. On a gun run at 180 knots you aim in one place and the rounds curve around and hit the target behind the point you are actually shooting at. The M60s had an ejection port on the right side of the weapon to eject the cartridge casing. If you did not watch it while on a gun run, you could be shooting forward, turn the gun towards the rear and – if not done correctly –the empty casing would blow back into the gun at a certain point. This could cause the gun to jam: what we called a "wind jam." If that happened you had all kinds of problems. It was difficult to get the bolt open and to get the gun back into operation again. We might be pulling G-forces because of turns being made at the end of a gun run.

By the time I got back I was ready and raring to go. I helped the crew chief work on the helicopter, whatever he needed, oil, cleaning the chin bubble or the windscreens (which the gunner was supposed to do anyway). After hours and after they no longer required the duty driver there in the squadron, I would go down to the flight line and work with the crew chief with whom I had flown that day. I would spend the evening working with him. After a day's flying we would often work all night to get the helo back in an up status.

Within a week or so of my training flights starting, we shot up a place called Monkey Mountain. It was alive with monkeys. We did some runs and were actually testing the helicopters. The NATOPS crew chief (the squadron safety crew chief) said we would go up and do gun runs so he could see how I handled the machine gun, make sure I could prevent wind jams, and handle the weapon properly in flight. I did all right and did not have any problems while shooting up Monkey Mountain. We were shooting rockets as well. The copilot was also getting shooting experience while testing the helicopter, and I was getting plenty of gun time. Anyway, when we got back the NATOPS crew chief cleared me for operational flights.

The next morning we were put on medevac duty and once again we flew over the runway, got our briefing as to what was going on at the time and then settled into the bunkers and waited. Sure enough, about an hour later the bell rang and we ran out to the helicopter. Once out at the helicopter, the gunner did not do much. The crew chief unhooked the main rotor tie-downs, and swung it free. By that time the copilot had arrived and took over. During that time the gunner and the crew chief waited. The copilot would now be turning up the helicopter and at the same time trying to get his seat harness on. By the time he would be in his seat harness, I would be closing the door for him then I would climb into my side of the helicopter. At this time the pilot would arrive and while he would be putting his harness on the crew chief would close his door, like a chauffeur. That done, the crew chief would get in the back, and the two medevac transport aircraft had lifted off and were gone. The gunships, being smaller and not as powerful, would soon follow. We would lift off and head down the runway for takeoff. We would cross the I Corps River and head out for whatever the mission called for.

I remember them saying that the medevac was out in Elephant Valley. By now I knew where Elephant Valley was, as I was far more familiar with my immediate surroundings because of the time spent in CH-46s. The pilot told us we were going into a hot "LZ" (landing zone), which meant that the transport helicopter was going into an area that was under fire. We would be distracting that fire from the helicopter going in to pick up the wounded. That was the whole job of the gunship. We had to draw fire away from the medevac helicopter and suppress the fire. About 15 minutes later we were flying over Elephant Valley – the helicopter I was in was flying chase at 1,500 feet while the lead helicopter was at 1,000 feet. We could see what was going on down below and we were also listening to the briefing the infantry people on the ground were giving us. They were saying, "From the smoke, 12 o'clock, 100 yards, we are taking incoming mortar fire," and so they carried on. This is what we needed at the start of the rocket run. The helicopter flying at 1,000 would perch and go in. Once he was done with his gun run, we would start in. When we lifted out of a gun run, the pilot lifted off to the right because the crew chief's machine gun was not prone to any wind jams and he could also see better. The crew chief would then fire down at the target and towards the back to cover the helicopter's tail. By then the chase helicopter, which was us in this case, would be perched at 1,500 feet, and would be rolling in with rockets. When firing, the rockets had a hell of a concussion. The pilot would fire them out of the pods. Now, I was the gunner and I was sticking out of the helicopter by at least a foot, leaning over because the machine gun sticks out. The crew chief and I would be firing forward: we would be firing 200-round bursts in unison. When the rockets were not firing, we were putting down a base of fire. We could not fire machine guns while firing rockets because the machine-gun rounds could hit the rockets, which meant that they would explode in midair. The pilot came in and rolled off to the right and when he did, the crew chief continued firing, all the way round.

By this time the crew chief would run out of ammunition. I would drop another 200 rounds into the crew chief's box. It was hooked on to the side of the machine gun and then fed into the weapon. That meant that the machine gun was out of action for only a few seconds before the drill was completed. I would slide across the floor and cut my knee on spend ammo links, though I never felt it at the time. This was the "real McCoy": we were in a real shootout. Within two or three turns around we had suppressed all the fire off the drop zone. The gooks had had enough. They had either run away or were waiting for us to leave. We kept up our base fire and got fire control instructions from the ground. In the meantime, the medevac birds had gone in and picked up the wounded, lifted off and were on their way back to Da Nang. Now the 46 picks up altitude quite quickly, and once it was above 1,000 feet it was reasonably safe. We carried on hitting the target, until the grunts were satisfied that they were out of danger. This is when we turned around and headed for Marble Mountain.

Our first job, once back, was to refuel and then rearm the helicopter. This took about 15 minutes. All the machine guns were loaded again, all the rockets were replaced in the tubes and then we would taxi over to the medevac bunker. Once back at the medevac bunker we would again sit and wait, and also clean out the helos. Sometimes we were back in the air within half an hour to do another medevac.

Once we were in the helicopter and lifting off, the pilot would nose over the bird and we would get going. At this point the crew chief and the gunner started arming the machine guns. To arm an M60 you put the barrel in and put the latch down that locked the barrel into the receiver. The next to be armed were the rocket pods. We would lean over and out of the helo, and connect a wire plug into the pod. This was actually a harness that went into the top of the pod and was screwed down. We then armed our own machine guns – that just meant putting a belt of ammunition on to the feed tray, and closing the feed cover.

This time we were off to another area of Elephant Valley. The grunts had uncovered a tunnel and then taken some casualties. We flew in, the low birds picked up the casualties and once again we shot up the area. By the end of the day, my ammunition expenditure from my own gun had been about 1,500 rounds. That in itself was nothing unusual for a day. I do not know how many rockets we had fired. The crew chief had fired even more. Once the gun run was over and the pilot turned out of it, the crew chief would be out of ammunition and he would be waiting for the gunner to drop another box in.

That afternoon, while on another medevac, the pilot pulled off to the left side, which was my side. Circumstances dictated this because we were up against the mountain on one side and therefore could not turn to the right. As he turned I put down a base of fire and then stopped firing because I did not want wind-jamming problems, turned the gun back and continued firing. When we got back to the hangar, Kubus, the NATOPS crew chief, told me that I had qualified and would carry on flying on the regular flights. I had done all right that day. I was very pleased to hear this and thanked him. I had been in actual shooting situations, taken and returned fire, four times that day.

Every day was not to be like this. I had to drive the truck during the day and that meant I would volunteer for medevac duty at night. I was out on medevac duty almost every night. Some might ask: "What about weekends?"

There were no weekends in Vietnam, just day in and day out. There was no Sunday, and no Monday: the days just run together. We were on call all the time. When did we sleep? We did not sleep that much. If we were on medevac duty, we might get about three hours' sleep a night. It would be a broken sleep as well, because sooner or later the medevac bell would go off. We would go out into the darkness and wind up the helicopter. It was quite eerie doing medevac at night. We would lift off the runway and go out over the I Corps river area – it was dark, black and we flew at a very low level. When we went out to a medevac, it was not uncommon for there suddenly to be a stream of green tracers going past us. The gooners were having a go at us, but we could not stop because our priority was the medevac and to get the wounded personnel out of the drop zone. If it was a permanent routine – meaning a dead man – we would not go out at night, and the grunts would just have to hold him until we could get out there during the day when things had settled a little. We would never risk a helicopter at night for a body, but for a live marine there was no limit to what we would do. All said and done, that is how I spent most of my time when I was not driving. I would work on the helicopter with the crew chief, learning about them. I was never good mechanically but I was trying to learn something. For what? Well, at that time I didn't really know.

Within a month or so of starting to fly with HML-167, I was racking up missions left and right. It was incredible. I would be working on a truck during the day and they would scramble a "Mission 80," which was alert. They might have a couple of helicopters sitting there with no mission to fly. The crew chiefs were kept down at the hangars and all of a sudden they would say, " Right, there is a problem out in Arizona Territory, let's go." That was it. I would jump into my flight suit, and run out to the helicopter with my machine gun, which I kept handy. The bird had already been pre-flighted and armed, so it was just a matter of the pilot coming out, turning up, and away we would go. We knew that if we were scrambled on a Mission 80 we were going into a shooting situation and this was quite interesting.

Another very interesting mission we had was called "Black Hammer," which was always flown at night. This was similar to Mission 80, only with roving gun birds and a Huey Slick armed with a high-powered searchlight. We often flew with an army OH-6 Loach, and all their pilots had different call signs. Two of the call signs that stick out in my mind the most are "The Mad Hatter" and "Night Scholar." Whenever I heard one of these call signs was flying, the shit would hit the fan. The Loach is a small helicopter with an observer in the back. The observer would be checking the area out with an infrared scope. He always found bunkers, tunnel complexes or gooks right out on the trails where there was no cover for them. When he had caught them in the open, they did not know they had been spotted until the big spotlight from the Slick was flashed into the area they were in. Then the two gunships, trailing higher – between 1,000 and 1,500 feet – started their attack. As soon as the spotlight was on, the first helicopter rolled in hot with rockets, aiming for where the spotlight was focusing on the ground. Sometimes we would actually see gooks starting to run for it, but it was too late because the rockets were on their way. Alternatively they would stand and fight, but by this time the first helicopter had pulled off its rocket run and the second helicopter would come in with machine guns. Now, with six forward firing machine guns, we were putting out between 4,000 and 5,000 rounds of ammunition per minute. The noise was incredible, and to see it from the helicopter with all the tracers going down was absolutely spectacular. There was only one tracer for every five rounds. The Loach would fly in an arc with the light beam on the area the observer was looking at through his infrared scope. In the meantime, we would keep firing at the illuminated area and back to wherever we saw muzzle flashes or tracers coming at us. One way or another, the gooks' bacon was fried, and the only way they could get away or to escape us was if they got into the tunnel or bunker complex.

Every time we flew with these Loach guys we would have contact, sooner or later, sometimes two and three times a night. The Loach crews were absolutely fearless. To say the least, they earned a lot of respect from us.

Every time the helicopter went on a mission over the I Corps River, we racked up a combat mission. It did not mean that we actually shot at anything, although this was almost a daily occurrence in the gunships. If we did not shoot during the day or in the evening of a particular day, we could end up in a shooting situation three or four time the following day, in a 24-hour period.

One afternoon we were called out to the Arizona Territory on a Mission 80. I remember being in the helicopter at the time when the crew chief came running and said: "Right, let's get ready to turn up … we are going out to the Arizona Territory." Gary Hughes was the crew chief I flew with the most. He had olive skin, dark eyes with very sharp facial features and was of medium height. Gary was one of the two most able crew chiefs that I ever flew with. He was always patient, quiet and professional in all that he did. The other was Mike Swiatecki. (last name probably misspelled). The pilots then arrived, turned up the helicopter and we got inside. We taxied out to the runway, pushed the nose over and flew down it. At that time we started arming the machine guns and rocket pods. I would always have a feeling of elation whenever gaining speed down the runway and it was always a rush to arm our weapons for the expected fight to come. It was something that would always excite me.

We got out over the I Corps River and the pilot said there was an area full of gooners that had been cornered in Arizona Territory, and we were going to nail them. The Cobra gunships were already out there giving them hell, but they were just about out of ammunition so we were going to take over the attack.

The lead bird went up to 1,500 feet and the chase bird got up to 2,500 feet. In so doing we had a longer run-in for what we were going to be doing. When we came to the area, we could see where the Cobras were firing and we could see fire coming back up at them. They had quite a good anti-aircraft battery going at the time. The Cobras cleared the airspace, and we rolled in hot and started shooting. I can remember the pilot could not pull off to the right, so he was pulling off to the left and it was up to me, the gunner, to carry on shooting. I was laying down a good burst of fire coming in and then I would stop firing until I could get the machine gun turned around and start firing again. Well, on the third or fourth gun run I had a wind jam. I guess I had become a little over-anxious and so jammed the machine gun. I grabbed the M16 off the wall, because I could not get the machine gun cleared, and while kneeling inside the helicopter I would fire long bursts. I was letting 20 rounds go at once. The brass on the ejection port of the M60 was on the right-hand side, and it was flying all over the inside of the helicopter because I was also inside. This was not so bad, except the fact that while using the M16 on one gun run, the helicopter suddenly became unstable. I thought the pilots had taken hits and that this was the big one we were going in. I put in another magazine and fired another burst, then another magazine. Then I heard the copilot saying over the intercom "That is enough, Barr! Stop firing, stop firing!" What was happening was that the hot brass casings were being ejected from the M16, hitting the back of the pilot's helmet and then going down inside the back of his flying suit. He was not wearing any skivvies (underwear), and the hot casings were burning the hell out of him. This was bad news, because I had us nearly taken out. The copilot's hands were all over the controls, his feet were kicking and that brought the helicopter into an unstable mode. By this time the pilot, First Lieutenant Yannessa, had the helicopter under control again and once he pulled around, we received extra support from our chase helicopter. When we got up to the perch, I was able to clear the machine gun again. That was one case of how I nearly brought down my own helicopter! The lighter side of the war is funny now, because we got away with it. The copilot on that flight – I will not mention his name – was from then on razzed by other pilots for being taken out by hot brass from his own gunner.

The helicopter had taken a few hits as well that afternoon. It was not uncommon to come back in and find the tail boom and other places in the helicopter had been hit. This was OK as long as nothing vital had been damaged. As far as the pilots were concerned, when we got down the copilot said to me, "Fucking hell, Corporal Barr, what the hell were you trying to do to us up there?" "Laying down fire, Sir," I replied. I doubt that I had been doing anything positive, but I was making a hell of a lot of noise and that made me feel better. Lieutenant Yannessa later told me that I had a confirmed kill on that one. I thought that we were going in, and was going to go down shooting. Thankfully it did not work out that way, and in the end it had worked out very well for all concerned. The pilots walked off chuckling about it all, although the copilot was walking kind off gingerly, because his ass and neck had been burnt where the hot brass had ended up at the bottom of his flight suit.

The pilots' seats were bulletproof, and they were quite heavy. The crew chief and gunner had nothing at the back, except that we sat over the ammunition. One thing we worried about was having our balls shot off if we took a hit through the bottom of the helicopter. We joked about this a lot, but it was a fear in everybody's mind. It was not uncommon to be flying over an area when all of sudden bullets would come flying up through the air, all too close to the helicopter. We would look at each other and know exactly what the other guy was thinking. We could have gotten the mother of all hemorrhoids or, even more alarming, lost our wedding tackle.

Whenever we were driving out in the city of Da Nang, we would come up to a stop sign or intersection and stop. Kids would jump out and say, "Do you want to fuck my mother? She is a virgin." "Sure," we would say: "I'm sure she is a very nice girl." We would then tell the kids to fuck off. At other times they would jump out and shout, "To give them money," which of course, we didn't.

It was a cruel land. They despised us, and I for one didn't care for them. We were not over there to win their hearts and minds, to hell with their hearts and minds, to hell with them. If they had been like their counterparts in the north, I might have had respect for them and have felt differently about them.

But all they were after was what they could get out of the GIs. I am sure that all this could have been different had their leadership been better, with true ideals rather than being as corrupt as they were.

I do not remember having any positive feelings towards the Vietnamese people at any time while in Vietnam. People were crammed together wherever they had a town. Shops and housing were one on two, and most of them didn't have good sanitation. The women would squat alongside the road and smile. They had "beetle nut" running down the corners of their mouths. I was told beetle nut had a drug in it that relieved the pain emanating from their bad teeth, but this probably caused even further decay. When they smiled their teeth were black and their tongues were black from beetle nut. When they spoke to us it was like looking into a black hole, which was their mouth.

While I was on convoy with the motor pool we did not stop to chat with the local Vietnamese. Then, as far as our daily routine in the helicopters was concerned, we did not have anything to do with the villagers, but I did have some dealings with the local people while driving for the squadron.

Most of the time I drove a truck during the day, but then the time came when they told me they had somebody else to drive the truck, somebody who had a license and did not want to fly. They then asked me whether I wanted to fly full time. I immediately accepted. I also worked on the helicopter with the crew chief. This went on for about three months, as they were short of crew chiefs until that December. They asked me, "Dave, do you think you could take a NATOPS crew chief test?" I told them I would do it, but did not think I would pass a written test: to which they replied, "Don't worry about it, let's just do the practical application." This was done with a NATOPS pilot and crew chief and once again the crew chief was Kubus, a medium height, curly-haired individual who had a slightly bent and shuffling walk. I wonder how he got through boot camp? By then, we had become very good friends as well. I remember that Kubus drilled me while doing the helicopter pre-flight on everything I needed to know about this, that and the other things. Then, of course, the pilot gave me a going-over. The difference between what had happened before and what would now happen was the fact that I would be sitting in the back of the Huey on the right side and we would be doing Mission 80.

It was not an hour later that we received the alarm. We ran out to the helicopter and prepared everything before the pilot and copilot arrived. The copilot came first and told us that we had a shoot-um-up out in Arizona

Territory again. The Arizona Territory was known as a free-fire zone, meaning that anything went, all was fair game. The pilot came, we turned up and were on our way.

Once there, our targets were some Viet Cong (VC) out in the open, and that's when the shooting started, with the pilot now pulling off on my right side. If you are in the lead, the crew chief also has to observe the "chase" aircraft. You look back and say: "Chase at six o'clock," "Chase at nine o'clock low," "Chase at three o'clock high." The pilot then knows that his maneuvers are limited depending on where the "chase" helicopter is, so as to avoid any chance of a collision. These VC were caught out in the open by the observation post in the area, and we went out and did a number on them. I do not know how many people were shot that day or any other day. We only received a positive feedback in one instance, and I will be coming to that soon.

Once the mission was over, and we were flying back to Da Nang, Kubus said to me: "Go out and recycle the rocket pod". What does this mean? You have to climb out of the helicopter on to the suppression kit (while flying, mind you), and go to the back of the rocket pod, which was a good five feet from the door or any other security. I held on to the suppression kit, leant over, holding on with one hand only and then I had to recycle the pod itself, then put it back on to the number at which it had stopped firing rockets. The reason this is done is that the pod had broken down and was making bad contact. By recycling it, the contact points were cleaned. Then I had to turn around, still while flying, go back to the helicopter door and crawl inside. We did not wear gunner's belts – they would didn't give one a great since of security, as you could just slip right out of them. I remember going out there without a safety harness at all, as there wasn't time to belt up before the next run in. If you slipped, well bad luck, away you went, yet I never heard of anyone falling off the helicopter. No wonder we held on for dear life!

Having done that, and finally getting back on the ground, we did a post-flight. The pilot drilled me a bit and the NATOPS pilot said, "Well done, Dave, congratulations." The helicopter I took over was TV-29. The Huey gunships of HM-167 had a red and black checkerboard on the front nose panel. Our mascot was a mongoose and our call sign was "Comprise!" As explanation, the mongoose eats Cobras and other snakes. The other gunship squadron at Marble Mountain was an AH-1G Cobra squadron so there was always friendly rivalry between our squadron and their squadron. There was never a problem between the crew chiefs and the airplane captains because their airplane captains did not fly in the helicopters. This was a point of irritation with those guys as well. Ken Prewitt was in that squadron (Kenny and I are friends to this day). The crew chiefs worked on them but did not go up in the air and do any fighting, only the pilots did, and they were officers. In the case of Huey gunships, the crewman worked on the helicopter and he also flew on it, so that helicopter was his life. I took over TV29 from Gary Hughes, who was going home.

A mission that sticks out in my mind was one that took place in early November, just days after I became crew chief. By this time I had also become a full corporal. We were flying south of the Arizona Territory in the Qua Son Mountains. It was raining cats and dogs and very foggy when we received a call for an emergency extraction of a recon team. They were in big trouble. So, with two CH-46s from HMM-263 (their call sign was "Peach Bush" – how they came up with that call sign I will never know), we flew out to the Qua Son Mountains. This was an area that was very mountainous and the mountains just went straight up, rock and jungle. We could see and hear the recon team taking incoming fire. They had been holding out there on their own for a few hours, and by this time their ammunition was practically gone. The "Peach Bush" helicopter could not land, so they dropped a ladder out the back and had the marines climbing the ladder as we were rolling in hot on the target. We watched them going up the ladder, and this amazed me because it was the first time I was actually seeing it from a gunship. The last man got on to the bottom of the ladder and the helicopter took off while those marines were still shooting away with one hand and holding on to the ladder with the other. I could see why they were the pride of the United States Marine Corps. As we flew away, "Peach Bush" flew into a cloudbank and we did not see that helicopter again.

We flew around, shooting up different targets, until our ammunition was depleted. By this time "Peach Bush" should have been well on its way to dropping off the recon team back at first recon headquarters, but there was absolutely no communication between the helicopter and our pilots. The other Peach Bush aircraft called and said there was a problem. For all intents and purposes the helicopter had just disappeared. We did not know where it went after it had flown into the cloudbank. Most likely the pilot had become disorientated and crashed into the side of the mountain. We did not know whether there were survivors or not. There was nothing in the Qua Son area besides the steep river valley and the mountains, which were straight up and down.

We returned to Marble Mountain, refueled and rearmed. It was now very late in the afternoon and we were then told to stand down. I did whatever maintenance was required on the helicopter and then we waited for any sign of communication from the helicopter that had picked up the recon team. The next morning we received word that another recon team had found it. It had smashed into the side of the mountain, killing everybody on board, including a lieutenant colonel from First Recon Battalion. The total of dead from the crash was 15, which included the five members of the helicopter crew.

The next morning we flew out to cover the recon team as they bagged up the bodies that had crashed with the helicopter. When everything was bagged up, another Peach Bush helicopter flew over with a jungle penetrator, and lowered a hook. The guys on the ground would hook up a body bag and this was taken into the helicopter until the miserable job was done, which took all day. We then handed off our mission with a couple of Cobras, which had flown out to take over from us when we ran low on fuel. It was a sad and miserable job to be sure, watching those body bags being lifted into the CH-46.

The cause of the crash was disorientation. It was assumed that the pilot became confused when he flew into the cloudbank. You can look through the chin bubble or windscreen of a helicopter and you just won't have any sense of up or down, left or right. The pilot must not have watched the artificial horizon on his instrument panel. He should have flown entirely on instruments. If he had been flying on instruments he should have known that his heading would take him into the mountain. Once the cyclic is pushed forward, the CH-46s in Vietnam could fly faster, with a cruising speed of around 120 knots. In an aerial accident, fifteen marines were lost coming out of a hot zone, and we still had to fly in that area in the future, in similar or worse conditions. We would be there again and again; day or night, in good or bad weather and the monsoons were now in full swing. That meant we would have three months of clouds, heavy rains and occasionally typhoons, which were something else.

During a typhoon, the US Army does not fly. It has nothing to do with them trying to get out of flying in foul weather, as they were as dedicated as anyone else in the service. The problem was they did not have droop stoops on their main rotor blades. A droop stoop is something that steadies and prevents the main rotor blade from dipping down and hitting the tail boom or the ground when rotating in high wind. So in high winds the US Army could not fly, and we then had to fly their medevacs as well. Flying in very high winds is not fun. Taking off in a helicopter when there is a 40-knot wind blowing is difficult, and then flying out over the I Corps River at night and doing a medevac when you cannot see in front of you is very demanding. The pilot would be glued to the artificial horizon and the ball, which would indicate the aircraft's flight attitude and tail alignment. He had to keep the ball within certain parameters or the helicopter would be flying sideways or off-center.

So, all through the month of December we flew day and night and, to my great relief, I had nothing to do with the trucks or motor transport. However, I was not really an aviation mechanic either. I could do the minor work, keeping the helicopter clean, greased, and checked over, but when something major had to be done, I was not capable (or authorized) to do it. At one time I almost killed a friend of mine named Gaha and the two pilots. (I think he later earned the Silver Star for something he did in a slick.) Gaha needed me to help him with tightening down a friction collar on the stack up to the controls on the main rotor. He got called away to do some other job. I also had to safety-wire it. I tightened it down, which was not a particularly difficult job, but I forgot to safety-wire it. That safety-wire or rather the lack of it, was not spotted on the pre-flight and the next day, when they flew the helicopter they had a hell of a beat (where the helicopter bounces up and down), so returned to base. They then realized that the friction collar, which holds down the whole bottom end of the controls for the main rotor, was only two threads away from flying off. The result would have been the helicopter going down. That afternoon the short-timers (people with 30 days or less in country) came to me and said, "Candy Barr [my nickname], you are a lousy mechanic." I thought to myself, No Shit. I also thought they were going to kick my ass up around my shoulders, which, I must say, I deserved. "We don't want to fly any more than is necessary, because we are short-timers. So you come back with a down or shot-up bird, then sign one of ours off, and away you go." I said, with great relief, "DONE!"

In return, for any crew chief that worked on my helicopter, I would fly for him. This was a trade=off for them helping me. It was also a way of making the airways a lot safer when it came to mechanical malfunctions. I was no longer doing heavy maintenance on the helicopter. I was always willing to fly and I was OK as a crew chief when it came to being in an operational situation.

About midway through December we got into another good shoot-out. Once again it was in the Qua Son area. I remember that my machine gun broke down altogether. The operating rod broke, and there was nothing I could do. I then hauled out the M16 and started shooting. I remember that the pilot was a Lieutenant Mike Morschauser. He was a graduate of the US Naval Academy Class of 1968, and a very good pilot. We were rolling hot, coming in lower and lower and at one point were only 200 feet above the ground. We were right there and could just pick our targets. We also knew that our targets could pick us much more easily at that height. Anyway, during the whole skirmish, I didn't watch what I was doing, and planted about six rounds through the helicopter skids. I saw a target out on the side so I fired at it, putting a couple of rounds through the blades as we turned. We could not see the blades and as the M60 was on a mount, we could only fire at a certain height, just below the blades. Subsequently I shot our own skids and our own blades. According to the grunts on a distant hilltop, we did a good job. Everybody was in an elated mood when we got back. A Major MacPhearson came out and asked about all the holes in the helicopter. I told him we were in a real shoot-out and when he asked how high we were I let my mouth run off without putting my brain in gear and told him we were below 500 feet. That is when he told Lieutenant Morschauser to report to his office. Lieutenant Morschauser was one of our best pilots, and was unerring in all that he did when behind the controls of a gunship. I later found out that the lieutenant had been restricted to flying on slicks, which meant a lot less action. For a man of his ability it was a waste, and I felt it was all due to my big mouth. I went to him and apologized, which he accepted as only an officer and a gentleman would, but I'm sure he did not want to fly with Corporal Candy Barr again.

Anyway, around New Year's time Bob Hope came to town. He came to entertain the boys. It was the same show they had done in Saigon round about Christmas day and now they were in Da Nang for New Year. Bob Hope was to perform on New Year's Eve and Lieutenant Morschauser ended up pulling duty on a gunship because we thought it would be a pretty good night for shooting, as well as being entertained by Bob Hope. I received two tickets but did not know who gave them to me. Because I had volunteered to fly that night, I gave them to two other guys, not knowing that Lieutenant Morschauser was going to fly as well. Sure enough, when I got down to the flight line I heard Lieutenant Morschauser saying, "Hell, I tried to get rid of Barr with those tickets, and I end up flying with him tonight. He was the one who got me grounded last time." I stood in front of him and said, "Sir, I am sorry, I will give you the best performance I can." He looked at me and realized that he was not acting like an officer and a gentleman. He said, "Right, let's go and pre-flight the helicopter." No more was said. The evening came and we were put on night medevacs. We flew over to the medevac bunker and relieved the crew there. I can remember that it was fairly quiet until about ten o'clock, when the bell rang. We ran out to the helicopter and started winding up. About this time the copilot arrived and Lieutenant Morschauser arrived shortly afterwards. The 46s had already taken off and we left shortly afterwards, arming the machine guns out over the runway while on our way to the Qua Son Mountains.

It was raining like a cow peeing on a flat rock and we were flying just above treetop level, as the clouds were too thick for us to climb above. We could see nothing except the occasional stream of tracers while on our way to the mountains. At a certain point we were told by radio to gain altitude. We climbed to 2,000 feet to get over the mountain peaks and we could see where a flare had been lit down below. It was obviously the medevac. It was a "dust off" medevac," meaning an army medevac. We went down, and immediately started taking fire from the surrounding area. I remember seeing the eerie glow of the clearing lights on the CH-46 as she went down into the drop zone while under fire. I could see her 50 calibre machine guns blazing away out of the two sides of the helicopter as we started rolling hot. We were in a fairly restricted area so our gun runs had to be short and it was just about this time that the low bird had picked up the "dust off" medevac. The clouds came down even lower, and we became unstable. It felt as if the pilots were becoming disorientated. Whether or not they were I don't know, but about this time I took the M79 grenade launcher (we had a box of flares) climbed out on to the skid (I was on a gunner's belt) and started firing flares. I would fire and eject the spent casing and the gunner would lean out and shove a new flare round in. I could not actually see the blade tips from inside the helicopter, whereas from outside I could see them from the glow of the clearing light, and I fired the flares under the blades. I thereby illuminated the area around us so that the pilot could start getting his bearings. He could just barely make out the mountains and other obstacles in our way. I leaned back over with the gun, and the gunner pulled out the spent shell casing and put a new round in. I then closed it up and fired again. This weapon is very versatile and has many different types of 40M rounds that it can fire. It was not an explosive round, but a flare with a little parachute on it. By the time we had fired 15 rounds, the pilots had enough light to see what they were doing. Though the pilots didn't say anything, I feel, maybe wrongly, that we were without positive direction in the same area we had lost the Peach Bush helicopter the previous month. We then gained altitude quickly, as our ordinance load was much lighter and enabled us to get up to 4,500 feet. We had been told that we would clear all peaks in that area if we flew in an easterly direction. Lieutenant Morschauser duly brought the helicopter around to a safe heading.

The 46 medevac helicopters had a lot of power. They had climbed straight up to 6,000 feet, and were long gone to the Da Nang hospital. We were now in a position to start flying east, which we did, and then we got back on course to our Marble Mountain base.

I remember that when we were done with these missions I would tune the Aerial Direction Finder (ADF) into the Voice of America broadcasting from Da Nang and we would listen to the music, but it would also point you in the direction from where the station was broadcasting. I remember that particular night they played a James Taylor song: "Fire and Rain". It was a beautiful song and quite strange, because James Taylor had lost the love of his life in a plane crash. It was a great relief to be flying home, though a couple of times that night we felt that we were at the end of the line, as we thought it was the big one. We had been flying totally blind, we did not know where our chase helicopter was, we were totally socked in clouds and we had fire coming up regularly from the ground. It was a fitting end to the year 1970 by the time we landed back at Marble Mountain. We landed after twelve o'clock, so it was now January 1971.

We flew day and night if the helicopter was in an up status all the time. Almost from the start, I flew lead or chase with a fellow named Mike Swiatecki. His helicopter was TV-17 and he called it "The Muff Diver." We had colorful names on the helicopters! My first was TV-29, and it was called "Pecker Tracks." Then I had TV-13, which I labeled on the side "The Greasy Rider" because I was always dirty. Depending on the seniority of the pilot flying it, Mike's helicopter would be in the lead, or mine. I flew a lot of the time with Lieutenant Yanessa, or if not him, Lieutenanat Dougherty.

Life was an endless cycle of up and down and work. Never let us forget the ever-present sound of rotor blades beating the air.

We did have respect for the North Vietnamese, the reason being their determination and dedication to their Ideology. If the South Vietnamese people had had half that, we would have been out of Vietnam in a few years and that would have been the end of it.

The North Vietnamese were the direct opposite. They cared about their cause and their cause came first. Their cause was to cast the Americans out and reunite North and South. In the end, with the help of our liberal politicians, the news media, the liberal populace of the United States and the poor performance of the South Vietnamese forces, they did exactly that.

There was another crew chief I had flown quite a bit with but cannot remember his last name – his first name was Don. Don was from Texas. He was a good solid marine, and that is all he ever wanted to be. He did his job well. He was a good crew chief and a good mechanic. I remember once when we were in the mess hall, we noticed that there were more and more black faces joining the Marine Corps. Why, I do not know. By February 1971 there was a lot of racial trouble on Marble Mountain, especially on the marine side of the base. The blacks did what was referred to as "the dap," which was used as the black power sign. They would tap their hands together and dance around everywhere. Well, this was funny for about five minutes. These people were not usually combat troops, although they all had training. They were truck drivers or some other rear echelon-type MOS. I remember that there was nothing but trouble and animosity with these people. There were many race riots in the enlisted men's club and going back a little, the night of the Marine Corps birthday – November 10, 1970. I was the youngest marine at Marble Mountain. The oldest marine, a lieutenant colonel at Marine Air Group 16, gave the youngest marine a piece of cake. I thought this was great. I was receiving the cake as the youngest guy in the whole Marine Air Group. It was not ten minutes after the ceremony when a major fight broke out. The MPs had to fire tear gas into the enlisted men's club. The whites were fighting with blacks. The blacks were in gangs, knuckle knocking, pushing the whites around. The whites reacted: we ended up with a riot and there were stabbings. My racial ideas were changing very quickly. All I, and many others, saw on the black side was jive blacks, not marines. To me the Marine Corps was becoming black and white, not the crimson, red and green machine.

I remember that Don and I had been out on a night of medevacs and we had had a very rough night. When we got back the gunnery sergeant on the flight line told us to go and get something to eat at the mess hall. Now Sunday morning was always steak and eggs. This was Sunday morning, and what a treat. We walked the half mile or so to the mess hall and got into the chow line. I remember there was a bunch of blacks standing in front of Don and me, knuckle knocking, the dap. The long and the short of it was that one of them butted in front of Don, and that was too much. Don grabbed the fellow and pulled him out the line and told him to get to the back of the line where he belonged. This is when the fight started. The cook took hot grease and threw it in another fellow's face. It was a pretty messy fight. In the end Don and I went back to the flight line – so much for our steak and eggs. We were a little more bruised up than earlier, but we felt good because we had also struck a few blows for what the Marine Corps used to be and was fast moving away from. We were then put on a Mission 80. The pilots came on to the flight line shortly after that, and we then had to go and fly a mission to Elephant Valley. Some infantry guys were in trouble and we went out to give them close air support, meaning we had to fire very close to our own troops. This can be nerve-racking because it is so easy to kill or wound one of your own people. When we arrived back at Marble Mountain, we rearmed. Our helicopter had taken a lot of stress in the shooting, pulling G-force. Elephant Valley is very steep, up and down, so it is more difficult for the helicopter pulling off than when flying in a place like Arizona Territory, which was southwest of Da Nang and much flatter.

Anyway, we then stood down for the rest of the day so we could work on the helicopters. The MPs came out to the flight line and told Don to go with them. I saw Don the next day when he down to the flight line checkout. He was on his way to Freedom Hill. Don had been in Vietnam for more than a year, to my knowledge; he was serving extra time. He was to be shipped back to United States, to be put out of the Marine Corps on an undesirable discharge. The Marine Corps was losing a good marine for the sake of that incident. So it was that very day I said to myself: "To hell with the Marine Corps. When my time is up, I'm getting out. This is not the Marine Corps that the drill instructors had taught me to love and respect." It was moving away from that very quickly, into a reverse discrimination-type situation and my feelings about blacks, almost from that time on, went through rapid changes. I was like many other white men in the Marine Corps who cared for its traditions and its history. I was now concerned that it was no longer the Marine Corps we had been taught about by our drill instructors and all the old marines I knew.

There is one other marine that I would like to talk about. Top Alfred was a master gunnery sergeant, supervising the entire hangar. He was in charge of the maintenance, ordinance, airframes and virtually everything to do with the helicopters. Top (a nickname for a master gunnery sergeant or first sergeant) Alfred was a veteran of the Second World War and also Korea. Top Alfred had been wounded in the Second World War, having been on a number of beach landings. He had been helicopter air crew on his second tour in Korea. He had been wounded in Vietnam when he crashed in a helicopter on his first tour. Before Korea he had been in the infantry, but since he left Korea he had been in the aviation department. Top Alfred was a solid marine, and the epitome of the title: "Master Gunnery Sergeant US Marine Corps." I remember Top

Alfred would fly every now and again. About three or four times per month he would go up regularly with me. There was no pretence about him. When he came out as a gunner, his rank fell away. He cleaned the chin bubbles, worked on the machine guns, cleaned loose brass, loaded – he did whatever was required of him as a gunner to help the crew chief, right down to fastening the cowling. I can remember that while flying, he would be right there at my side, as quick as lightning, his long frame and craggy face bent over the ammo can as he expertly reloaded my internal gun. Some of the gun runs, going in and coming out, would expend as much as 400 rounds of ammunition out of one gun. It could all be done in one second if your gunner was on top of things and Top Alfred was the epitome of the expression "A good gunner." I do not know what his first name was, but he was someone I had grown to respect very much during my time in HML-167. He left Vietnam in March 1971, went home to the United States and retired from the Marine Corps after 30 years of solid good military service, with three wars behind him. I remember the day he left the flight line: after saying goodbye to us there was a tear in his eye. I am sure that he felt the same as most of us about the way things were starting to change in the Marine Corps: changing for the worse.

There was another time when we were up – I was with Lieutenant Yannessa on a Mission 80 and taking fire from a few places. He came rolling in hot, as we were taking fire, and he was moving the tail to get them all. I was watching the tail rotor alignment ball and it was out, which would mean brass would hit the tail rotor and we'd need a tail rotor change. Once back at base, sure enough, there was a spent casing dent in the tail rotor. He walked away and was back in half an hour with a bottle of Johnny Walker Red. Good on you, sir! I shared it with the night crew while they changed the tail rotor. The next morning I was found – I had passed out – and relieved for the morning, while the crew went up with another crew chief.

Then there was a Major MacPhearson. He was the squadron safety officer, a bald-headed heavy-set major; I can remember one day he said, "Corporal Barr, we have a special mission to fly. I want you to drop the rocket pods off the gunship and take on an extra 5,000 rounds of ammunition for both the internal and external guns." There are, of course, four external guns. I did as he instructed, and it lightened our load considerably. I remember taking off from the runway. The copilot for this flight was Lieutenant Colonel Blank. Blank was the squadron commander and would fly every now and then on special missions, sometimes performing as the operational commander when our helicopter supported infantry in different areas. We were flying quite low over the water up the I Corps and other rivers. This particular afternoon we were very exposed at times, and suddenly the infantry would see us from the riverbank. They would tell us to come up the riverbank and over a specific target. We would pop over the riverbank and come down hot (shooting) on a designated target. By this time smoke had been put up by the infantry so we knew where it was safe to fire ordinance. In a matter of 30 minutes we expended nearly 20,000 rounds of 7.62 ammunition. These missions were always exciting because everything was done at super-low altitude and the gun barrels were smoking all the time. The din coming from the machine guns when all six were fired at the same time was something that is hard to comprehend. Major MacPhearson was, to say the least, a top-notch pilot. But so much for flying at 500 feet. Do as I say, not as I do!

There was one other pilot with whom I flew quite a bit, and the two of us got on very well. He was Lieutenant Dougherty. One of the missions we flew was a Mission 80. We were called out early in the morning and told that there were gooners shooting at medevac helicopters from HM-262 as they crossed a lake. (I think it was Spider Lake but I'm not certain.) The lake was located just below the north side of the Qua Son Mountains. When we found their boats, they were, as usual, very crowded – and this was a big mistake for the gooners.

We got the helicopters in the air, reached the lake and sure enough, there they were, but by this time they were almost on the other side of the lake. The lake was not that big, but their little sampans were not very fast either. We started rolling in hot with rockets, then suddenly we started taking fire from the far side of the bank. I raised my gun up and started covering us. As I was hammering away something felt loose, and all of a sudden the internal machine gun came free from its mount. I was still trying to suppress fire and keep from hitting the main rotor blades (It simply wouldn't do if I'd shot up our skids for a second time). Lieutenant Dougherty was turning the helicopter hard this way and that. There were targets everywhere and I was doing all I could to stay on one target or another. The lead aircraft was flown by Yannessa and he was using flechette rockets, like we were. That meant the enemy must have looked like pin cushions after we finished with them. After this, Yannessa got the nickname "Nails."

I soon ran out of ammunition, and while the gunner was tied up on the other side, I reloaded and got the gun back in the mount. I had started firing again when, once again, it came off the mount. Then the weapon ran away, meaning I couldn't stop it from firing and, by this time, my hand was out on the front of the gas tubes, my glove was smoking and my hand was on fire. I was just trying to keep the rounds from the machine gun on the target and also trying to keep it from shooting us out of the air altogether. I heard Lieutenant Dougherty as he pulled off again: "Stop, hold your fire, Barr, hold your fire, fucking hell, hold your fire!" I was just doing everything to hold the gun and finally it ran out of ammunition. I dropped it to the floor shaking my hand and trying to get my smoking, very hot glove off my hand. At this time he said, "What the hell is going on back there?" I told him I had had a runaway gun and asked him if he wanted fire from that side of the helicopter or not? I almost shoved my smoking hand in his face! Then he could have all the fire that he wanted. I also told him that I did not shoot the chase helicopter down because I could see what I was doing. This was a pretty hairy few moments.

It was about this time we ran short of ordnance, but by now the Cobra gunships were on the way to finish the job. We later found out that our score of kills from the two helicopters was approximately 120 gooners. They were floating in the lake. There were also the ones that we shot at in the bush, so we will never know how many we really got that day.

We flew back and once we landed we discovered holes in the rocket pods and a couple of holes in the blades. This did not impress Lieutenant Dougherty, but he knew the situation and nothing more was said about it. I looked back at the tail rotor and found out that he had not kept the helicopter's tail properly lined up. When we fired brass, it went back and hit the tail, which meant I had to change one of the rotor blades in the tail as well. When this happened, the pilot had to buy the crew chief a bottle of whisky because it meant a lot of work for him. The long and short of it was that Lieutenant Dougherty showed up at the flight line with a bottle of (I think) Johnny Walker Red Label. The beer was terrible (Falstaff beer – yuck)!

I was drinking too much as well. Whenever we had time off we drank. I remember once I went into one of the hooches. I was dead drunk and it was the wrong hooch. I then got into trouble with one of the guys there and we started fighting. I was doing very well at close quarters: I could see the guy, so I grabbed him and knocked the shit out of him. Then the rest of the people in the hooch threw us out because we were tearing the place up. Once outside, I could not see him. He was coming at me from all sides. The long and the short of it was I came up short in this fight. This happened at the end of February and I remember going on the flight line the next morning with a black eye. It was swollen and completely closed. Now, on the doors of the pilot and copilot of the helicopter I had a sign, which read: "Crew Chief, Dead Eye Barr". I was looking the helicopter over before we went out that morning. I was feeling hung over and miserable, and my pride was wounded. I then saw that somebody with a sense of humor had crossed out "dead eye," and written "closed eye" above it. So now I was crew chief "closed eye Barr." I left it on the helicopter door for quite some time.

I was grounded after that incident and was not able to fly for three days. This was the first time I had had three days off with nothing to do. Major MacPhearson wanted me down. I had totaled one 150 hours flying for February, which was an incredible amount of flight hours for a crew chief. A crew chief had significant stress, not only while flying but once on the ground doing required minor maintenance. Maintenance included anything from greasing to cleaning up the helicopter and taking samples of fuel and oil. Basically, this was all I was qualified to do. So I just took it easy for three days. I stayed in the hooch and more or less drank a lot.

Then in March I was back in the flight line, and I was told: "Well, Barr, we are going to send you on a 'Huss' trip." I asked them what that was, and they told me it was a trip to Karot in Thailand. It would take three days. It was not a proper four-and-a-half day R&R. This was the first and only time I had time off, except for the black eye, since I had arrived in Vietnam. I had a little extra money, so I was keen to go.

That afternoon we were flown to Karot in Thailand. It was a big air force base, and we flew there in a C-130. There we were given a briefing before we could leave the base. They told us not to go into the villages in rickshaws and to be careful of VD in the whorehouses. If they did not show us a VD card, we were not to screw the girl. If the girl did show a VD card and had not had a check-up in the last three days, don't screw the girl. We were told a long list of "don't do this and don't do that." We were again warned about the Black Syph that the Thai girls could have as well. We just did not care! We were impatient to go.

Two other guys and I (one from 262 and one from 263 Helicopter Squadrons) then made our way to the hotel and got stuck into the booze. The barman immediately asked us if we wanted girls and we said no, we wanted to go to a whorehouse. He told us he knew of a very good whorehouse, so we got into a cab and went to It. There was a two-way mirror – we could see through it, but they could not see us. There were lovely Thai girls sitting on a bench.

They looked very nice but we were also very drunk by this time, so anything looked good. We picked them by number. In this instance I picked number twelve. I remembered I was hornier than a ten-peckered billy goat by this time. I lifted her on the bench and got her pants off and got on the job. This also meant I was no longer a virgin, as this was the first time I had a real piece of ass in my whole life. Kris and I used to pet, but I respected her. It was now time to get laid – in a whorehouse in Thailand. When we came out it was time to change partners, so I took another girl. We had to pay $5 per girl: I think that was 100 bot in Thai money. For 100 bot we could have the girl for 24 hours, and all we had to do was feed her. We then went back to the hotel room.

The next day, well, more fun and games. We had breakfast and then off we went to another whorehouse. We picked out some more girls there, whores, prostitutes, or whatever you want to call them. By now we were drunker than rats, and I can remember we decided to go back to the hotel by rickshaw, although we had been told not to do this. As far as I was concerned, to hell with the briefing, let's ride these rickshaws anyway. Rickshaws are like three-wheeled bicycles. So down the road we went, me and the guy from 262. We were lean marines and while riding along I said, "let's play *Ben Hur.*" I stood up with a bottle of beer in my hand and hit the driver on the back of his head, saying: "Come on, you dip shit, move out." By this time the other guys were up and shouting and smacking their drivers on the back of the head as well. The whores must have thought we were out of our bloody minds. Anyway, we were riding through the streets of Karote and *Ben Hur* was being relived again and again. It was great fun.

We went through one intersection and my friend's rickshaw was in front of us, when suddenly a bus came through the intersection and hit the lead rickshaw. I saw the rickshaw, my friend's prostitute and the driver go flying through the air, ass over kettle, and land on the ground. The rickshaw we were in just managed to stop and I got the whore out. The driver then beat a hasty retreat and got out of the way. He did not wait to see what the crazy American in the back of the rickshaw would do. I went to my buddy and said, "Come on, let's get another rickshaw and go back to the hotel and have some fun." All he said was, "Fuck you, your rickshaw and your silly games." It was at this juncture that the four of us got into a taxi, which was also a frightening experience, and back to the hotel we went.

Once at the hotel safe and sound, we carried on with more drinking and making general asses of ourselves. That day passed into evening and the next morning it was time to face the music again, with swollen heads and hung-over bodies. We went back to the air force base, where we boarded a C-130 and returned to Vietnam. I was back on the flight line by 4:00 pm that afternoon. I had taken a few pictures of all the fun with my Polaroid, which the guys on the flight line expected. I was put on night medevacs that evening, and so the work began again.

It was March 1970, and I was back to routine, back to life in a helicopter. My whole life revolved around that helicopter: maintenance, arming it and keeping it clean. Notwithstanding flying in it, we lived for and in and around the helicopter all the time. For 24 hours a day there was always the sound of helicopter blades beating.

On the lighter side of things, one morning we were called out to Arizona Territory. There was apparently a big shootout going on there, and the Cobras were already out there hammering away. Now, though, they were ready to come back and rearm while we were on our way out. I can remember that we came in from about 2,000 feet – we were going to have long gun runs. We could see from where the Cobras were taking fire. The grunts were directing fire from an observation post. We started our gun run, rolling in hot. Things were going well. We then had a good rocket run, backed off and made another rocket run. About halfway through that run, the rocket pod on my side of the helicopter packed up. This meant I had to get out of the helicopter, crawl to the back of the rocket pod and recycle it. We had come out of the rocket run, I had covered the tail and we were going back up. That meant I had about a minute or so to get the job done. I unhooked my gunner's belt and crawled on to the suppression kit, then to the back of the rocket pod. Now we were flying at about 80 or 90 knots, all the time gaining altitude. I got to the rocket pod and saw that it was stuck. I cycled the pod around and then did it again. Once finished, I got up and started to turn around. In the meantime we were taking quite a bit of fire from the ground. The pilot forgot I was out there (I forget who the pilot was). He brought the helicopter around sharp. As he did, he nearly threw me off the rocket pod. I would have been a goner, but I had a death grip on the suppression kit. When he came around, he started rolling in hot and firing rockets. In the meantime, while he was firing rockets I was straddling the rocket pod, facing forward, hanging on. The rocket exhaust was hitting me in the chest and on the front of my legs. It was burning holes through my flight suit. This was all very painful! I was doing everything possible to hold on because by this time our speed was over 120 knots. Then he fired some more rockets from the other pod, followed by some from the pod I was hanging on to. I was taking all this on my chest and once at the bottom of the run, he turned off to the right. It was everything I could do to hold on out there. It felt as if I was holding on to a bucking horse, and I'm not much of a cowboy. As he was pulling off I remember seeing his profile. I couldn't hear him, as I wasn't hooked up to the intercom while outside the helicopter. He was saying: "Fire, Corporal Barr, fire, Corporal Barr, shoot, shoot. What the hell is going on back there." I was waving my one arm around trying to catch his attention as if to say: "Here I am, outside the helicopter, you dumb ass." Finally the gunner tapped him on the shoulder and pointed back. He looked back and saw me waving. All he said was. "Oh shit!" and pulled around to the left real quick – rounds were flying everywhere, coming up at us. He nearly launched me off the rocket pod when he turned around to the left, but when he did that the gunner was able to put down a base of fire. Once the run was finished and we started to gain altitude again, I was able to crawl back into the helicopter. My jumpsuit looked like Swiss cheese. It was covered in burn holes. I was just lucky that the visor on my helmet had been down, or my pretty face would have been burnt all over and not just on the bottom half.

In the end the Lieutenant Dougherty and the co-pilot and the gunner were laughing about it. I crawled in and I must say I was a bit shaken. I was just so glad to be alive, and here were these three cackling coyotes, looking at me. The officers and gentlemen all had smirks on their faces. Zummie – he was a metal smith I believe – was one of the best gunners in the squadron, and he had a wary smile on his face as well. Anyway, in the next 15 minutes or so, we finished off the rest of the ammunition for both guns and rockets, and then returned to Marble Mountain. We later found out that according to the grunts we had scored quite a few kills. We had also put the anti-aircraft weapons out of action. There was no particular damage to the helicopter and this was a great relief, but I know it was very close at times because we heard rounds cracking as they flew past while I was sitting on the rocket pod. If they had hit me, it would have been the end of me.

In the meantime, by the time we got back to base the whole incident was just a big joke … typical military sense of humor. Looking back on it today, it actually frightens me, but that day we just laughed and carried on to the next mission. I guess that was one of the things that made the Marine Corps what it was – the spirit, and the fact that we could laugh at the closeness of death and carry on. We did not have too many guys dropping out of flying, because all flying was voluntary. If you did not want to fly, that was it. They would find something else for you to do, whether it was in the squadron or not, but you did not have to fly unless you really wanted to. I do not remember many guys quitting –only a couple during the year that I was there.

I remember the pilots let me fly the helicopter on test hops. If we were changing the engine, we would fly a test flight to try it out. If it was at night and there was no other particular air traffic around except medevacs coming in and out of Marble Mountain, they would let the crew chief fly. We would do touch and go. This meant we flew down the runway, lifted the helicopter off and flew out over the ocean. This was very gratifying. I could never get the helicopter to hover. I was not good pilot material because my coordination was not that good. To be able to fly a helicopter, you had to have good control with both hands and feet. Your left hand does something, your right hand does something else at the same time and both feet are needed to control the tail against the torque of the main rotor.

The squadron used to have gas wars at night, one against the other. One squadron would go over to the other squadron's living area and throw a gas grenade into the middle of their hooch area. We would gas the guys in the middle of the night while they were sleeping. This was always great fun. We would watch them stumble out of their hooches in the middle of the night, cursing, hollering, snot flying out of their noses, vomiting, rubbing their eyes. Inevitably they would find out which squadron had done it and then they themselves would gas that squadron at another time. I was usually one of the culprits that liked to do all the gassing and it was great fun, watching the other guys being gassed all the time – it always amused us.

There was something else I liked to do while flying in the helicopter. At six o'clock in the morning they would say: "Good morning, Vietnam," over the radio. Reflecting back on the movie, *Good Morning Vietnam*, about a disc jockey in Saigon, it was just like that. We would be flying along, maybe coming back from a medevac. We would be listening to the ADF, listening to rock and roll and jive in the helicopter. We could still hear what the pilot was saying – the pilot could not monitor all the radios, the way the crew chief and gunner could. At the same time we would be freezing our asses off in the back of the helicopter. There was a big door at the back. It must have been about five feet across and four feet high, and it was always open. We sat at the back and the wind blew in on us. If it was raining, the rain would blow in and then we would really freeze our tails off. Listening to the radio was one of the few pleasures we had while in flight. I used to sit there with the butt of the machine gun touching my right leg, looking down at the barrels and rocket pods, then down at the ground, looking to see if we were going to take any fire. I remember feeling very exhilarated. It made me feel on top of the world. We were the type of marines our drill instructor had taught us about in the last few days before we graduated from boot camp, and I was very proud of this fact. However, I was also becoming very aware of what the future held for me in the Marine Corps with the black and white situation as it was. It was becoming worse all the time, at Marble Mountain and everywhere else as well. The dapping people were being mugged at night and riots and other things used to happen on a regular basis in the enlisted men's club.

The beer we drank at the enlisted men's club was Falstaff beer. Falstaff was the world's worst beer, if I recollect properly. We used to have a joke about the beer: we said it must have formaldehyde in it because we never had worse hangovers than when drinking Falstaff beer.

Life in the helicopter was a ceaseless up and down. When it rained we were soaked and then froze. During one particular typhoon, in March 1970 if I recollect right, we had to fly very low to the ground. We picked up fire and had to return it if we could. If we took fire from a village, we sprayed the village. It is too bad that innocent people were probably hurt. We had to suppress their fire. We weren't worried about winning hearts and minds. They were down there housing the enemy, taking care of them, so they suffered as well. The civil population was caught right in the middle of the conflict. They were in a position where they were dammed if they did, and damned if they didn't.

Flying during a typhoon was very dangerous because we flew in one direction for so long, then turned, turned again, and if a pilot did not keep track of what he was doing, we could run into the side of a mountain. Sometimes there were hurricane-force winds and we could not get the helicopters off the ground. When the wind got down to 40 or 50 knots, which meant it was gale force, then we would fly. I can tell you that flying out on a medevac in that type of wind was frightening beyond words. We would sit in the back of the helicopter just waiting to run into something, be it a power line because we were so low, or the side of a hill, anything. We knew other aircraft were out there. We would, however, fly medevacs for the army, as I stated earlier.

Our group (MAG-16) was also awarded the Navy Unit Commendation and the Vietnamese Cross of Gallantry Unit Citation for flying during the typhoon in October 1970. This particular typhoon created much flooding throughout the 1 Corps Amphibious Operational Area (AOA), and marine helicopters were credited with saving numerous Vietnamese lives. Lieutenant Yannessa was the pilot, and we had been up flying most of the day, in very foul weather. We were coming back in to base on instruments, and by radio control from the conning tower. The closer to base the worse it got. It was also late afternoon and getting dark, and we couldn't see where we were at all. We knew we had to be very close to the base and Marble Mountain. Lieutenant Yannessa told me years later that he asked, "Could I see anything, as his vision was distorted because of the Plexiglas and the fog?" I said, "Yes, we have the runway up ahead of us." He said he caught something out of the corner of his eye – it was me, holding on with one hand in his door, the other holding the intercom, one foot on the leading edge of the skid. I was leaning out, so as to have no obstructions guiding him on to the runway and not into Marble Mountain. He said I had scared the crap out of him. It scared me too, but the thought of running into the mountain made it a better option than just sitting there hoping for the best.

There were no modern facilities at the base. We almost always showered in cold water and the toilets were long drops. One night a staff sergeant went down to the staff NCO shower. It was pitch black down there. He went in and fished around for the string that was attached to the light inside the shower. He found it and turned on the light. Now I can't tell you how big the cobra was, but the man himself was six feet tall and this cobra was standing there looking him right in the face with flared hood – so the story went. So he turned the light off again and beat a retreat from the shower, at an incredible speed. He went back with other staff NCOs and they shot the hell out of the shower. The staff NCOs had hot water, but that meant an end to their hot water as well as an end to the snake. It was a huge cobra. A lot of snakes had been washed down in the rivers and into the ocean, because of the floods. They would then swim back and come up the beach – and we were right on the beach at Marble Mountain.

There were snakes, cockroaches and everything else you could think of. There were even cockroaches in our food.

Now, getting back to the snakes, one day I was sitting on the toilet in the early morning, when a bamboo viper (I believe that is what they were called), slid past in front of my boots and carried on. Now, if I had been constipated at the time, that little incident would have cleaned me out because if a bamboo viper bites you, you're dead. It is one of the more deadly snakes around. They are only about one foot long –very small but deadly.

I remember the CH-53's evacuating civilians from certain areas. One day we saw a water buffalo flying out in the back of a CH-53 at about 2,000 feet. Then we saw a gooner going after the water buffalo. They hit the ground, and that was the end of them. The water buffalo is a very sacred animal. On the lighter side of things, we were flying in one of the more troubled spots, near the Qua Son Mountains, which were full of tunnels, bunkers, caves and whatnot. As nothing was happening one day when we were flying out there, and we were impatient for something to begin, Mike Swiatecki got permission to shoot a water buffalo. There should have not been any civilian population around there – the water buffalo obviously belonged to the VC, the NVA, or whoever was out there. Swiatecki shot the animal and lo and behold, the whole hillside lit up. There were people down there, and they started shooting at us. There were a lot of bullets flying through the air – we really had done the wrong thing this time! The people there believed that they could replace their wives and children more easily than they could a water buffalo. We had really fouled up the family prize possession, and this was a mighty big family. There were rounds and tracers flying everywhere and both our helicopters took hits that day.

I guess one of the closest times I got to being shot down was on a night medevac. We were really shooting up the area and we took part of an airburst in the tail boom of our helicopter. For some reason, it exploded before it hit us. Had it hit us, we would have gone down. When it did explode, it took a big chunk out of the tail boom and knocked the helicopter for a loop as well. We were just lucky that the pilot was Lieutenant Yanessa, and he regained control of the helicopter fast. Lieutenant Yanessa was another of those very special people: one had no trouble going into any situation with him, as he was competent, quick to make decisions and flew with a professional fervor that is rarely seen. Of all the pilots that I flew with in Vietnam, I flew the most with Lieutenant Yannessa. Lieutenant Dougherty was another pilot I flew with a lot. He was of the same caliber as Lieutenant Yannessa. Lieutenant Dougherty was killed in 1975, while flying a Harrier jump jet from an aircraft carrier. Somehow the jet capsized and crashed, killing a real leader of marines. That was a sad loss to the Marine Corps. He left behind a wife and a small boy.

In the movies one always sees helicopters being shot down. Helicopters were shot down, but we did not lose that many helicopters in my squadron – I think there were four – during my year in Vietnam. I was not shot down, because we were good both as gunner and as crew chief. The gunners that flew with me did their jobs the way they were supposed to, and our helicopters were not shot down. The pilots were the very best. Their officer candidate school was, I believe, a year and their flight school was also a year.

March was a very difficult month for me. I was flying a lot of hours because there were many operations on at the time. We flew north as far as Hue and sometimes points even further north, near Khe Sanh. We always ended up in shooting situations when we would take and return fire. One particular night, while out on medevac, we had been called to the south of Marble Mountain, where the Republic of Korea Marine Corps (ROKMC) were shooting it out with a large force of Vietnamese. They wanted close air support and medevacs, so the medevac helicopter went in. Somehow I got my fire directions wrong. I was not able to tell our red traces from the green traces of the communist block. This particular night I was very fatigued and I ended up shooting at a bunch of Koreans. I remember them coming over the radio telling us to stop firing and told us they no longer required our air support. The chase medevac helicopter, CH-46, then came right into the zone and picked up a bunch of wounded. I do not know whether any had been killed, but I do know that I wounded some of their troops. I had put down a good 200 rounds on the pull-off before we were told to cease firing. We finished what we were doing, and when we got back to base I was given a very good chewing out by the pilot. He asked me what my excuse was, and I told him I did not have one. I had got my bearings confused, and I was not going to make any excuses. If they wanted to ground me for this, they just had to do it. Our squadron CO saw fit to say no more about the incident. It was one of the unfortunate aspects of war, something that happens with close air support. He said I had also done a very good job as a motivated crew chief up to that point and did not see any reason for disciplinary actions, but as he said, I now had to live with what I had done. I felt terrible about the whole incident. My heart was literally in my stomach. The pain I felt deep down inside, knowing that I had wounded and very possibly killed Allied troops, was incredibly difficult for me to accept. I did accept it though – I was in the air again the next evening for the night medevacs. We flew practically the entire night, and hardly had a break from shooting during the next 24-hour period. That was our job: the gunship drew fire away from friendly troops and extinguished hostile fire. In so doing, the troops on the ground would have room to breathe, put in their sweep line and make their final attack. We also drew fire away from medevac aircraft, resupply aircraft or insertion aircraft. We did our job and we did it well.

Someone might say, "Hey Dave, you are color-blind". Well, when I took my flight physical, I asked the corps man to give me a chance to fly. I told him that I did not think being color-blind would be a problem. We know the result there, but that was the only problem. You might ask, "How did you tell the difference between red, yellow and green smoke?" They would always say they were putting colored smoke out, and that would be the only smoke. I would spot it, even camouflage and things like that. In general terms, I could spot things before the pilots did. So in many cases where I was concerned, being color-blind was an attribute and not a drawback. This particular night with the Koreans was definitely a drawback, but I was also very tired, although not on the verge of collapse. I was always ready to go and I never shirked my duty. If a guy was short-timed and did not want to go out on something like a Black Hammer at night, or a night medevac (the most dangerous missions were at night) I would always take his place. He would work on my helicopter. Many times when I got back and the helicopter did not require any maintenance at all, I was immediately put on a Mission 80, medevac duty during the day. If it was a slow day and we only had three medevacs in 12 hours, we could get up to six hours broken sleep. Then we might not, depending on the situation. Some times it was a case of picking up a medevac, taking the wounded back to Da Nang, and doing it again, just up and down. We could sometimes be down within one and half hours from the time we took off. A 12-hour period could be anywhere from three to five hour's worth of work. If we started to take fire, we would stay with it.

I found out that we had been put in for a citation of some sort for the medevac we had flown on the night of December 31, 1970. The pilots had also been put in for an award (I don't know what), by the mission commander, who flew in a CH-46. He had put Lieutenant Morschauser and the copilot in, and Lieutenant Morschauser put me and the gunner in for the Single Mission Air Medal. My award was for my actions when I got out of the helicopter as I had done, firing flares to light our way in the dense rain of that evening. To say the least, finding out about this made me feel about 10 feet tall. I was in for a real award. You would say: "What is in an award? What will it get you, a cup of coffee in a restaurant?" It was not that. It was a sense of accomplishment, and a record had been made of it. I was very proud of this. When I went home to Kristine and my family, especially my dad, I could show that I had been cited for gallantry and that I had performed my duty above and beyond the normal call. At the time I did not think anything of it – it was just a night's work. It had been a frightening and scary night, to be sure. It was a night when I thought I would meet my Maker and I'm sure everybody else in the helicopter had the same thoughts. God in his greatness decided to let us continue, and that is why I am here today. This made me feel very good because I had not thought much about it after that, except for the fact that I was doing my duty and that was all that really counted. I was there fighting a war.

What other awards had I been given by the time I left Vietnam?

Well, I had my Vietnam Service Ribbon and the General Service Ribbon. Then of course, by the time I had finished flying I also had my Air Medals, although at that time in March I was not sure how many Air Medals I had – but the number was growing at an alarming rate. I was flying day in and day out. I knew my time was just about over in Vietnam and they were not letting guys put in for more time there The word was that the Marine Corps was due to pull out in June 1971, and my time was to be completed in April 1971.

The time went by and we got to April. On April 15 I remember flying night medevacs, and once again it was a pretty hairy night – but it was all in a day's work, so to speak. When we got back to the flight line, the squadron sergeant major came out with a few of the guys and said, "Corporal Barr, you are leaving Vietnam tomorrow and we will be turning your wings upside down." They turned the patch with the Combat Aircrew Wings on my flight suit upside down. My time as a crew chief was over and my time in Vietnam was drawing to a close. I did my post-flight check on the helicopter for the last time. I would be leaving Vietnam the next day as the orders had come through. It was an expected surprise. I felt very empty, because a chapter in my life was closing. I knew I would return to motor transport because I did not have Aviation MOS, even though I was a crew chief. I was leaving behind guys with whom I had gone through many things, Mike Swiatecki, for example, who still had another month in Vietnam. I had had so many incredible and dangerous experiences with Mike. How I would miss him. I had been trained by the very patient, always calm and ever steady Gary Hughes. Other guys had already gone home because their time was up, and now it was my turn. I was excited by the fact that I would be going home a Vietnam veteran, a real marine to my family and my girlfriend Kris. I had worn her high school ring on my little finger all through Vietnam. I was proud of what I had done and the life I had lived. I was a marine and had done a marine's duty for other marines. To hell with the Vietnamese, and the US government.

I also found out that I had racked up fifty-seven Air Medals, and the squadron commander told me that this was a very high number indeed. An Air Medal means twenty combat missions flown, although that did not necessarily mean that I took fire every time. I had done exceptionally well and the squadron commander, Lieutenant Colonel Blank, now shook my hand and said, "Corporal Barr, very well done!" It was with pride in my heart and good feeling that the next morning I said goodbye to my friends and left for Freedom Hill in Da Nang.

Once at Freedom Hill I checked in at the air terminal, which was just a big corrugated tin building with some benches in it. I ran into Staff Sergeant Drill Instructor Lewis. I went up to him, stood to attention in front of him and said, "Staff Sergeant Lewis, Corporal Barr reporting as ordered, sir." He looked up at me, stuck out his hand and said, "How are you doing, Barr?" "Very well, sir," I replied. "I'm on my way back home. I am the marine that you told us to be and that you taught us to be." He looked at me and said, "Well, you still look like a sack of shit tied in the middle." We both just smiled. It was true. My military bearing left a lot to be desired. Again he just smiled, and I smiled back. I did not know whether he was going to reach over and smack me or choke me, but in the end still smiling, he said, "Well, congratulations, obviously something we taught you rubbed off, you survived." I replied, "It was not something, it was a lot." I never saw that man again.

That afternoon we boarded a Northwest Orient airline and flew from Freedom Hill at Da Nang Air Base to Kadena Air Force Base in Okinawa, where we were trucked up to Camp Hansen. There we were given shots, debriefed in the sense that we were told we were going home now, told to take it easy, not get into any barroom brawls and not to show our frustration on the civilians. Then of course there were the race riots. The Black problem was becoming worse and worse. They were dapping and growing bolder. When I say bolder, I mean just more arrogant. My mind was definitely made up now, I would not make the Marine Corps my career. If this was what the Marine Corps was going to be, it was not my place. It seemed that everything had turned around and I will discuss that later.

4

The End of the Marine Corps

On April 19 we flew from Okinawa to Yokota in Japan, and then to Norton Air Force Base in San Bernardino. We collected our bags at this base and then they said: "Gentlemen, job well done, good luck. There is a bus waiting for those of you reporting for duty at Camp Pendleton." That meant that those guys were getting out of the Marine Corps on "early outs." They had almost served their time, and with only a few months left they were just going to be put out of the Marine Corps early. The rest of us, like myself, who still had a year or more left in the marines, were given 30 days' leave and told to report to our respective duty stations. My duty station was to be at Camp Pendleton, base motor transport. I had leave and I was excited beyond words. I was going home.

On the bus taking us home, the first thing we saw were civilians standing out there with signs saying: " Marines go to hell," "Baby killers," and other meaningless stupidity. We did not even bother to give them the finger. The bus took us into San Bernardino, where I caught another bus, a Greyhound bus, to the Puente off-ramp, in Baldwin Park. I put my seabag on my shoulder, walked through the underpass and the first person I ran into was Mr Lorenzo. He was working on his gate. I got a big welcome from him, as well as a big hug. Then Dean Lorenzo came out, and his wife Cress, my childhood friend. We were all shaking hands and hugging one another. I remember the great feeling of pride that I was someone, I had done something, I had been somewhere: I had been through war. I was 19 years and seven days old and I had been in Vietnam a year.

I walked on home and Mom and Dad were not there. They had gone to a movie, so I put my seabag down and decided to go over and see Kris. I then went back to Mr Lorenzo and asked whether I could borrow his car. This was not a problem to him. He gave me the keys to a '64 Ford and told me to go. I got into the car, still in my dress green uniform and drove across West Covina to meet Kris. She had not received word that I was coming.

Upon arriving I knocked on the door and Kris came to answer the door – her mouth dropped open. I had expected her to rush into my arms and give me a big kiss but she didn't. Her father turned off the television and got up. Bill was a big man – he grabbed me and gave me a big bear hug, and asked me how I was doing. By now Kris was on the telephone speaking to some other guy. I had interrupted the telephone conversation. Her brother came out and gave me a hug. Kris was off the telephone by now. Anyway, we sat talking for about 10 minutes, and then I said I wanted to see whether my mom and dad were home. I asked Kris to go with me, so we could talk. We got out to the car and she immediately started telling me about another boyfriend, and this and that. She told me she did not agree with the war. She was at college now and it had opened her eyes to many things. My heart was sinking by the minute. All the pride and elation I had felt when she had opened the door was quickly evaporating.

We drove to my place across town, went inside, still talking, and this time my mom and dad walked in the front door. We all embraced each other, hugged one another – it was a very touching moment, to say the least. But I could not feel what I wanted to feel in my heart, being able to grab hold of my mother and father again, touch them and give them a big hug and a kiss, because my whole world was sliding out from underneath me. I was losing the love of my life.

I took Kris home again, then went back home and had a few beers with my dad. Then I crawled wearily into bed. I had not had a hero's welcome from Kris, on the ride back to her house our conversation was negative, and I was only to see her once more. Welcome home.

My leave was a miserable, drunken affair. I was drunk the whole time. I got into trouble with my mother and father, and they did not particularly want me around the house. As far as the rest of the neighborhood was concerned, my reception was a good one, as was the reception from my friends. There were no problems or animosity. Funny how animosity ended the whole Vietnam affair – if you were in the marines it was like being a second-class citizen. This did not bother me. At the end of my 30-day leave I was happy to be going back to Camp Pendleton, and I'm sure my mom and dad were happy I was returning, too.

At the end of May I reported to Base Motor Transport in Camp Pendleton. I had to go through the rigmarole of having to check in. I was given more shots and assigned to a barrack.

Base Motor Transport was the biggest motor transport unit at Camp Pendleton. We drove civilian soft-skin vehicles, as opposed to tactical vehicles.

My job was to work with an old man named Ralph, who was a civilian, doing general repair. We fixed tailgates, replaced boards on truck sides, on the floor and things like that. This was boring and disgusting to me. Then one day they had us out and wanted us to do a physical fitness test. My physical fitness left something to be desired and I barely passed the test. I was now smoking a lot and drinking every night. It was the only thing to do.

Then there was a new dimension to the equation. There was the black and white problem in Camp Pendleton, and it was growing at an alarming rate. There were fights, almost on a nightly basis, in the EM club. If there were white girls in the club, there were always the blacks around them, trying to jive and make trouble, This would inevitably end up in a good fight. It was not a happy time. If you got into trouble with the blacks, you were actually singled out and punished, if not put out of the Marine Corps on a undesirable discharge (that was the whites, not the blacks). They did not do anything as far as the blacks were concerned. They were dapping and running around with Black Panthers on the backs of their jackets after hours, when they did not have to wear their uniforms. This was fine for them, but the whites could not do anything like that. They could not identify with anything like that: It was strictly forbidden, so it was a one-sided affair. The dapping in the mess hall and chow line was such that anybody who had pride in being a white man was on edge. They would knock knuckles together, butting into lines and generally making assholes of themselves, as only people with no shame can do. Like a lot of other people, the pride I had had in the Marine Corps was quickly ebbing. It was no longer the Marine Corps we had been taught about. This was a totally different concept. In my view, and in that of many other people, it was now something created for the blacks. As far as we were concerned, the standard of the US Marine Corps was on its way down the toilet. Guys like me, Vietnam veterans, the people who were the carry-over until the next war, the next generation of marines, were getting out of the service. To hell with the Marine Corps! In my opinion, this was not what it was all about. We were discriminated against because we were white. A lot of the blacks were lazy, and they were always on light duty. They did not want to shave, their hair was long but we were made to have our weekly haircuts. In my opinion everything was for the blacks, and I could not understand this. I was also made to feel ashamed of the fact that I had flown in Vietnam. I remembered standing in an inspection once with the numerals "57," meaning 57 air medals, displayed on a service ribbon; and I also wore my wings. When the major came by to inspect me he said, "My gosh, what have we got here? How in the heck did you manage this?" I told him that I had flown in Vietnam and had not worked on trucks. I caught quite a ribbing from then on from the other enlisted men in the barracks. They called me "Wings" until finally one day I just stopped wearing them. They did not seem to mean much anyway. The American public was ashamed of me, the racial problem was growing, and the guys around me in the barracks did not seem particularly to care for the fact that I had combat aircrew wings.

I was also very miserable inside, and this stemmed from the welcome I had received from Kris. This did not even consist of a kiss. I saw her once more while on my leave and I tried to do something to rectify the things that had gone wrong, to try and get our relationship back together again. It did not work, because she did not want anything to do with me. I returned her ring because she was no longer my steady girl. The most heartbreaking thing was that just after I reported back to Camp Pendleton, I received a letter from her. This letter was addressed to me in Vietnam and it had now caught up with me. In it she said how much she still loved me, and she also told me what a great time we would have once I returned from Vietnam. A nice time indeed!

It seemed from the moment I stepped off that aircraft and drove out from the air force base at San Bernardino, my time and life in the United States deteriorated. The government was not for us, and did not give a damn either. It was for expedience and a vote. The news media were against us too. It was not just the Marine Corps, it was the whole military situation in the United States. It stank. It was as if they were ashamed of us. What right did these people have to be ashamed of us? What right? "Don't take a chance, don't go to Vietnam. You are a fool to go over there."

I was beginning to feel that America was rotten, and I was becoming very dissatisfied with everything American. It seemed as if every man who stood up for something conservative or middle of the road was shouted down by the media and all the other liberals, who seemed to have so much verbal power. I was 19 years old, and could not legally buy a beer outside the Marine Corps base. I could not legally buy at the Marine Corps base either; we were just lucky the Marine Corps turned a blind eye to it. Life was becoming very miserable.

I was still heartbroken over Kris, and everything else around me, the whole foundation of what the marines were all about, had been shaken to ruin. Everything was black and white, and mostly black, yet they were the most unproductive marines. In Vietnam, I had seen two black marines in the whole marine air group that had flown as gunners. They were truly marines, and caught hell from other blacks. In that whole time there was also one black pilot. He was a responsible pilot, not a ball-buster like Lieutenant Morschauser or Fred McCorkle or Lieutenant Doherty. He was a good and safe pilot with whom to fly, but he was only one. Things were just going wrong. It would seem that new standards were being made and these were low standards. They were not standards of pride and dignity. They were not standards that had to do with past traditions of the Marine Corps. They were standards that accommodated another race of people, instead of another race accommodating itself to the existing standards of the Marine Corps. I do not know what things are like today, but this was the way things were in 1971.

For the next few months I worked at Base Motors, doing everything from working with old man Ralph to driving the truck on weekends. I became buddies with a guy in the admin section. Among other duties he did orders. One night while sitting in the pub, I said to him, "Could you get me a set of orders to go up to El Torro Marine Base, so that I can get a little closer to aviation again?" He said he would see what he could do.

It was also about this time that I bought a Triumph motorcycle. I had some money burning a hole in my pocket and so decided to start riding motorcycles again – the old free and easy, easy rider type of thing. It was a little Triumph TR6, and my dad and I fixed it up. I started to ride this at weekends when I was home. By now I was going home almost every weekend. This was not to my parents' delight, because I was not a fun person to be around at that time. After I got the Triumph on the road, the guy in the admin section that I had become friends with had a set of orders cut for me. I was to go to El Toro Marine Base and report to one of the motor pools there. I thought this was great, thanked him and then took him out for a good night on the town. He certainly deserved that. I also got a week's leave out of it, so I got on the motorcycle and made a trip through Southern Nevada, Utah and Arizona. This was the first motorcycle trip I had ever made. That Triumph wanted to shake and beat me to death!

The ride was plagued with problems, plus a not very serious accident when I had too much to drink. It was, however, good to just go away. When I arrived home, I put the motorcycle away and drove down to El Toro Marine Base, where I reported for duty. There I ran into one of the pilots from Vietnam, Captain Blair. He asked me why I was going into trucks again. I told him that I had been in trucks for the past few months and it was disgusting. I wanted to fly again. He agreed, and said he would try and organize it for me. He called a squadron commander, a Major Lee of Helicopter Marine Heavy (HMH) 363 and asked him whether he could use a flight line technician. Captain Blair realized as well as I did that I did not know my ass from a hole in the ground as far as being a mechanic was concerned. Being a mechanic on a Huey was one thing. The CH-53 was another ball game altogether. Major Lee asked for me to be sent over, and said he would see whether he could get me into the squadron. I went to Marine Corps Air Station Helicopter Santa Ana (MCASH) and reported into HMH-363. There, Major Lee welcomed me aboard. He said I could do some on-the-job training and possibly get on to flight skins within a few weeks on CH-53.

This was great. This also meant flight pay, which was about another 60 dollars a month. This was top-notch stuff. Being a corporal at that time, I would be making about 300 dollars a month on flight pay. This was big time.

We had the same problem in the air wing that we had in the Base Motor Transport and elsewhere. There were the black marines and there were the white marines, but there was a totally different set of rules for each. We had no blacks flying in 363 except one. His name was Jake, and he was a theologian as well. Jake and I flew together regularly; we got along just fine. He was there to work and do his duty, not be an asshole, dapping and carrying on. I remember a bunch of blacks coming by once and they wanted to dap with him in the middle of the street. He told them to go to hell. He was not going to dap, he was a marine. That created a bad situation, but Jake was a man of conviction, and was very much one with God.

The same thing happened in the EM club. If there were any white women around, a fight would ensue and this could lead to a riot. It happened that people were stabbed. Things were sure changing in the Marine Corps.

I remember trying to get on to flight skins. I was a tentative crew chief. I was operational. They gave me a helicopter, number 68. I did not know what to do with it. A CH-53 was a gargantuan flying mechanical machine. The blade span is 88 feet, on the main rotor It would stand two stories high and is about 90 feet long, from main rotor blade tip to tail rotor blade tip. It had two huge turbine engines that powered into the main gearbox. To say it was a mechanical nightmare was to understate the case. It wasn't long before it was well known among the flight line mechanics that there was no hope of me ever doing a real mechanic's job on these helos. We came to an accommodation I would fly for the guys who did not want to fly, especially night flights. If it were a weekend, I would fly the whole weekend for them. They in turn, when not flying, would help me work on the helicopter.

There, too, it was not all misery as far as the Marine Corps was concerned. There were also some funny times. I remember my last Marine Corps Birthday – November 10, 1971. Kenny Prewett and I had renewed our relationship. Gary Hughes, a good friend of mine while in Vietnam was there as well. Kenny was in the CH-46 squadron and was now flying. We all went to the staff NCO club. This was big enough to allow all ranks into their club for the marine birthday. There were officers at the birthday, and many girlfriends and wives. We had to stand in line for an hour to get something to eat and there was Corporal McArthur with quite a bit of food on his plate. He had macaroni salad and a few other things and he was as drunk as a pig, as were all the rest of us. We were all sitting eating, all dressed in our green uniforms. McArthur came up to the table and said: "Hey, look what I've got here." There was a girl sitting close by, and the plate of macaroni salad ended up upside down in her lap; so much for her nice party dress (she was wearing a dark-colored dress). Shortly after we found ourselves being thrown out of the staff NCO club. At least Kenny and I had eaten. Conduct not becoming to marines.

We went to the EM club where there was a big fight – a little more fun. Then to top the evening off, Ken and I (it was very late by then and all the other coyotes had packed up and gone home) went up to the base duty officer's building. He was a major. Ken said, "Let's go and say good evening to the major." I said to him, "What do you want to say good evening to the major for, we will just get into trouble." Anyway, we were drunk, and we decided to go. We got to the door and the duty NCO said, "What do you two clowns want?" We said we had something to report to the major and we were told to wait while he fetched him. The building was alive with military police (MPs), and they were all awake because guys had been getting into fights all around the base.

Kenny saw the major approaching, stuck his head in the door and said, "Hey Major Malfunction, fuck you!" I immediately got the cue, turned around and started running, running like we had never run before. MPs were coming out of the building like angry hornets out of a disturbed nest, with batons and mean looks on their faces. I knew we were in big trouble now. The MPs were gaining on us and I wondered how we could get rid of them, but by then we knew what to do. It had been raining quite hard that day and there was a field that was covered in mud so, still in our uniforms, we ran across that field, slipping and falling in the mud, groveling around. We knew that the MPs would not be inclined to follow us, not with their spit shine shoes and nice uniforms. We crossed the field and skirmished over to the barracks. Kenny was staying in a private room, which housed two guys. The barracks I lived in housed 40 guys. Once in the room, we proceeded to drink the last of the beer and when that was gone, we looked for something else to drink. There was beer into which we had been flipping cigarette butts. We thought we would strain it through a stocking. We had a girl's nylon stocking there and strained the beer into a glass. It looked pretty mean but we were pretty thirsty as well. We ended up taking a few sips, and this made us sick as dogs. We were throwing up all over the place and making a general mess of the room we were in.

When I woke up the next morning, my head was pounding, my tongue was stuck to the roof of my mouth and I felt like the southbound end of a northbound mule. I realized we had gone a bit far the night before. There was mud caked all over my uniform. It was in my hair and under my fingernails. My shoes looked like I had been out in the boondocks, which in fact we had. Kenny looked the same – he was on the floor next to me. We were in great misery. I got up and brushed off as best I could and wandered off to my barracks to clean up. We were lucky it was a Saturday.

I flew a lot. We sometimes flew up to San Francisco, Las Vegas and other points far away. Reserve pilots flew these distances to get their flight time up.

About January 1972 I bought my first Harley Davidson motorcycle. It was about a week after a friend of mine who had a Harley Davidson Sportster let me ride it; he was also in the marines. That was it! I sold the Triumph in short order and bought a 1200cc 1961 Harley Davidson Panhead. I immediately started stripping the bike down to the bare frame. I wanted to build a super-looking chopper out of this thing. I wanted to be an easy rider. I spent the next few months chroming this and that, painting it – and by May I had the bike put together again and was riding it. I was working the bugs out and there were plenty of those, given my limited ability as a mechanic.

Back to the Marine Corps. I remember doing a deployment to a place called Fallon, Nevada. It was up near the Carson City, Reno area. The entire squadron flew up there – we were to deploy infantry into the desert around there for a big exercise. Fallon, Nevada had a navy base, believe it or not, and they had helicopters stationed there. We were doing different maneuvers during the day, and sometimes we could have the night off.

On one particular night a couple of guys and I stole a jeep from Special Services. It was freezing cold, as well as wet and misty. We got hold of a couple of cases of beer, got into the open jeep and down the road we went, having a gay old time. We got into Carson City. I have never been much of a gambler, but one of the nice things about these gambling places is that you can get a good meal quite cheap and you also can get free booze while you gamble. I bought a roll of nickels – five-cent pieces – and went around the different slot machines, playing a slot machine every now and then and grabbing a beer when the waitress came around. They were certainly not making a good investment with us. On my second roll of nickels, the machine started doing funny things, and nickels started flying all over the place. I have never seen as many nickels in my life. I did not know what to do. I scooped them all into a bag and the jackpot was about $50 worth of nickels. Holy mackerel, this was a lot of money! We then decided to go and eat. We had a nice big chicken dinner there in the casino and we still had a lot of money left after that.

We decided that we would carry on driving around, so got back into the jeep. We got some more booze and off we went. I was shouting at one road sign: it said "Mustang Ranch, exit one mile." I then realized what it was, and said to the guys, "Hey guys, Mustang Ranch is the biggest whorehouse in the United States." We then decided to go and see what it was all about.

We drove through the main gate. It was an electrified gate and we had to identify ourselves before they would let us in. We said we were from the United States Marine Corps, and the gate opened. We were wet, freezing cold and had mud on our shoes, because earlier the jeep had left the road and we had to push it back. Anyway, we trotted into the main foyer. There were a lot of mobile units hooked together, and the girls would stand up when people walked in. The madam would say, "Company, girls," and they would all start flocking around us. There were tall girls and short girls; there were big girls and small girls. There must have been about 15 girls there – girls with black hair, girls with blond hair, girls with red hair – all kinds of girls, all clad in skimpy outfits. One girl brought me a beer; exactly what I needed. The other guys and I had a look of absolute bliss on our faces. I still had most of my winnings, so paying for this was not going to be much of a problem. The chicken dinner had been quite cheap.

The other two fellows paired off with some girls and so did I. Mine was a lovely girl as well. We went back into a room and she said: "What type of party do you want, marine?" I had never been spoken to like this before. I told her what I wanted; she told me what it would cost. It was $10, and I thought it was good value for money – but I will leave what went on up to the reader's imagination! We did our thing and left the room. My buddies came out a few minutes later and all of us were smiling like possums eating shit. They gave us another beer and said: "All right, marines, thanks for coming along. We will give the entire squadron a night on the house if they will give our girls a ride in one of those big helicopters we see flying around here." Someone had to go and see Major Lee about this. Think of all the fun we could have!

We got back into the Special Services jeep and off we went. The next morning I requested permission to see Major Lee. I was having memories of my drill instructors, and asking for water. I got as far as my squadron sergeant major, and he said: "Barr, what the fuck are you up to? What do you want? Whatever it is, I am not interested." I told him I had a golden opportunity to promote good morale for the entire squadron. He asked me what I was talking about. I told him what the madam at the Mustang Ranch had said about a night on the house if her girls could get a ride in one of our helicopters. He said he would speak to the major. He went to see the major – and that was the end of it. Major Lee obviously did not have the same idea about how to promote good morale as we did.

We deployed back to Santa Ana Marine Corps Air Station within a few days, and left paradise behind. This broke our hearts. Word had got around about the free night at the Mustang Ranch and Major Lee had become a very unpopular person.

At this time I was living with a girl, because I could not stand the barracks – the drunks, all the noise and everything else. She was getting ready to go back to South Dakota for her sister's wedding. That was the end of that little relationship, but it had served its purpose because it had kept me out of the barracks for six months. There was nothing but trouble in the barracks as far as the drunks and the noise emanating from them was concerned. Towards the end of my time I was very outspoken about my racial ideologies and whenever there was trouble in the EM Club, or anywhere else, I was often involved.

My time in the Marine Corps was drawing to a close, and I did not know what I wanted to do once I got out. I knew that I would ride my motorcycle back to New York to see my buddy, Gary Hughes. We had been very good friends: he was also the first crew chief that I had flown with in HML-167. Gary was a solid guy, who had left the Marine Corps a few months before I did.

I wanted nothing to do with the Marine Corps. My feelings were the same about the United States government as well: it stank. I was tired of the whole mess and once I had received my separation pay, which was about $300,

I thought I would see Garry. This gave me a good excuse. I had to get the marines, Vietnam, and all the black racial problems out of my system. Kris was still bothering me as well. I was not doing very well.

I went to the career planner to start checking out of the squadron. He said: "Barr, I will recommend in your record that you reenlist, but I do not advise it. You should get out of the Marine Corps." When I checked out I had to say goodbye to Major Lee. This was protocol. He sat up right at his desk, big, solid, squared off, and with the look of a professional leader. He didn't mince words. He said I was doing the right thing by getting out, because the Marine Corps was not made for people like me. He said: "You are a marine, and it is fast becoming a place where what we were taught is becoming obsolete." He looked at me intently for a moment, and said, "Dismissed". He was quite right. I do not know what the Marine Corps is like today, but back then it was not the Marine Corps our drill instructors had taught us about. So I checked out of the squadron and then had 10 days in which to goof around.

Every morning I went over to El Toro Marine Base. There we would have "muster" at about 10:00 a.m. and then would have the rest of the day off. That meant we could go and get drunk. That's how I passed those 10 days. Then, on June 29, they told us to get haircuts for the last time, which we grudgingly did. If we did not do this, they would not let us out of the Marine Corps: rather, they would let us out but they would not pay us. We still looked like skinheads.

We received our papers as well as our final check and saying: "Right, see you later," I got into my car (an Oldsmobile that I had bought from my parents when I had returned from Vietnam), and drove out the front gate. There was an MP at the front gate. I waved my papers at him and said: "I'm out, free, fuck the Marine Corps." He only said: "Go on, get out of here, man." I drove out of the main gate of El Toro Marine Base. I was now a civilian.

I had covered a lot of ground and come a long way over the last three years, as I reflected while driving home to West Covina. I took off my uniform, sat down with a beer and started to get drunk. I knew my mom and dad were glad to see me get the hell out: they were glad I was going to make the motorcycle ride to New York. That night I loaded the Harley Davidson in a drunken stupor and passed out. That is how I ended my three years in the United States Marine Corps, drunk and very empty. I was miserable inside – there was nothing there: I had no positive feelings for the country I lived in; I had no positive feelings for myself; I did not know what I was going to do. From that point forward I was to face that question many times in my life.

At 08:00 a.m. the next morning I started up and headed for points east: first obstacle the Mojave desert. I blistered my face, but managed to make it to Utah that night. Then it was cooler traveling. I felt good being out on the road, as if I was being set free, and starting all over again, and truly I was.

After a matter of days I was in South Dakota and visited my friend Cheryl Hewett. I shared an apartment with her and her brother, while in the marines. We had a good week together, and then I headed off, eventually reaching my next destination: Gary Hughes, in upstate New York. Gary was not a man of any outward emotion. With Gary, all was steady and thought out, just like in the days when we were in the squadron together. I was sure that his future would be one of success. He wasn't a man to make many mistakes. He took after his father Chuck Hughes, who was a police officer in Potsdam, NY. I got along champion with him, as well. He had been in the army in Europe in the Second World War, and been involved in some heavy fighting in his service time. Gary's Mom was a tall, quiet woman, who had her finger on all that went on around her in their home. She made me feel as if I was one of the family, and was a great cook to boot.

After this visit, I headed back to Detroit, Michigan, and visited my Aunt Della. She was in her seventies and not doing well. I worked for her son for a week or so, and then was on my way south, heading for North Carolina. As I was leaving Detroit I caught a rainstorm, and it stayed with me for the next four days. It was a truly miserable time. I was not as prepared as I should have been. I had no tent, no rain gear, so was soaked the whole time. I slept under picnic table in parks, with a blanket over the top. The Harley gave me trouble off and on. Fortunately it was nothing big. The main problem with this machine was it was a hard starter. It would work my ass off whenever it was cold. Or whenever there was a crowd!

I worked for a couple weeks in North Carolina while staying with my cousin, who had recently moved back there. I was able to get the Harley serviced and ready for the next leg of the journey, plus I also put some money back in my pocket. I had started out with only $300.00, so things were tight on this trip, to be sure.

When I left my cousin Joe and headed for Canada, I crossed the border just out of Platzburg, NY. It was only a hop, skip and a jump on to Montreal, in Quebec. Here, I needed some welding done on a broken oil line. I rode round the Great Lakes, and was very impressed by the beauty of what I was seeing in Canada. However, I was still having troubles with the HD. The charging system was on the blink, and I had carburetor problems, but was able to carry on.

When I got west of the Great Lakes the land started to open out, and become flat, more like plains. It was always cool by Californian standards, and it also rained a lot. One week in Winnipeg, Manitoba, I was getting some oil, and a fellow said that If I wanted to stay for a few days and work on the HD I was welcome. This was very much the Canadian spirit that I found right across the country.

There was only one thing that marred my time in Canada and that was when I was traveling across Saskatchewan. I rounded a gentle curve in the highway, and passing a truck was a car. We were going to crash head-on when I decided to get off the road and go down into the ditch, which was bordered by a barbed wire fence. I was bouncing along, just barely holding my own, and eventually brought the machine's speed down from 60 mph to about 10 mph. I was able to get it back up on to the shoulder. I got my rifle out – I had been carrying it as protection for when I was sleeping out. But I had to stop myself, as I would have killed whoever it was that had run me off the road. I knew it wasn't intentional – we all make mistakes driving – what angered me so was not that they had run me off, it was the fact that they didn't stop. What if I had hit the wire, or crashed? What a coward.

The days went by with small problems with the HD, always hard starting. When I made it into Banff in Alberta, I had been through some of the most beautiful country that I had ever seen in my life.

Money was getting pretty tight. I was down to something like $50.00, and still had 2,000 miles to go by my route. That night I slept in a cemetery in Banff. I must admit that it was quiet, all were at peace.

I had a stop in a small town in British Columbia for the repair of a burnt valve in the rear cylinder, and on I went. I was just lining it for home now, hoping that the motorcycle would hold up.

It was in early September that I arrived home. I had ridden something like10,000 miles. That was my first real big motorcycle journey. Now what was I to do? The trip had been good for the head, but what now? With reality setting in one had to work. A friend who was in the marines with me said that the Texaco refinery was hiring. I went down to Long Beach, put in an application and was accepted. This was the first – and probably the only – time in my life that I could say that I had a job with a real future to it.

After our training I was assigned to the hydrogen producing complex. It was interesting work, being involved in producing gasoline. It was a unit that had a high turnover, as there was always something to do. There was a lot of overtime as well. I moved up to operator quickly. I liked what I was doing. We worked shift work, a week on days, a week swing shift, a week graveyard. I was making good money, and I bought a brand new 1972 Harley Davidson Super Glide. I had the Oldsmobile car and a nice apartment. I had what every young single man should have to be happy, or so society tells us.

In fact I was miserable. I would look at the people on the freeway in the morning, battling the traffic, and coming home in the afternoon. They were just going through the days of their lives, and time was slipping away. What for? For retirement? If they were happy, great. For me it just wasn't the way. I knew in my heart of hearts that God had not put me on the earth just to try to make myself comfortable, then one day retire and die.

I also was still very disenchanted about the United States. I didn't see anything that I could identify with. I couldn't get Vietnam out of my system. There, I had a purpose. War is extreme, and those extremes were, for me, supporting the marines that were in the field, no matter what. The people that I flew with were of a very dedicated frame of mind. They lived hard, flew a lot, and asked little for themselves. In civilian life, I felt that I was just living for myself, and that didn't seem reason enough for me to carry on this way. I needed a purpose, a cause to be a part of, and I was looking for this when the Yom Kippur War started in the Middle East. There was a major gas shortage, although we worked right on through at the refinery, never stopping production. Because of this war, Israel was a place that I started to read about. They were the underdogs, and seemed to fight their fight with ideals. The more I read, the more I thought that that would be a good place to go, and find out for myself what was happening. It was in late 1973 that I made the decision to go to Israel. Not on a vacation, but quit work, and just head out. I felt that I was being stifled in America. I just wanted to be away from it.

I then battled through the rest of 1973 and into 1974. I was becoming more and more discontented with the United States, I could not stand the rat race, the freeways, going to work and all the people living next to you – on both sides and above you in the apartment building. I could hear everything that they were doing. There was the constant roar of a freeway and all this was really getting to me. I asked myself: "What is life, what is the meaning of all this, why do people do this all their lives and one day die?" I thought Israel was the one place which, in all the books I had read, had a high level of ideals;

where life had a meaning other than the material things around you. I started laying plans in the early part of 1974, not only to go to Europe but to go on to Israel.

I started to save money. I paid off the Harley. I wanted to fly again, but did not want to spend the money for lessons. Skydiving seemed to be just the right thing to do. In June 1973 I went out to Elsinore, California, signed a waiver that said that they were not responsible for death or injury, and did three to four hours' ground training. We then went out to an old Howard Topwing airplane, which was leaking oil and smelling of avgas. The pilot made us get inside and started up. The plane belched smoke and vibrated worst that my motorcycle as it roared into life.

We went down a dirt runway, bouncing as we went. The lake was coming up. We couldn't see it but knew that it was getting close. With a last big bounce the plane was airborne, and the lake was under us. It seemed just a short time, and we were at 2,500 feet. Wayne Walker, our instructor, got us out on the step one by one, and off we went. I was too afraid even to know what was going on around me. All of a sudden I was floating under the old converted military canopy. It was beautiful to hang suspended in such a manner: to look out over the world.

Within minutes we were on the ground, and the zap wagon was there to pick us up. We were given first jump course certificates. I got on my motorcycle and headed home. I felt that this was a sport for me. I am still skydiving to this day, and love it as much as a motorcycle.

I went back time and again to skydive. I purchased my own rig, a 7 TU Lopo parachute. I got it cheap, as it had more holes in it than you could shake a stick at. I taped the holes up, and just used it. When a new hole appeared – more tape.

I was still very tense with the sport. Finally after about 35 jumps I became more relaxed, and started to enjoy myself. I had just kept forcing myself to go until one day it all just seemed to come right. I made a jump with a guy named Bob Sinclair, bald, craggy face, with rotting uneven teeth. At the time he was about 55 years old and had about 2,000 jumps in all, using converted military parachutes. He was one of the pioneers of the sport, to say the least. This was my first jump where I was pinned by somebody else. From that moment on skydiving has been a part of my life, one way or the other, be it military or civilian.

5
Going to Israel

In July 1974, in the very early morning, I sat and I started my first diary. I can remember the absolute loneliness that I was starting to experience. My mom and dad were still in bed and I was embarking on a great adventure, something totally different. I had traveled with the Marine Corps to Vietnam and now I was really leaving, to go to a foreign country on my own. There would be no ties to Uncle Sam, nobody to take care of me. I was on a one-way ticket to London, England. I was saying goodbye to my mom and dad and I knew that my tentative, ultimate, aim was Israel, and very possibly the army. My feelings were those of deep pain, of separation from my mom and dad again, of not really knowing what was ahead of me. But everything has its price. I am not a Jew and my ultimate goal was the land of the Jews, the land of Zion. My feeling of desolation within me – hurt, loneliness, emptiness – was settling in. I can remember my mom getting up that morning. She had a bit of a tear in her eye. Then my dad got up. We had breakfast and made small talk. I know my dad understood what I was doing – it seemed my dad always understood me. He had a feeling for what I wanted to do in life, whether it was Vietnam or anything else, in fact I think he understood me better than I understood myself. My mom had a hard time understanding. She wanted me to find a nice girl, get married and have a family, like moms always do. Mom, being a gentle woman, would always have a hard time understanding her son wanting to run off on his own to a foreign country on the other side of the planet, in order to find some meaning in life that he could not find at home.

A woman friend named Kay arrived. I asked her to stay outside while my mom and dad and I parted and, of course, it was the same as when I left for Vietnam. On my part, anyway, there were tears shed. The pain I felt in my heart was a very deep and rending one because I could not say when I would be back. It was not a situation where I could say to Mom and Dad: "Well, I'm going off on a bit of a trip and a little bit of a vacation. I'll be back in a few months." I knew that I might not be back for years. At the same time I knew I was embarking on one of the greatest adventures of my life.

Mom and Dad held back their emotions as I walked out the door. They were true to their generation, strong and stoic in every respect. Kay drove me to the airport and I bid her goodbye. We had had a few beers on the way to lighten the mood. Why did I have someone else take me to the airport? Well, after having had my mom and dad take me to the staging area for departure to Vietnam in 1970, I did not want to experience that kind of parting again. It was very difficult for me to control myself.

Having checked in I walked into the departures terminal. When the aircraft took off I started to feel better. I began to feel a sense of freedom – my life was going to change very radically, as of right now!

We flew to O'Hare airport in Chicago, Illinois, and changed planes for Heathrow, London, England. At Heathrow I went through customs. When I got out of the airport I started walking, in no particular direction other than out of the airport. I had been walking in the rain when a fellow in a Mini pulled up alongside me and said, "Do you need a lift?" My first thoughts were: "Is there something wrong with this guy, is he queer?" I decided that whether he was queer or not, it was damn cold and wet out, so I'd take a ride. I was heading for London because it was all I really knew of England. As we were going down the road I said, "Which way is London?" to which he replied, "Oh, London is that way, you are on the wrong motorway." I asked him where he was heading, and he said he was going to his family in Cardiff, South Wales. He invited me to come along and stay the night, and said he would show me some of the sights, including some Roman ruins. I accepted the invitation, as I did not really have any particular direction. I was on a one-way ticket with $300 in my pocket. That was all I had, plus what was in my pack.

We made it to South Wales through the English countryside. I can remember that it was staggering to me to see everybody driving on the opposite side of the road. This was a shock! The countryside, with all the old buildings, was beautiful and I was getting a sense of history that I had never seen before. There were real ruins – it was history, and we have very little of that in the United States.

Once in Cardiff, we went to a couple of pubs, then some Roman ruins and then we went to Tiger Bay, which at one time was the roughest seaport in Europe. I remember all this very clearly because it was my first night overseas, and I was on my own. I was footloose and fancy-free! We went back to the man's house and I had a very good night's sleep. The next morning he took me to one of the highways leading to North Wales.

I remember knocking around various places in England during that month.

I went to Scotland and clearly remember one adventure I had in Blackpool. I was looking for work there, possibly washing dishes in one of the hotels in the resort area. All this brings to mind a joke that was going around at the time. "Why does Blackpool have all the donkeys and Liverpool all the Paddies?" (Irishmen.) The answer to that one is: "Because Blackpool had first choice."

In Blackpool I went from hotel to hotel and from pub to pub to find a position washing dishes, or whatever. I wasn't having any luck. In one, a fellow came up to me and said: "Listen mate, you look like you could do with a pint of beer!" Well, a pint sounded pretty good to me, so we sat down and started drinking. It came out that he was a tradesman of some kind and on vacation on his own. He seemed likeable enough. We got chatting and he bought me another pint. I told him that I should leave. He disagreed, and said he would treat me because he had nobody there. One pint led to another, and eventually it was time for the pub to close for the afternoon break.

We went off somewhere, got of a couple six-packs of beer, went and sat down in an alley and started drinking. By this time we were really getting drunk and then it was time for the pubs to open again. The six-packs were gone by then. I hadn't eaten since the previous day.

We rolled back into the pub and one beer led to another. I remember there was some dancing going on in another little section of the pub and we ended up there. I can't remember what happened to my new friend at this point – the events are a little blurry. I remember an attractive young woman, but then in my state anything would have been attractive! I went up to her and asked her to dance. I am sure I was trying to be polite but I don't know how I came across. She did not accept my invitation to dance: in fact she said, "Why don't you just get the fuck off away from me, you make me sick!" At that point I thought I would really make her sick, so I stuck my fingers down my throat and threw up a gallon of beer all over her dress. The next thing I knew, I was being knocked all over the place – by whom I don't know. I obviously could not help myself, so I found myself out in the middle of the street. I looked around and my pack hit me right in the face, so with my wounded pride I staggered to my feet, put my pack on my back and wandered off into the rainy night.

What happened next is pretty blurred, but I remember walking down the street and coming upon a Peugot car. It looked pretty inviting, so I fished around the doors and sure enough, one was open. Now this was England and maybe people don't steal like they do in other places in the world. I crawled in and passed out. The next thing I remember: it was daylight and there was a bobby tugging at my foot, saying, "Come on, man, out you go." I got out and there was a family standing around the car, looking at me. I had mud all over my boots, so obviously there was mud on the seat. The car must have smelt of musty beer. "What were you doing in there?" the bobby asked. I told him it had been raining the previous night and it seemed like a good place to sleep, especially as I didn't have a lot of money. He told me I was going down to the station with him, and the first thing I thought was that it was still early, and possibly I would get a nice egg and bacon breakfast. At the station, he filled out a report and I said. "Well, it's time for breakfast," to which he replied. "Oh no, it's a bit late for that, mate." "Tell you what," he said, "We could put you inside for 24 hours, but perhaps another suggestion would be better. Would you be willing to leave Blackpool?" I said I would, because I didn't see much of a future in the town for myself as a dishwasher. We drove to the outskirts of town, and he pointed the way to London. I hitched all the way that day, and ended up sleeping in Hyde Park that night. From London I headed for a place called Bournemouth, on the south coast. It was a vacation area, and I had heard in London that it was a good place to go to find work.

I got a job in the Durley Dean Hotel. I was finally a dishwasher. I worked from morning until dark with a room and food provided, so naturally I was gobbling like there was no tomorrow. There was a very nice waitress employed there whom I walked home at night. We went to a discotheque and I remember seeing some of the British nightlife. It was quite fun – plus I wasn't drunk and in trouble.

After weeks of working, I made enough money to go skydiving. I heard that there was a drop zone at Thruxton aerodrome, which is several miles north of Bournemouth. When I arrived on the Friday it was raining pretty hard. I met some British soldiers from the Red Devils. They are the equivalent of our Golden Knights US Army parachute team. We all started boozing it up in the pub all Friday night and Saturday – we slept there side by side. It was all very good camaraderie from one to another. The fact is that we were all soldiers and soldiers have a feeling for one another that is not generally shared by civilians.

Sunday morning dawned, bright and clear. I had drunk up most of my spare money, and was getting ready to hit the road. The Red Devils said, "No way, mate, you are not going anywhere without making a couple of jumps with us." They paid for two jumps. All in all, we had a grand time, except we all ended up lying under the trees because the spot was bad.

That afternoon I bid farewell to all and made my way to London, where I stayed with Joe, an Irish fellow that I had met at the drop zone. He took me out for some fish and chips. I had been warned in the past about the fish in London, and – wouldn't you know it? – I got food poisoning. Joe, one of the funniest men I have ever met, was never short of a joke. His red face would light up after telling a good one. At the sight of another person laughing, he would laugh harder. He lived with his mother.

There was a cemetery at the end of their street. He took me out there and showed me the grave of his late wife. This explained the sadness that I always saw behind the humor. After a few days convalescing I bid a sad farewell to Joe and Mrs Gallagher, and headed for Dover and the Continent.

I made my way across the English Channel on a Sealink ferry to Ostende, Belgium. I arrived late in the evening, and started walking out of Ostende. It was raining very hard, I had not changed any money, and I was hungry. Food on the ferry was way too expensive for me. I found an old abandoned house and thought I would go down to the cellar because the doors were open. I will never forget the growl and the pair of mean red eyes that I saw down there. I don't know what it was, but all I could think was that it was a demon. I had not been drinking either! I got the hell out the cellar very quickly and decided I would sleep up in the house, which was leaking from one end to the other. The rats were noisy as they scurried back and forth through the old house.

I made my way down to Germany. Hitchhiking was terrible in Europe, so I got a train to Italy and knocked around there a while. The weather was much better there than it had been further north. The trains were so cheap I couldn't believe it. I took a train all the way through Italy to Sicily, then I went back to Rome. I had enough money left to fly from Rome to Israel. I might add that before I flew out of Rome, I rented a moped and went all over – the catacombs, the Coliseum –wandering around on my own. I was on my own tour, with my own little handbook. I saw the Vatican – I will never forget going into the Vatican! It was such a massive thing, and it was the most staggering building I have ever been in in my life. It was artwork that verged on infinity. To say the least, I was finding out that I was not much of a tourist. For me to go from one interesting place to another is not attractive. Plus it is expensive!

From Rome I flew to Israel and arrived there on August 24, 1974. I had made it to the Holy Land, my destination. As to what was to happen here, well it was anybody's guess!

I arrived on *Shabbat* and everything was closed. *Shabbat*, or the Sabbath (Saturday) is a holy day of rest in Israel. This is the first commandment given to man by God. Jewish Sabbath symbolizes the creation of the world by God, and the Biblical commandment is to sanctify this day and not work, following God's act after the completion of the Creation in six days. *Shabbat* is not only used for rest and refraining from work: from Biblical times it has been seen as a day of holy joy.

I made my way to a fleabag hotel down Allenby Avenue in Tel Aviv. I had arrived in Israel with only $20 in my pocket and I drank that up that night, in celebration for arriving in Israel. The next day was Sunday, the first day of the week and I went to the *Sochnut* (the Jewish agency which operated to help the return to Israel of more than 3,000,000 people, founded over 450 communities throughout the country, taught more than 300,000 children (youth *Aliyah*), and has established more than 1,500 educational and cultural institutions). The agency assigned me to a kibbutz out in what is known as the "*Ramot Menashe*" (*ramat* meaning hill) area. *Ramot Menashe* was the land of the tribe of Manasseh. It is the strip of rolling hills separating the southern part of the Carmel ridge, on the northern slopes of Samaria. The region (located between Yokneam and Kibbutz Gilad, the most beautiful in our country), has recently been declared by UNESCO as a Biosphere Reserve – a space that maintains a perfect balance between man and nature for future generations. This is one of two reserves in Israel where there are many springs and a number of perennial streams, such as the river Justice.

The kibbutz was called Ramat Hashofet. *Ramat Hashofet* is the Hebrew for "The Hill of the Judge." I managed to get down to the bus station with all my gear: the *Sochnut* had provided a bus ticket to the kibbutz. I thought we were going quite far north because the trip took about two hours, but in fact there were just a lot of stops in between. I arrived at the kibbutz and will never forget the sight that greeted me. The view stretched across the valley of Israel to Nazareth.

I checked in with the head of the volunteers, a woman named Goldie, who was a concentration camp survivor. I was to be on an *ulpan*, which is a school that teaches Hebrew. This meant that I would have to work so many hours a day, and learn in the school how to speak Hebrew. The class had already been in progress for a month and I am no academic whiz (as I've established earlier in this book), so I got stuck in the very next day, trying to catch up.

We worked in the mornings and had classes in the afternoon. The work I was doing was in what they called the *minsara*, or the wood factory, where we made orange crates. It was there I met a friend that I have to this very day, a fellow named Peter Koff. Peter was tall, lean, well educated and very liberal. He was handsome, with curly black hair, gray intelligent eyes, and sharp Semitic features. Peter was from South Africa. We were at the end of a big machine where the boxes came out and were being cut in half with a great saw. It was very noisy. We would stamp the end of the box on to the main body of the box, and throw it to the next guy, who would stamp the other end on, and then he would throw it to the guy at the bottom of the steel table, who would stack them together, wire them up in stacks of five and off the table they would go. This was not very stimulating, especially when everyone pictures being in Israel working in the fields. After about an hour the drudgery and the boredom of the job set in. This is what we did for four hours per day for one week and six hours per day the following week. Sometimes to give us a break, Pete and I would jam the machine. The *kibbutznik* mechanic would come and have to unjam it, this putting him in a bad mood, because he suspected foul play. After hours we also had our study time. The national working week in Israel is six days.

Now as far as learning Hebrew is concerned, I learned the alphabet and certain parts of grammar, but I never caught up with the class. To say the least, most of the kids there had some type of college background, which I had not, so I was kind of the odd man out. They were all naïve liberals, and I was very conservative.

I did my best to learn on my own after hours, and a few of the *kibbutzniks* were helpful with my learning of Hebrew, but in general most of the Israelis were selfish about the Hebrew language. They did not want to speak Hebrew because they wanted to learn English and did not care less about anyone else's Hebrew. If a person was from a country in South America, say, or a European country where English was not the first language, they learned Hebrew quite quickly, because that was the language everyone used. But if a person spoke English as a first language, it did not work in your favor.

We worked in the *minsara* until January, when the *ulpan* finished. During that time I had been making enquiries about immigrating, the army, etc, and had been coming up fairly blank. At one point, when I went down to try and join the army I was told I had to become an Israeli citizen before I could enlist. Now being a non-Jew and trying to do something like that is very difficult. I then went to *Misrad Hapnim*, the immigration bureau, and what followed was all quite interesting.

This was in Afula, where the *Misrad Hapnim* for our area was located. The man completed all the papers but asked for proof of my Judaism. I told him a story of having served in Vietnam, that my mom and dad did not want to see me in the army in Israel, so they were not prepared to help me in any way and would send no proof over that I was Jewish. He then asked why I looked like an Irishman and I told him my father was Irish and my mother Jewish, which still makes me Jewish. At the time I was very convincing.

I would go back to the offices every other week to see what progress had been made, but the officer always asked for proof of Judaism. That is when I blew my cork. I used reverse psychology and did what an Israeli would do, used *chutzpah*, which means cheek! I started ranting and raving like an Israeli, saying I had come here to serve Israel and help the country by doing my patriotic service in the army. I asked him how he could deny me that right and asked him what he wanted of me. At that time Kathy Ben Aron, the daughter of Shlomo Ben Aron, helped me. Shlomo was himself the head of the kibbutz and a famous figure in the making of the state of Israel. Kathy knew me from the kibbutz, and like any Israeli she was more than ready to take a side and get involved in the argument. She confirmed that I was a very good worker and a conscientious person. Kathy then asked the officer, "What the hell is wrong with you? Let him migrate."

The immigration officer gave in. He telephoned Jerusalem and they agreed to let me immigrate. It was actually a very big moment in my life and it is impossible to describe what I felt, but at that moment I knew that I was to realize my dream of going into the army. The officer said he would send the papers through, which he did, and within a couple of weeks I received my *teudat zehut*, which is a personal identity booklet. When this book arrived I went straight down to the army administration centre and got a date for a physical. It was set for January 2, 1975.

What would I have done if I had not been accepted? I never really thought about not being accepted – I certainly worried about it sometimes, but once I put my mind to it, I just had to find the way to do it. I don't know what I would have done had I not been accepted, there just was not any contingency plan.

On January 2, I went straight to Haifa. Now January 1 was New Year's Day and then, and on New Year's Eve, I had been on a pretty good binge with other volunteers in the kibbutz. We had some mighty whopping good parties, so I had quite a hangover when I went into the administration center. I nearly had a fit when the doctor told me I had a heart murmur and palpitations. I knew it was true but refused to believe it. There had never been anything wrong with my heart. He told me they were actually going to fail me on the physical. Needless to say, I was shattered. My whole world had just caved in on me. I left the center in a very low mood, made my way back to the bus station and then to the kibbutz.

I decided that my drinking had caused me to fail the physical, so I stopped drinking, and for the next two months I worked out very hard. Pete Koff and I ran three to four miles per day, did pull-ups, push-ups, and sit-ups but absolutely no alcohol. I cannot remember the exact date, but I think it was in April that I went and had my next physical. It was a different doctor this time and after testing my heart and blood pressure, said the previous guy must have been crazy to say I had a heart murmur and palpitations, because there was nothing wrong with my heart. Naturally I was greatly relieved to hear that I was 100 percent fit for duty as an operational soldier.

My next step was to have a date assigned for induction. I was assigned to go into the army on May 5, and left the administration center in a very good mood. I was on top of the world because I was actually going into the Israeli army. This meant that my previous two years of planning was now really starting to take shape. The new beginning was in sight.

The morning of May 5 eventually arrived. I got up at about 5:00 a.m., and said goodbye to Elsa and Fred and all the people who had given me a farewell party the night before. All the volunteers had been at the party. I got on the bus and left for Haifa, arriving at the army building at about 7:00 a.m.

I was called out of the line and told that there were problems with my American citizenship and going into the army. I had an audience with a stern-looking woman who told me, as she leaned across her desk, that I could lose my citizenship. My reply was, "Well, if I lose it, I lose it. I came over here to serve Israel, so if my ideas mean anything, I have to go along with what I feel." Once again I was right back to the old feeling that what I was doing was right, and there was no backup contingency plan for not being able to accomplish my goal. She then signed some other papers and I was processed through with everybody else. At the time that I was taken to her office I can remember thinking: "Oh boy, here we go again," and my spirit just sank. What problem did we have now? When I came out of the office, I knew everything was on. We were told to board buses and head for Bakum, which was the army induction center.

I kept hearing people saying in Hebrew, *mau mau*. This meant all the

Moroccans, the jailbirds, the real negative ends of Israeli society were inducted into the army in May. My spirits were still very high when we boarded the buses and drove out of Haifa. It kept reminding me of the day in June 1969 when I joined the marines, and boarding the bus at Los Angeles induction center to be driven to San Diego, This time I was on my way to Bakum, to be put into uniform in the Israeli army. I could actually say I was in the army again, and to me it was a very momentous day. It was a goal attained. It wasn't just for the sake of doing it, it was for being a part of something that I felt was worthwhile, not only for myself but for this struggling country of high ideals. I knew what I had read, plus now what I had experienced up to this time in Israel. I knew in my heart of hearts that this was right for me.

We arrived in Bakum in the late afternoon, and the fun began. We had to run from one place to the next and every time somebody looked around, which was all the time, they would tell us to run around this tent or this pole, fuck around here and do this or that, instead of hitting us. All of it meant punishment. We were run over to some buildings and were issued with uniforms. Our civilian clothing and belongings were not taken away, but put into bags. It was not as in the marines where our things were sent away. We kept everything with us but were not allowed to use it.

They were not shouting at us, or hitting us. Terror was not a tactic of discipline. We were then processed for the different units and I felt I would like to go into tanks. I felt it was an interesting way to get around during training and operations and not have to walk or run. Though I was not a mechanic I did like machines. We had been over 24 hours without sleep, as well, and we were all dead tired. I was also realizing that these guys were not interested in doing what they were told. In the marines we screwed up everything that we did, but we were at least trying to do it right. That had no relevance to anything for these characters.

When we finally got our heads down, we had been going non-stop for more than 40 hours, after a particularly long session of being run around the tents, with people tripping over the tie-downs and stakes. I was to find out that nothing in the Israeli army was to be gained without pain. I met with tank officers and they were happy to accept me into the tank regiment. This was great!!!

The next day, through the grapevine someone in the paratroopers somehow found out I had been in the marines. A sergeant from the paratroopers approached me, and said there were some officers who wanted to interview me while they were interviewing people for the paratroopers. Red lights were flashing in my head, warning something bad was about to happen. I told him I was not interested because I had already been accepted into the tanks, to which he replied, "You will not like tanks, but come and see these people anyway." It was more or less an order, so I went and reported, and had an interview for half an hour. My Hebrew was still not very good, although with great effort it was improving all the time. I am not a linguist, my hearing has not been great after Vietnam and I am quite tone deaf, so it is very difficult for me speaking a new language. I could, however, understand what they were saying. They asked me to strip a M16 and they also asked me to do a few other things. Finally, the head man there, whose rank was *magad*, which is a battalion commander (the rank is actually equal to that of a lieutenant colonel), said that they would like me to go into the Israeli paratroopers and not the tanks. I tried to be polite, and told him those nice people had already accepted me into the tanks. I did not want to go into the paratroopers. I had already heard how they ran and marched, how their life was a never-ending, colossal, training exercise. I was just not interested in that. He replied that they wanted me to go into the paratroopers as a volunteer and once again I told him I had been accepted into the tanks. He told me forcefully to forget about the people in tanks, because I had just "volunteered" to go into the paratroopers. I was now a very worried soul. I honestly didn't know if I had what it takes to be a paratrooper, in Israel. I was to be in Battalion 809, Israeli Parachute Brigade.

> Short history: Battalion 890 –"Rattlesnake"
> The first paratrooper battalion in the Israeli Defense Force (IDF), it was founded in 1950 and began to take its place as one of the spearhead units, like the legendary 101 unit. The regiment's first commander was Ariel Sharon (the greatest Israeli field commander and eventually 11th Prime Minister).
>
> From the early 50s to the present day the regiment participated in all the battles of the IDF including retaliations, incidents such as fighting the battle of the Chinese Farm, other incidents in the Lebanon Wars and more.

We then went over to another area where I was issued with a pair of red boots: I had to return the black boots already issued to me. I was now wondering about the quality of the people around me. The people were real greenhorns, but they were not just greenhorns. A lot of them were real shitbirds as people to start with. I was with a better class of shitbirds at the time, because of being in the paras, who were volunteers. The last two days I had spent with people of very low caliber. They would steal anything from you: they were fighting amongst themselves – it was a mean place. I still could not say much for the quality of the people that I was with. The boys being inducted as paratroopers were a hard bunch to get along with. They were all people from the city, and city people are more difficult to get along with than country people or people living on a kibbutz. *Kibbutzniks* tend to have a better education, and a far higher level of ideas and motivation, both for their army units, and for their sense of patriotism.

The next day was spent running around poles, doing odd things, being processed here and there. Finally, we did a five- to six-mile run. We went through the trash heaps and other obstacles around the base, just to see who could keep up with the instructors. I was in pretty good physical condition from working out on the kibbutz, but these guys were like gazelles. The next day. we were sworn into the army as Israeli soldiers in front of an army monument. For better or worse, I was truly in the army.

In serving on the kibbutz, I had a great privilege – I guess due to my idealistic state. I attended a seminar in Jerusalem (which also happened to be my first trip to Jerusalem, the Holy City). The seminar covered the Holocaust and the beginning of Israel as a state, and we also toured Yad Vashem. I recall that we were all in a very high state of idealism as we went through the Yad Vashem memorial. *Yad Vashem* means "Hand and Name". It is a memorial to the 6,000,000 who died in the Holocaust. There was a large bar of gold made from metal taken from human teeth, and all kinds of relics from the Warsaw ghetto, the concentration camps, and the Holocaust itself. We also went through the military cemetery on top of the mountain, very close to Yad Vashem. I can remember a very strong stirring in my heart. This was Israel, a country that had a right to exist. We also went to the Wailing Wall, the last visible remains of the Temple and the pinnacle of Judaism, which – so we were told – goes about 150 feet down under the ground. Devout Jews wail by the wall, pray to God and put little notes in the cracks in the stones.

In early June 1975, months and what seems an eternity later, we also had a ceremony at the Wailing Wall. The ceremony we had was with the paratroopers, and it was here that we received a copy of the *Tanakh* – the Hebrew Bible – and our M16 rifles for the first time. We had actually had the rifles before that but not the formal ceremony itself, called "Swearing at the Western Wall." We got there from Sha'ar HaGai, besieged during the War of Independence, from which a road about six miles long in a narrow valley leads to Jerusalem. The song *Bab el Wad* (the Arabic name of this place) describes the difficulties during the battle for Jerusalem and is the most famous sad song one will ever hear in Israel.

We climbed to Jerusalem through the Tomb of Samuel, the traditional burial site of the biblical prophet Samuel, atop a steep hill at an elevation of 908 meters (Israel uses the metric system of measurements – in the States, this would be nearly 3,000 feet) above sea level. It is situated to the north of Jerusalem. We passed through Ramot, an Israeli neighborhood that was under construction. On the site of Samuel's Tomb is a building containing a mosque. This was originally a church, built in the eighteenth century. The tomb itself is in an underground chamber, where a small synagogue is located. From Ramot we continued to Ammunition Hill (Giva'at Hatahmoshet) – a memorial site and museum commemorating the 182 Israeli soldiers who fell during the Six-Day War. A bloody battle was waged on Ammunition Hill, which was ultimately taken by Israeli soldiers, and opened the way to Israel's capture of the Old City. The task of capturing the hill was given to 3 company, 66th Battalion of the Israeli Parachute Brigades.

In 1987, Ammunition Hill was declared a national memorial site. It was a powerful ceremony, which took place at night, with lit torches. The rabbis chanted and there was a speech about the meaning of what the prophet Isaiah said in the End of Days prophecy: "And he shall judge among the nations, and shall rebuke many people: and they shall beat their swords into plowshares, and their spears into pruning hooks: nation shall not lift up sword against nation, neither shall they learn war any more," thereby raising our motivation level. As the ceremony finished and the dignitaries left, we realized that the rifles were mixed up and then of course, punishment, and mass confusion to figure out whose rifle was whose, in a company of a bit over 100 men.

Our base was Sanur, a Palestinian village in Samaria, between Nablus and Jenin. It is a place I will never forget as long as I live. The base itself was a Jordanian army base before the Six Day War. After the Six Day War the IDF transferred basic paratrooper training to this site, on the side of a hill. From the gate it was 700 meters (2,300 feet) up a paved road to the top, just straight up, and we were forever going up and down it, being punished for some sin that we had committed.

Punishment was *onesh.* When we arrived there we had two weeks of just plain miserable life. We were called out at all hours of the morning and night and put into the fireman's carry position. I do not recollect being carried on anyone's back at this particular stage so I was always carrying somebody. Two guys were with me throughout the basic training: one was Zachme Surriel, who was a short stocky Yemenite, and the other was a fellow named Hiflah Mordechai. God rest his soul. These guys seemed to fit on my shoulders just perfectly and that is why I always ended up carrying them. They did not get their balls crushed by my shoulders as I was lugging them around – sometimes for long periods. This may sound funny, but it is something that the Israelis do all the time. The fireman's carry is for punishment, but also has to do with training soldiers to be ready to carry a wounded comrade as a matter of survival.

They were building us up one way and tearing us down another, which means we had very little sleep. The day started at 4:00 a.m. sharp, and continued right through until midnight. Sometimes they would even wake us up when we should be sleeping. Sometimes they would let us go to sleep early and then later we would spend two hours in punishment running up and down the hill, from the top to the bottom. Then there was the obstacle course. I must say the marines had a pretty tough obstacle course, but there was nothing like the *maslul*, their obstacle course.

The course itself was 600 meters (656 yards) long. It had everything from climbing ropes to poles for crawling up and swinging from – you name it. We had to wear our tin-pot American helmets, carry an M16, 10 magazines of ammunition and two bottles of water. We first had to run 500 meters (547 yards) down a tarred road to the obstacle course. It was 600 meters (656 yards) through the obstacle course and then another 500 meters (547 yards) afterwards. We ran this in the morning and in the afternoon and this was not known as physical fitness, this was just running the *maslul*.

I thought my heart would quit and that I would die. In all my life I have never drunk so much water. To say we drank 10 one-liter (1 ¾ pints) bottles of water a day is really not out of line. The whole thing was a real grind.

They tried hard with the food. In the morning it was hard-boiled eggs, bread and tomatoes. In the afternoon we had our main meal, and many times we got hard-boiled eggs, bread, and tomatoes in the evening, with possibly a salad.

En mesihin beshat aa'ruha means in Hebrew "No talking at dinner while eating." This was the command we had to obey, This was in the laws of Judaism dealing with human behavior during and after the meal. Of course silence during meals did not happen. Guys always found reasons to break it. So when I was asked to pass the salt at the table, I refused, and answered: "Do not talk while dining!" They kept asking me to talk. I wasn't going to speak. This would lead to trouble with the squad leaders and *onesh* would ensue.

Saltshakers were not used. The salt was put in a little pile on the table and everybody stuck their fingers into it. Hygiene was not high on their list. We had to use a lot of salt because we were soaking wet with sweat within half an hour of getting up in the morning.

I can remember going to bed wet with perspiration on many occasions. We were so fatigued we just did not care. We just crept into our sacks (sleeping bags). During the time I was in the Israeli army, there was no such thing as a mattress or a blanket, and boy, did these sleeping bags stink after a while. They smelt like the inside of a garbage bag.

We were tired all the time: so tired that at times my teeth ached. I could see that my state of physical fitness was on its way down. We had classes during the day and I battled to keep my eyes open. Sometimes the instructors would make us run a few 100 yards around some pole or something. They would make us go *ehad al ehad*, which means one on one in the fireman's carry. They would do this for about 10 minutes. However, they did not like to take time out of the training day to punish us. They would just write in on their little shit-list, and they would get us that night when we were sleeping. The whole idea was to punish the platoon at night, on our time and not on theirs!

One punishment was called *tirturim* – and for that, our commanders were specialized. Once during a weapons lesson some men fell asleep. We were standing in pairs facing each other, slapping each other. The guys were pretending they were hitting one another, but in fact were only stroking each other. Nehemiah Elisha, an Indian fellow, was standing opposite me and got a very strong slap in the face from me, which was a shock. He didn't expect it. When it was Nehemiah's turn, he was standing in front of me, hands behind his back. Then I felt a strong punch in the face. I was biting my lips as it was a strong punch.

So we would have classes in the morning, off and on, and sometimes in the late morning or late afternoon we would have two hours of what they call *madoss*, which meant sport, but it wasn't. It was just grim, hard exercise, and it seemed never-ending: push-ups, squat thrusts, running. They would say we were just going for a run, as if we hadn't already been running off and on all day.

I don't know how many kilometers we ran a day – usually between five and 10 (three to six miles) or more during the course of the day. They always told us they would not risk a helicopter to pick someone up when we could carry the person out of the danger area ourselves, and if you did not have a stretcher you would have to do it one on one in the fireman's carry.

The dropout rate was pretty high. In those first two weeks we had a large number of guys that we shipped straight back to Bakum for reassignment. They had no stomach for it. There were people coming in all the time from Bakum and people being shipped out daily. After the first two weeks we had a *mahlaka*, which is a platoon. I was in *mahlaka ahat*, which is platoon number one. We were to be a cohesive unit as such for the next 14 months, which was supposed to be the duration of our basic training.

I often thought: "How would I compare training in the Marine Corps to the Israeli army?" The Israeli army was grim; the hours were longer by far than in the marines. The marines would go from 4:00 a.m. to 9:00 p.m. The marines were good about letting us sleep. Here we were under pressure all the time: the Israeli army was physically far more demanding. The marines did not have us in a one on one position all the time: we slept better, and the food, I must admit, was superior to that of the Israeli army – which is not saying much. It seemed as if I was in a world of my own most of the time, because I did not understand everything they were saying. I knew that when they said *ratz* or *gash*, they meant: "Move your ass." We were always being punished for something. *sararote*, which meant sins, and *onesh* – I learnt those words because that was the precommand for anything we were going to get punished for. I didn't understand why the fellows were laughing at me when they heard me replying to the commands. This is one funny story: as part of the training and martial teachings, along with physical exercise we had weapons lessons, generally conducted in the sheds, which were lean-tos. The lessons required disassembly and assembly of different types of weapons many times. There was a lot of repetition. Everything was timed, day or night.

We had to repeat everything the instructors said when doing outside training. My Hebrew vocabulary was still very limited, and I could not understand at all what I was repeating I was just parroting what I thought I'd heard. One funny sentence was when the commander said: "Do not put the blanket on the bed that way." When I repeated it, it sounded like: "Your sister is the opposite."

They gave us seven minutes to go up and down the hill. The words *mizdar conenut* meant a readiness inspection in seven minutes. It is a sentence that will live with me for the rest of my life because it meant you got up from a dead sleep, and within seven minutes you had to be on the road and ready to go to war. But it was not war, which I feel would have been preferable. We started long periods of punishment for the sins of the day.

We started with about 33 recruits. Of the 33, only 12 of the original guys passed at the end of the 14 months. At this particular time the training started to pick up. The first two weeks were nothing compared to the following 14 months. I thought I was miserable with that – well it was nothing, because it just became worse and worse. The days were long. It might be asked : "Why 14 months basic training? Why so long?" It was not so much basic training. In the Israeli army (in the paratroopers) you are operational after five months, because by this time the infantry training and parachute-jump course is complete. However, they did not consider us properly trained as a *hayal cravie*, which is an operational soldier of the front line. You are operational if war comes and you are sent into the front line.

Nonetheless the training is 12 months and then a two-month NCO course, and we were under the gun all the time.

In the Israeli army, every three or four weeks they give you *Shabbat* off, which is Friday afternoon, all day Saturday, and we had to report back and start training again on Sunday. We needed this time to go and do laundry, get cleaned up and have some undisturbed rest. In that training nothing is undisturbed. You are on the go seven days a week, even on *Shabbat*. When you are lying around during the day, they would take us for this or that detail. When there were three stars in the sky and the *Shabbat* was over, they would tell us to start paying for our sins of the Sabbath. We were talking out of line, did not move fast enough when called out, or some other problem from *Yom* (day) *Shabbat*. No matter what we did, we were still wrong, and generally the troop leaders were right in punishing us. I had never seen such an unruly bunch of people to be trained as these.

On the other hand, where the Marine Corps was concerned, we had no time off for the ten weeks we were in boot camp, none at all. We had a little time to relax on Sunday, but they still kept us going. After church we had to write letters, or polish boots and brass. We also went out for a long exercise period, so the day was a full one. I must admit, once the Israelis said "stand down," if you were in camp that Friday afternoon and Saturday they did not hassle us the way the marines did, and every three to four weeks we were allowed to go home for the Friday afternoon and Saturday.

Being what they called a *hayal boded*, a lonely soldier with no family in the country, I went back to the kibbutz. I must admit the elders at Kibbutz Ramat Hashofet were good to me. They allowed me to keep a room there, for which the army gave them a pittance. It really was *not* worth their while. They did it out of the goodness of their hearts. They gave me that room for the whole time I was in the army and they could have made a lot more money out of it if they had volunteers or students in the room, because those people would have been productive on the kibbutz. All my laundry was done for me – this was done on Saturdays for army personnel. Kibbutz Ramat Hashofet was my home, and it was a place I loved very much. To this day I have affectionate memories of it.

After a few weeks of basic training we went on our first long forced march. This time we started out with our packs, but I cannot remember how much weight we were carrying, probably about 35 lbs, with rifle, magazines and everything else. We also had big American tin-pot helmets. We marched fast from our base at Sanur to the Kule Hills, located near the city of Modi'in. We were only doing this in platoon strength, not in company strength yet. We wore a harness, meaning a belt (no vest), with a pair of straps connected to a belt that had magazine pouches suspended on it, and bound together with shoelaces. These carried our magazines, grenades (which we had not received yet) and water bottles. When a march is done in company strength it is a lot more difficult. In platoon strength we went out at night and marched over the hills – mind you, this was very hard, rocky country to march in – and we went over hills, on goat paths, over thornbushes and everything else, the distance being about 30 miles. On the last two miles we started to run, carrying the stretcher, and sometimes there would be as many as four men to relieve us, sometimes only two. I remember one troop leader in particular, Yoel Nitzani, who was to be a friend to this very day. The other was Lieutenant Peled, who was our platoon lieutenant. Peled was a runner, he could just take off and go. I used to hate to see the sight of his backside working because I knew I would be at my wits' end within minutes, trying to keep up with him. I came to respect Yuval Peled very much. He was the very essence of an infantry platoon lieutenant. He led by example, never wavered, and never showed any emotion about anything. One never knew what he was thinking.

Personal memories and impressions by our commander, Yuval Peled: "Platoon 1! Once you have learned all the secrets of camouflage, each of you has 30 minutes to disguise himself on the hill behind us: 30 minutes – move!" This order was given at the end of basic training in camouflage. After half an hour, Sergeant Nitzani went to check the results of the exercise. A few minutes later he came back, laughing and said to me, "Peled, come and see! " I followed him. On the way we passed some soldiers, hiding in the bushes with straw on their heads, then Nitzani pointed to a tree that stood on the slope and said, "Look!" I looked on the ground, but at first I did not see anything, then Nitzani said: "In the tree." I looked up at the tree and hardly identified a figure of a man who turned himself with arms and legs into branches! Yes, it was Scott. He did what he was taught at the marines camouflage course, which was probably more meaningful than what I had taught.

My first impression of Dave was at the first meeting with the platoon, at the basic training. The platoon sergeant had arranged the men in three rows. David was placed in the front row and I, as a young officer, went down the line with the soldiers on my left. As I approached him I heard a bang on the weapon, such that terrified me. I looked left and saw David standing at "present arms, " which he learned in the marines: the salute when the officer walks by. It was the same when we taught the men to do *pazatsta* (dropping to the ground from a standing position), where he showed another drop technique for fighting in built-up areas and other differences – David was able to teach me a few things also.

We ran for miles, to get back to the base. We had cuts on our shoulders, our shoulders were rubbed raw, and I had my first taste of a real forced march, which I never had in the Marine Corps. It was a real all-night march. These forced marches were to be almost a monthly ritual from that time on and the distance would be up to 50 miles at a time, with a lot more weight than we were carrying at the moment.

The next day we would be told to clean up. They would roust us around and run us in the fireman's carry. We had not slept in well over 24 hours. Finally some buses arrived. When we saw these buses we thought: "Holy mackerel, we are going home for the weekend." These were the most beautiful buses in the world, from the Egged bus company of Israel. We just wanted to get out of there. Finally the troop leaders would release us. We climbed into the buses in a state of weariness hard to conceive. They would take us out to Beit Liet, which is a place I will never forget.

From Beit Lid we would do tramping, which is hitchhiking, to various places. Now as a soldier in uniform, I could get on a bus without paying, which is a consideration from the Egged bus company. I made my way to the kibbutz for my first real weekend of liberty, and I remember all I could do was lie down on my bed and relax for the first few hours. Then I had a shower and went to dinner, which was always a very nice occasion. The residents would have a little talk for about five minutes and then they would wish everybody a good appetite and *Shabbat, shalom*, and everybody got stuck into the chicken and schnitzel.

6
Basic Training, Israel

At the kibbutz, I would always sit with the volunteers in the *heder ochel* (cafeteria). These volunteers were from all over the world. My Hebrew was improving all the time, the hard way. I was also learning a grade of Hebrew that was spoken in the army, like the whole new vocabulary that I learned when I went into the marines (not at times good).

As I've mentioned earlier, *Shabbat* is the weekly day of rest, holy to the Jewish people. This is a covenant between God and the nation of Israel. Saturday (*Shabbat*) starts at sunset on Friday, as the Jewish calendar is a lunar one. All work is stopped and we rest both mind and body from the difficulties of the week.

On Friday night we stayed at the base when we gathered for a special meal and began singing hymns in the honor of *Shabbat*. Essential work for the war effort, tolerating no delay, should, if necessary, continue even on Saturdays and holidays in Israel.

When we were sent home on *Shabbat*, we went with our M16s and a magazine. Unlike the marines, we had use of rifles from almost day one. On June 6, we had our first leave from Sanur and I had a weekend back in the kibbutz, which was appreciated. Sunday morning, June 8, I got up very early to leave the kibbutz, and caught a ride to Beit Liet, which was the jump-off point for the West Bank. I can remember sitting down to have a cup of tea, very early in the morning, somewhere around 06:00 a.m. I had just had a sip of tea, when all of a sudden shots were fired from across the road in a northerly direction. It looked like an Arab firing indiscriminately, spraying the area. I sprang from my seat and ran across the open area to get a clear line of fire on this guy. I jumped down beside another American, a fellow named Doug from 202 Battalion. We figured that there was more than one of these guys but we did not know where the others were. There was a jeep parked across the road, and I could see the terrorist from underneath, so I started to shoot at him. By this time the *Mishmar HaGvul*, the border police (usually known as the Magav), were on our left and all of us starting firing at the about the same time. To say the least, this Arab was not going to last long. Right in the middle of all this Doug's mouth in his narrow face was working: he yelled: "Grenade, grenade." I looked to my right, and between us there was a pineapple grenade. I very briefly contemplated jumping on it, but I wasn't ready to die right yet, so I grabbed the grenade and threw it back. With all the shooting going on, I cannot remember whether it exploded or not, but we did not find the grenade afterwards. I am not a good baseball player but with the strength I had that morning to survive being blown up, I could have thrown that grenade off into infinity.

The Arab terrorist was soon dispatched and we went over and inspected the body, which had a well-ventilated appearance. We then formed search teams to hunt down any others that might have been with him. We thought there were more. We hunted for the rest of the morning, but came up empty-handed.

This is an account of the incident from Joes Levich, one of the soldiers of our platoon.

> We were supposed to leave at 09:00 a.m. on Sunday morning and the first troops began to arrive. It was a pleasant summer day and we could relax and enjoy a cup of coffee and a snack. At 07:45 a.m. or so we were standing and eating sandwiches, enjoying a continuation of the Sabbath – until suddenly we heard shots from different directions and shouts from one of the officers. We formed into line and stormed towards the gunfire, firing ourselves. This turned the terrorist's fire and he threw a grenade at a group of soldiers at the crossroads – it was a major road junction and a popular hitchhiking station.
>
> Needless to say, the initial shock, fear and lack of experience caused most of us to lose time locating our cartridges. Someone beside us shouted: "Soldiers! Fire sprayed out, fight!" We took cover behind barrels filled with concrete, which separated the road from the parking area. We could see directly into the orchard, and from their building the border guard joined in the shooting, using a submachine gun. Between the barrels, we identified a terrorist standing in the ditch that separated the orchard and the road. He was spraying the area with a Carl Gustav sub-machine gun. We began to return fire while four of us took up a position behind a barrel. At one point someone shouted "Grenade!" and indeed there was a Zhino grenade lying on the ground about three meters (10 feet) from where we had taken shelter. David, who was there, sprang at it, and threw it back at the terrorist near the orchard. At last the firing stopped and we went forward and identified the terrorist's body. Someone shouted: "Get up, get in line and start moving

towards the orchard." This search was done in case there were more terrorists hiding in the orchard. We were then told to clear our weapons and we started back. The body of the dead terrorist was searched. There were now jeeps facing east and west. Out came three paratroop officers. We had not seen them in the firefight!

Half an hour later *mesocco* of GOC arrived – Yona Efrat, who questioned us. Then it was time to board buses and head for Sanur.

When we got back to the bus stop there was a busload of schoolgirls singing: *David, Meleh Israel.* They had heard about me throwing the grenade away before it killed us and they possibly also thought I was the guy who killed the terrorist, although I could not say in honesty that it was me. There were a lot of people shooting at the same time. It couldn't be said that my marksmanship was any better than anybody else's. What they were singing meant "David, King of Israel," and my head was about as big as a balloon. It was soon to be deflated. We were put on buses shortly afterwards and on our way to Sanur, where all the fun and games of basic training was to carry on. So much for *Meleh Israel*"!

The way to our military base passed near the railway station in the Palestinian city of Tul-Karem, established by the Turks during the First World War as part of the railway designed to cross the Sinai Peninsula to Egypt and the Suez Canal. Samaria is mentioned in the Bible many times. It is a major location of Bible stories from the times of King Solomon to the times of King Herod, from the First to the Second Temples. Samaria has a variety of landscapes, mountains, high ridges, wide valleys, springs, streams and spectacular views. It takes about 40 minutes on the bus, from Beit Liet to Sanur, but brings us to another world.

The reality of our lives was about to begin again. On arrival at Sanur we were immediately knocked down a peg or two. They said, "So you think that you are a real bunch of fighting soldiers after shooting up the bus stop?" The troop leaders went on to inform us that a jeep had apparently been shot up. The jeep turned out to belonged to some officer, so now the troop leaders were shitting to make us pay for this sin. They made us run all afternoon in *madoss* – physical fitness – all Sunday afternoon in the heat. That evening after dinner we were called out for training. There were times when I would ask myself,

"Why am I here among these people?" Can you imagine how lonely I felt at times, being a gentile amidst all the Jews, all those long noses? Some of them were dark, some of them were blond with blue eyes, but they all had one thing in common: they could argue and be miserable like no other race of people that I have ever been around. I do not say that in a mean or anti-Semitic sense because I have a very deep and strong feeling for the Jewish people. However, when I asked myself in the middle of the night as we were being punished, or when we were just sweating blood knowing that the next day would be the same miserable routine: "What am I doing here, why did I do this?" I would look to my inner self and always know why I was doing this. I had made a commitment that I was going to serve; I would morally and physically give my best to this country and its people, no matter what.

As far as loneliness was concerned, I was at times very lonely. Nobody really knew my secret – that I was a gentile – although I was often told that I looked more like an Irishman than a Jew and I would always come up with the answer that my mother was Jewish and my father Irish.

There was a very special young woman that worked among us taking care of our mental needs. Her name was Anat. She was like our mother, and a nurse and a psychologist and our sister as well. She had to listen to our troubles, visit soldiers in hospitals, at their home and whatever else was needed. She was *pikeyda plugatee* – the troop secretary.

A troop secretary raises the mood and makes basic training bearable. Her role as a troop secretary includes the distribution of newspapers, filling reports, printing documents and bringing packages sent to the soldiers She was there for motivation before *masa*, as a form of psychological help, or at least a sympathetic ear for the soldiers. Especially, we could just talk to her normally, without any crudity or roughness. She was also there as a bridge between the troops and the commanders, to persuade, and to solve problems.

The following is Anat's perspective on David, written 40 years later:

> I think it was at the induction center when were doing classifications in the Bakum that I first met him. He was quite different from all other soldiers – age, origins, language, personal history and his past as a fighter. He appeared as a "strange bird," but very intriguing and challenging.
>
> Compared to the rest of the soldiers who were completely in shock, he was organized, most disciplined, and had the endurance and ability to withstand the most difficult situations. Even now I hear the loud voice: "Yes,

sir!" The disruptions What does this mean? Does it refer to his poor Hebrew?to his words, the seriousness and responsibility he displayed all the time made it seem that David (as I read it), did not get tired … I remember clearly how amazing his behavior was in the light of some of the soldiers. I guess in his wildest dreams, he would not believe he would order a company of *Mainikim*, some of whom do not have any real responsibility for order and discipline.

After the incident of throwing a grenade at the crossroads, David was the hero of the day and we were all grateful to him for saving our lives.

Others who helped David establish himself and were very supportive were especially Yoel Nizani and Yuval Peled (his commanders), and of course the soldiers learned to accept him for the difference and responsibility, and all parties were impressed by it

One of the hottest memories burned in me is – David came to visit me at my home, and we went with my father to drink beer. My father was a soldier for many years (in the Jewish Brigade WWII British Army, and then the Israeli army). He felt fellowship with fighters, and greeted Scott with open arms.

It was very, very exciting when we met again two years ago after many years of not having seen each other. I was surprised by the closeness, love, warmth, curiosity and interest in the meeting they had. It not faded with the years!

I think it is a great privilege for us to know David-Scott-Bar.

The Israeli mentality, especially the May induction group mentality: I have never been around such a pack of liars in my life. They would lie about anything – not so much to one another, but to the people in charge, to the troop leaders, the troop sergeant, Yoel Nitzani. He knew all the tricks and there was nothing that could get past him.

Yoel Nitzani: our relationship was to become very close, even at times when we were being punished. There was an affinity between us, although we never showed it to the other troops. I would be punished right along with them. Yoel could see through everything. He would say to one of the guys during a class: "You're asleep! I saw you." Even though the man's head had been nodding down and his eyes were closed, he would deny sleeping. "You were asleep, I saw you." "No Sir, I did not sleep, on my mother I did not sleep." Everything was "On my mother." Another favorite saying of the Israeli soldiers to one another was, "Are you going somewhere, are you going to do something, was it you that did this?"

And the favorite reply was. "No, it was my sister." I still use the saying today because it is something I have always found quite humorous. They were a very hard bunch of boys to teach anything to. Through the centuries the Jews as a people have generally not been known as great soldiers, but as great educators. Now all of a sudden there was a Jewish nation and they intended making great soldiers out of these guys, whether they wanted to be great soldiers or not. It was a test of wills that went on through the whole basic training period. I must say that although the training was grim and difficult, it could have been made so much easier with a little sense of cooperation amongst these boys. The November induction group, which is the best one of them all, is made up of *kibbutzniks* and *moshavniks*. They get along and accomplish more in a lot less time, and with far less punishment.

The *kibbutzniks* had socialist ideals and values of human equality and sharing. Kibbutzniks played an important role in Israel's security forces. During the Six Day War, when Israel lost 800 soldiers, 200 of them were members of *kibbutzim*. The population from *kibbutzim* has decreased, and is now less than two percent of the total population in Israel. At one time 75 percent of the Israeli Air Force pilots were originally from the kibbutz movement. Kibbutz members served in key positions in the community and the country's leadership, and especially in the first decades of its existence these people made a very large contribution to the Palmach central defense and command staff and the army of the state. This contribution was reflected in the relatively large percentage of members of the kibbutzim population who became recruits for combat units and commanders.

The February and August induction groups are also a little better. They too are from *moshavs* (collective farms) in the country, whereas with the May induction, one could say they were for the most part shitbirds. They are the hardest ones to teach. Lucky me! I was right in the middle of it. Eventually I learnt to understand and have a genuine respect for these guys, although we used to argue and hassle over everything. Nothing can be done, one to the other, without arguing. There is just no easy way for these guys.

Maynik is another word for the *mau mau*. It is slang, like *kibbutznik*.

As training continued, these guys began to be pretty good rifle shots. We were starting to learn more about ourselves and working with each other. Our sense of teamwork was a funny thing – there was teamwork, but it was only created through extreme harassment. I used to see whole platoons yelling at each other! iI was incredible, way beyond the normal person's understanding.

Having been in the marines, with the old saying "gung ho," meaning "together," and working together as a team, to me it was such a foreign and alien way of doing things. These guys could actually work against each other, as a whole.

We were learning to march, but did not get very far with that. I don't think there is any army in the world that could possibly have been worse than the Israeli army at troop and stomp, left, right, left, right, column left, left, right. These guys were hopeless. It was simply impossible to teach them. It is called military parade: *targile seder* in Hebrew. I was never good in the Marine Corps, and I was always in trouble whenever we had parades, but these guys made me look like I was from the Fifth and Ive platoon, which is the Marine Corps Formal Drill platoon, on Fifth and Ive in Washington DC. They had no sense of left, right, column left. It was a laugh. All I could think about at the time was, "Hippity ho, mob go, hippity hop, mob stop," which my marine drill instructors used to say in the Marine Corps. We never really got too far with formation marching.

Commanders had a disdain for drill. It didn't serve a purpose, as far as they were concerned. It was easier just to run, and that is exactly what we did. We ran everywhere. We ran up hills, down hills, we ran to the mess hall, we ran to the toilet. We ran between the buildings and if the trainers caught someone walking they kicked your ass. Another thing I might add to that is that – unlike the Marine Corps, they did not hit us. We would have slapping contests where we would line up, one facing the other. One man would slap the other, then the other guy would slap him back. We would stand and slap each other back and forth. This was also known as another form of punishment, which was quite regular in our first days of basic training. We were to say the least, slap happy.

Sanur is a terrible place. As I mentioned earlier, it was a Jordanian army base before the Six Day War. The buildings were square-shaped and made of concrete, with no particular design. The toilets were open holes in the floor that were forever plugged up. There was no grass, no greenery, the countryside around it was scrub brush such as is found around Southern California. As I have described, it was situated on a steep slant and throughout our training from morning till night it was either *madoss,* or running up and down, in Hebrew "the treeg". The treeg was 700 meters (766 yards), up or down, depending on where we were. A lot of the time the troop handlers would make us carry someone in the fireman's carry, up the treeg for punishment. It was grim, and it felt as though your heart was going to explode in your chest by the time you got to the top. My physical fitness level was going down because of the lack of sleep.

What we didn't realise at the time was that they were making us hard mentally. They were bringing us the physical and mental reality of the hours we would keep in the war.

One very important thing is called *mizdar*, which means "inspection." Waking up every morning at 04:00 was followed by loud cries. We washed our faces and brushed our teeth, then we found ourselves jogging five kilometers to an abandoned Arab village with a small structure called "the well". Breakfast finished, we had morning roll call. It was an important ceremony at which we were told about things that would happen that day. Our beds were checked and our persons. Everything had to be in order; everything neat and tidy. Otherwise there would be punishment without explanations or common sense.

From the shout of "Listen!" at breakfast, there was pressure at all times. The tidying of the room or the tent, seemingly straightforward, was in practice, a very complicated task that required a lot of tinkering. The bed had to be made in the form of an envelope, arranged so that the blanket was tight enough for a five-shekel coin dropped on it to bounce back.

Washing the floor had to be done last so as not to get it dirty. Any dirt and it would have to be started all over again. No matter how hard we cleaned, dust would be found. There was always more dust: the bar above the door, at the foot of the bed rail, at the window.

Equipment was maintained as if it was from the nuclear reactor in Dimona.

Everything was done by time, and there was never enough.

There was real animosity between the military police and the rest of the soldiers, because one of the favorite pastimes for the military police was hunting soldiers who were "non-standard, " especially those who were not wearing a beret. They were loaded into a van and brought to judgment fast (so-called "Operation dressing"). "Hunting season" was their main activity, particularly on Friday when the soldiers were on their way home, thus ruining their vacation. They especially hated the paratroopers, who didn't listen to them and ran off when challenged. They didn't catch us because we ran so fast. We used to tell many stories about how we made fun of them. Against this background fights often broke out between different groups, ending in bruises, cuts and black eyes.

At the time we had done no platoon tactics. The days consisted of shooting, exercising, being punished and also the ever-present obstacle course. In the morning we had the obstacle course, a 500 meter (547 yards) run to it, 600 meters (656 yards) through it and another 500 meters (547 yards) afterwards, to the finish. This was done with a rifle, a webbing belt with magazines, dummy grenades, and canteens on it, and sometimes with an American army steel helmet on as well. It was hard.

Let's not forget the evening. The troop handlers would let us get to sleep, then wake us up and start punishing us for sins committed during the day (which we probably had already been punished for anyway). I cannot remember ever sleeping a full night during basic training, except on the beginning of the Sabbath. It always started out with the words: "*mizdar conenute*," which meant readiness inspection within seven minutes. You would get everything together for war, your rifle, grenades, water bottles and have it ready in seven minutes from a dead sleep, out on the grinder. I did not realize that I had it in me to do things like that! I remember in Vietnam the bell would ring and the helicopters would be turning in five minutes, but we had all our equipment out in the helicopter waiting for us – the rifles, machine guns – everything was mounted in the helicopter, some 50 meters (160 feet) away. Subsequently, the readiness meant a readiness for punishment. Sometimes the punishment was going to be five minutes, then they told you to get lost and go back to bed. Or the punishment could last more than an hour, and sometimes two hours. If the troops wanted to argue with the drill instructor, it could last all night. It did not often happen that we did not sleep all night, but it did happen.

Finally, in late June, we were to make our first trip to the field. This was not just a matter of getting into trucks and going. We were to go on foot, so we had a full day's training. We had our breakfast – and then of course we had to run the obstacle course, and then some classroom training, then we had more exercise and another obstacle course that afternoon, then finally dinner in the late afternoon. We got everything ready and threw our seabags into the trucks. The trucks left and we were allowed to rest until dark, about an hour. I had learned one thing from that last *masaw* (forced march), and that was to wrap up the insides of my thighs. During the march you rub them raw and it is incredibly painful. If you have never had a raw thigh you would not appreciate what I am telling you. I wrapped my thighs in elastic bandages. Funnily, I always liked to give my boots a good shine before going on one of these long marches. It just somehow made my feet feel better. It sounds totally illogical but I always did it.

We set out across the hills that evening at dusk. The night grew darker.

We marched and about midway through the night we were told to break out a stretcher. I do not remember the distance of the march but it was close to 40 miles. We marched all night long; and then of course we had the stretcher with a shitbird on it. He was having a pretty rough time because it does happen that the stretcher is dropped – when somebody trips over a rock, for example, one guy goes down, the other guys holding on let go and the guy in the stretcher gets flung out. No one feels pity for the one being carried.

Usually they put a small- to medium-sized person on the stretcher. There was never a shortage of shitbirds, but a seven7 kg (15 lb) radio joins him, plus his helmet, rifle and all his webbing as well, so in the end we were probably carrying close to 175 lb on that stretcher. Depending on circumstances, there might be two to four people as relief. The word is *leahleaf*, which means "change," "change with me." So one guy would come forward to the back or the front of the stretcher to the guy that wanted to change and in the meantime this thing was digging into your shoulders. We would be going up and down hills, over rocky trails – not along roads – and we were not wearing tennis shoes: we wore combat boots. It just went on and on. We were given two minutes every hour to stop and drink water.

We were on our way to a field somewhere, to start our infantry training. To this day I do not know exactly where it was. As we were struggling along through the night, I remember looking at the stars. One of the things that used to go through my mind on these marches was a picture of a commercial we had back in the United States of some girl jumping up out of this beautiful pool of water. She had all this cool water coming off of her and she was so beautiful. I thought about this in the misery of the night. My shoulders were killing me, my feet were killing me and my mouth was always dry. Whenever we had a stop, I would drink a whole liter (1 ¾ pints) of water: I'd just pump it out in sweat in the next hour of marching. My mouth was always on fire as well, like my feet.

On any of these marches your feet would swell, and going downhill was agony. It was better to go uphill and pull a heavy load. Going downhill, with your feet swollen up, your toes would be pushed against the front of the boot. My first two toenails were always crushed. Every time they grew back I would just crush them again. They would go black and blue, and I would pull them out.

By dawn the next day we were coming in to the new camp area, which had all been set up for us. We put the stretchers down and were given a welcome and told we were going home, but the work hadn't finished yet. We then had to put up our two-man tents, which were just two shelter halves.

I've been asked if we were not afraid of being attacked or ambushed on some of these marches, because we were on the West Bank in the middle of nowhere. The answer to that is that we did not even think about it, although the possibility was there, I suppose. We were all armed and had live ammunition, but at the same time we were so stuffed, and in so much pain, that you would thank the guy that shot you – anything to put an end to the misery. We still had not made a march in company formation, which was coming.

I was going to share a tent with a guy named Marcovitch. He was what we called a *kaskeshan*: he used to run his mouth all the time, and was often told to shut up.

> Markovich had been told by me that we slept very little and "still, David was sitting on his sleeping bag and writing his personal experience" (diary). "He didn't give up his nightly diary practice even when he had to go on guard later that night and almost did not sleep. Needless to say it did not affect his commitment or his performance."
>
> Jose Levich

However, he was a good lad and we became friends in basic training. We pitched our little tents. We had inspection. It just seemed endless. By this time it was about 12.00 noon, and finally we heard the buses coming. What a wonderful sound those buses made, with their diesel motors and Egged painted on the side. When they arrived they were most beautiful sight: the vehicles that were going to take us away for about 36 hours. Away from all the hassle – it meant rest, to be off our feet – it was a kind of sanctuary that moved.

Everybody put all their gear away. Those to be punished had lagged behind in the march. They were to remain in camp, the *maal.* This was where they would spend their *Shabbat.* Their feet were up in the air as soon as the buses started moving.

After we arrived back from *Shabbat* to start our formal training in the field, for the most part of the week we trained in the prone position. That also meant jumping into the prone position. The area was covered in thorns and rocks. To say the least, it was a shit of an area to train in, but it was very fitting for the Israeli paratroopers. We would be walking along, and troop leaders would say: "*Paza-tztot*!" which meant we were under fire and had to jump down into the prone position. The heels and inside of our hands filled up with sticker thorns. They got thick and swollen, but were also getting tough, as were our knees and elbows because we did a lot of crawling. We always kept our rifles off the ground, because they had to be kept clean at all times. After a while we would be on a full run and they would shout "Paza-tztot". We would hit the dirt without getting our rifles dirty, and start shooting.

It was amazing how coordinated we became and how we adapted to the terrain so as not to hurt ourselves. In the beginning everything – our knees, elbows and hips – was beat up, from hitting the ground.

The training day started at around 04:00 a.m. We would go out and do morning training, or dry runs as it was called, come back have breakfast. After breakfast we would go out and train for a while longer. Then we'd start live firing exercises. Everything we did was singular: it was open field fighting that we were learning at this time. We would go up the hill screaming "*Esh, esh*!" (which means "Fire!" in Hebrew). All the time we would be jumping down into the prone position, up and down, up and down, just like a bunch of jumping beans out of control, all the way up the hill. As soon as we were good enough at it, we would do it with live fire. Then we would have a lunch break. That break wasn't to sit around and relax, it was to get ready for inspection, so we cleaned our rifles and tried to look like some semblance of a military person, because we were normally filthy. There was never enough time to get a shave, but at least the equipment was clean, which for the Israelis was the bottom line.

In the afternoon, before we went back out for training we did an hour's physical fitness training: push-ups, squat-thrusts, jumping jacks, sit-ups, all in the dirt. We were sweating from the heat, and our uniforms were like cardboard, with an unpleasant aroma. Then we'd go on a three-mile run or longer. We did all this in regular combat boots, and we ran on asphalt, dirt roads, rocky paths. I was always near total collapse. I couldn't get enough water in a day. At the time they regulated what we drank. I did count: 10 liters (over two and a half gallons) of water a day was my average. The temperature was always around 100°F (38°C). Later in the basic training they let us drink as much as we wanted. We were wet with sweat from early morning until late at night. We only changed our uniforms once a week. To say we stank was to put it *mildly*.

When finished, no break – back out to the field for training again and dry runs, and last thing in the afternoon we would do a live fire exercise. We would then come back and have dinner. After dinner, we would go out and do whatever we did in the morning, and afternoon, a repeat of the day. This would carry on until about 9:00 p.m., 10:00p.m., or even 11:00 p.m.

We would come back, and of course would have to pay for our sins of the day. (I use the word sin because that is a translation from *sararote*, sin or wrongdoing, the word the troop handlers used).

We would first have an inspection and they would tell us to turn in. Sure enough, within an hour, just as you were deep in sleep, you'd hear "*Mizdar conenute,*" readiness inspection in seven minutes.

You'd fly out of the sleeping bag, put your boots on and get everything ready you'd need to go to war, within seven minutes. When we stood outside we knew that if we were having a readiness inspection, we were being punished for something. We would do the fireman's carry and run in circles around the tent area, or we would get stretchers and run around with somebody on the stretcher. Obviously, the guilty party was on the stretcher and he was known to get a boot in the ass every now and again from somebody who did not like him for causing the trouble.

I have been asked: "Why did you have punishment? What was the punishment for?" Well, the punishment could be for anything: for dirty rifles, dirty boots, dirty faces, lack of motivation in training. Of course it did not matter that we had only slept two hours the night before, it was still lack of motivation. By this stage too, the very soft guys had been weeded out. The people that were not going to make it at all through any of the basic training were gone. The nucleus of what the platoon was going to be by the time we finished our training was now in the field training. Another question I am asked is: "Why didn't the guys get stuck in and beat the hell out of the offender?" Jews beating Jews is not in their nature. I don't know how it is now, but at the time it wasn't the way.

It is time to talk about the rank structure. The *memcaf* was a squad leader, or the platoon corporals. The rank of corporal was *rabat*. They had done their basic training and had been through the NCOs course, which was 14 months combined. We had three of them. After that, there was a platoon sergeant, *samal*, and then, of course, the platoon lieutenant, *mem-mem*. Next in line we had the company first sergeant, known as *rasap*. He took care of all the administration. The company commander was the mempay, usually with the rank of captain.

Getting back to punishment, it could go on for two hours because the men would argue with each other. They would make comments that should not be made; they would just never shut their mouths. I would say, "Just shut your mouths and let's get this thing over with so that we can get some sleep." Oh no, no! We couldn't do it the easy way. It is never done the easy way. How I cursed them at times!

There was another very good word used all through this period, which is *zion*. The word means prick. It is quite obviously a slang word, and I used to hear it all the time. It meant that if you goofed up, you were going to get "All the *zion*," and that meant punishment and real good punishment at that. So quite often, when we heard the word *zion*, we knew there was trouble on the way.

We finally received our platoon weapons. I was given a MAG machine gun. We were issued with RPGs (these are anti-tank small rocket launchers), and 60mm mortars. This meant more responsibility in the platoon. From then on I only carried a machine gun, which weighed about 23 lb, in the field. I put the M16 away. The machine gun was a heavy piece of equipment and was known in military terms as an LMG, light machine gun. I do not know how anybody could call that a light machine gun. When we went to the mess hall we had to carry our rifles, when we went to the toilet we had to carry our rifles. In my case I had to carry the machine gun. The MAG went wherever I went. It had a 100-round charge bag of 7.62 mm ammunition mounted on the side, just to make it a bit heavier – over 25 lb.

When we went into the field on a three- to six-mile run, I ran with the machine gun. It became my wife. It was actually a very well-made weapon and I carried it with me until the day I finished active service in the Israeli paratroopers.

It took the whole platoon to help me clean the machine gun. I had to dole out parts to the guys and they did not want to clean them. With daily inspection and everything else, they had enough trouble keeping their own rifles clean. They did not need the extra work. I would have to argue and shout: they were just not interested. "*Zion*," they would say. It was such a hassle that I tried to do it all myself, but there were times when I had to force parts on to someone else. The MAG has a lot of parts to share out and clean. Of course the parts never came back clean. At inspection the *memcaf* would ask, "Why was the machine gun not cleaned? You didn't want to say which person did not clean his part, so inevitably everybody in the platoon would be punished.

There were times that I actually gave parts out and – don't ask me how it happened –they were lost. Now the machine gun was "US" (unserviceable) and I had to stand inspection. "Where is this part?" the instructor would ask me, and I would reply, "I don't know, sir." Naturally he would say, "What do you mean, don't know, you don't know where parts of *your* machine gun are?!!" I would just stammer and stutter: "I don't know, no excuse, sir." Then it would start, you could just see the trouble coming. I would then have to run around with the machine gun above my head shouting: "I've lost a part of my machine gun, I've lost a part of my machine gun," and this would go on and on. It was incredible, besides the embarrassment of losing a part of the machine gun. By now everybody was running and everyone knew who the shitbird was that lost the part from the machine gun.

This was not the end of being in the field. This was only the beginning. We looked forward – certainly not in excited anticipation– to 14 months of this grim training,.

On August 7, 1975, we started the day at about 6:00 a.m. after a very long day, as on August 6 we had only got to bed after 2:00 a.m. We had a heavy exercise period in the morning, a run of a few miles, then we broke down the camp. We were preparing ourselves for a big *masaw*, a 50-mile forced march.

I would be carrying 300 rounds of ammunition and the MAG machine gun, which weighed 23 lb, approximately 20 lb of ammo, plus water. It was heavy. This was to be our first march in company formation. We had four platoons in a company and the end platoon ran almost continually. The front platoon was the best position to be in, the further back you got the more running to keep up you had to do.

The *mempay* was leading the march, and everybody would follow him. As it was, we were given a five-minute talk to motivate us. We were marching back to Sanur – that in itself was enough to demoralize all of us.

We started to march round 5:00 p.m.in the afternoon. At this time of day it is still burning hot. We started off at a very fast pace. After an hour we stopped for two minutes to drink water, which was the routine. Every hour, a two-minute stop; and I always drank one bottle of water, plus salt tablets when issued. Then your platoon moves back one and the end platoon comes forward to be the first platoon. The next hour, the same thing – the end platoon always did the running, it just seemed as if you were running all the time. This was not a slow march: it was a fast march. Hour after hour, it just seemed to go on. Our feet were swollen, the sling on my machine gun would be eating into my neck and the pack, so heavy with all the ammunition, would be eating into my hips – it was actually taking the skin off my hips. The countryside was very bushy, with rough roads and a lot of rocks. The long and short of it is that it went on and on and on, and at stops you drank as much water as you could.

Around the 25-mile mark we stopped for what they called dinner. Everybody thought, "Wow, incredible!" When we got there, there was nothing to eat. Oh well, I suppose it was silly of us ever to believe what they were saying. In the end we did have about a 15-minute break. They made us lie down on our backs and stick our feet up in the air, to let some of the swelling go down. At this stage the guys were starting to get cramps and we were taking salt pills, because our bodies were drained of salt. I drank my bottle of water, and 15 minutes later we were on our feet and moving again.

The platoons were still shifting every hour. I can remember just pushing. Slower people always seemed to be in front of me. This meant we would be running to catch up more often, rather that just keeping closed up. Sometimes I studied the back of a person through all this. It is amazing how you concentrate on it. In the middle of the night, the boys were actually going to sleep on their feet, causing them to stumble and fall.

One particular guy – we called him *Hamor*, which means mule in Hebrew – his real name was Ruvin Abraham, fell over a ledge and landed a good 10 feet below. We heard him groaning down below. I though it was quite funny, in all this dire misery we were going through. Perhaps my sense of humor had finally hit an all-time low. We heard him rustling around below, so our platoon pulled out of the formation, went down to the ledge and got him back on his feet – and away we went again. He was Kurdish, and we used tell jokes about the Kurds that matched him exactly. Why can't *Hamore* be a zebra? Because he is a donkey (*hamor*). What has an IQ of 100? 100 Kurds. Two Kurds were killed in a car accident – two more in the reconstruction.

Now at the end of the company, we caught up and carried on through the night, stumbling and falling over the rocky road. Our legs were like lead. My feet were swollen and I knew my toenails were crushed once again. I could actually feel the front of the toenail being lifted off, especially going downhill and believe it or not, all this time we would be praying just to go uphill. Water was pouring off us all the time. Even my boots were wet. They looked as if I had been wading in water. My clothes were soaked through. The webbing that held the ammunition was soaking wet.

We pushed on. At sunrise we were about five miles from Sanur One of the boys fell out of formation, and the platoon had to pull out because of him. The *mem-mem* made us run in circles around this *ben zona* (son of a whore) until he was back in formation. Shaul Adaddi_- I will never forget him: he was a first-class worm. He was told to get back into formation, but he kept hollering that he could not go on and he was tired. No shit – we were all tired. He screamed that his thighs were raw. I jumped out of the formation and slapped the bullshit out of him. After this he was ready to continue. Pain, as I found out in the marines, is a great motivator.

We all got back into the company formation and carried on. When we were within about two miles of Sanur they stopped us and said; "Right, one on one," a good old *zion*, right to the end. So up into the fireman's carry we went for the last bit. Once we got moving, the platoon *samal* wanted us to start running. I had Heaflah on my back because he fitted well on my shoulders. He was about my size, but a bit thinner. Some people fit better on your shoulders than others. Away we went. To this day I do not know how we made it to the base. It is just beyond explaining to another person what my body felt like. I still had the machine gun, I still carried 300 rounds. As I carried him, Heaflah had his rifle plus his 10 magazines of ammunition and grenades. At one stage they stopped us and told us to swap and carry on. Well, Heaflah lasted 100 meters (109 yards) and then I had to carry him the rest of the way. I had never seen anything so beautiful as the gate of the base at Sanur, even though it is a hellhole of creation. Once through the gate they pulled us off to the side and told to put our loads down. We waited for everybody to catch up. Heaflah and I were among the first to get in.

We were marched up the hill to what was for a short time to be our living area again. We were told to get on to our backs, and move our legs to get the circulation going again. We heard the wonderful command to turn in dirty uniforms and head for the shower. Get ready to go home! We were going on a 36-hour liberty. There isn't much one can do with this small amount of time off, especially given the condition we were in. When we were ready, the beautiful Egged buses arrived. The Egged bus service has to be one of the greatest in the world. Not for its luxury, but for being able to go anywhere. And soldiers ride free.

We boarded the buses – that is, the boys who did not have punishment were allowed to go home. I was fortunately one of them. Those who had done something wrong or had been really bad on the march stayed that weekend. That was your reward: you could sit on that base. I went back to the kibbutz, got to my room, locked the world out, and went to sleep. Peace at last, as the pain flowed gently from my weary body.

Mike Swaitecki's Helo "The Muff Diver" loaded with two three-stage concussion bombs.

Mike Swaitecki's Helo the "Muff Diver" on a rocket run in Vietnam 1971. (Taken from Dave Barr's Helo the "Greasy Rider".)

Two rockets on their way to a hilltop target from Mike's Helo.

Two gunships on the roll taking off from Marble Mountain in Da Nang, Vietnam, 1970-71.

Mike Swaitecki in Dress Blues after he returned from Vietnam.

Bedouin women and a little girl collecting - what is precious - water in the Judean desert on the edge of our camp. This was tolerated because the Bedouins were pro-Israel – sometimes serving in the IDF.

Anti-tank training in the Negev Desert, 1976.

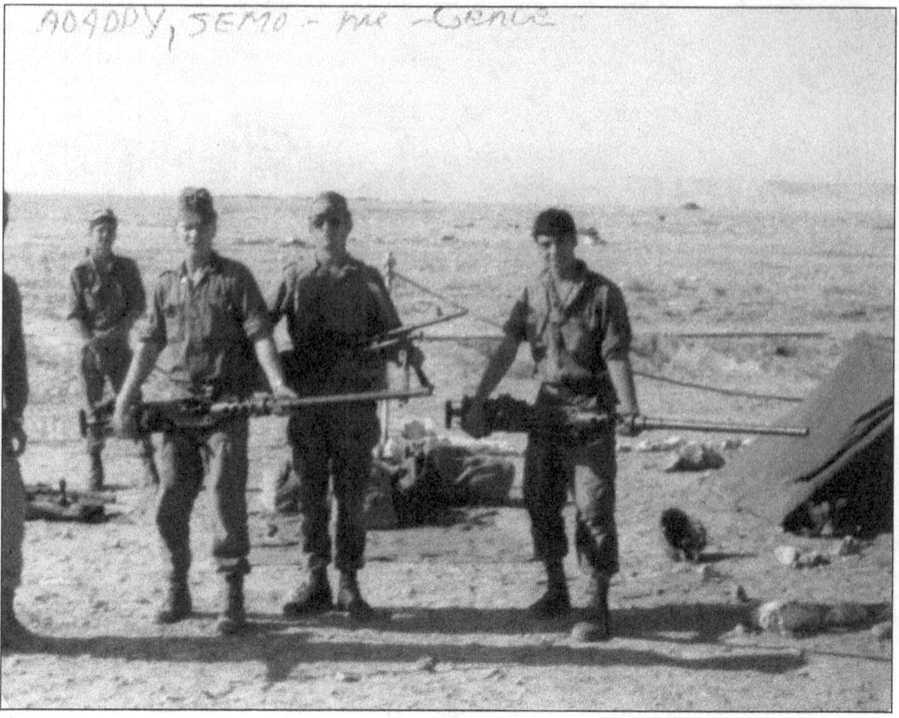

Showing off in the Negev Desert, 1976.

Heflock and Dave taking a break in the Judean Desert, 1976.

Dave and Heflock standing in front of shelter halves in the Judean Desert, 1976. This was the way they lived while in the field and training for months at a time.

The squad taking a break in the Judean Desert, 1975.

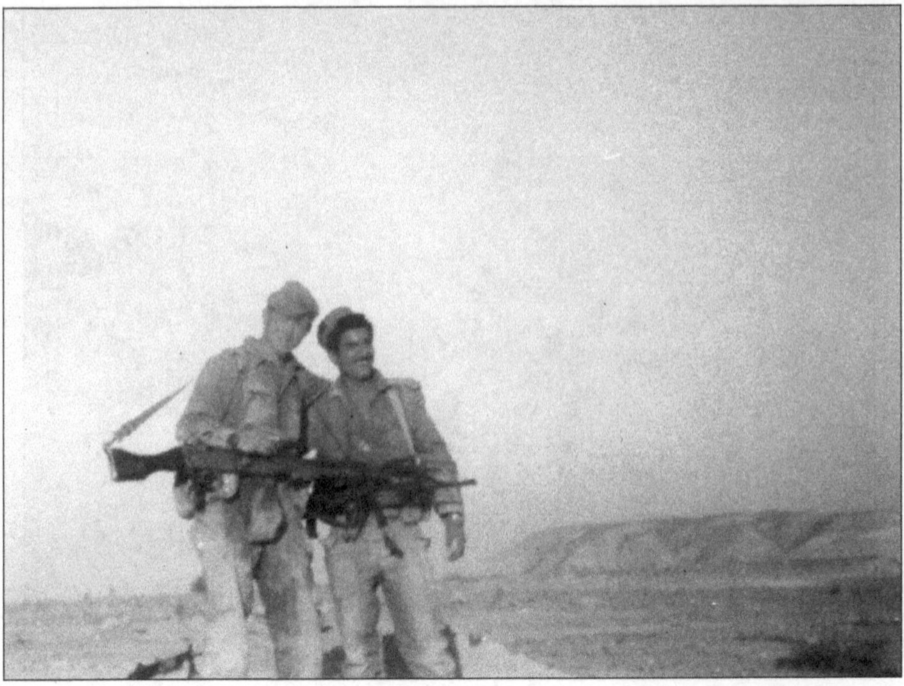

Dave and Zockme. Dave used to have to pick up Zockme in a fireman's carry when he was being punished. Both Zockme and Heflock fitted nicely on Dave's shoulders.

Dave during a MAG/LMG border patrol in the Golan Heights along the Syrian border.

Training in the Golan Heights in very cold weather. This is a Motzov (hilltop position).

Dave – in dirty uniform – on Graduation Day from the NCOs' course, July 1976.

In the end, that march took 16 hours. Imagine 16 hours, and we were carrying a lot of weight. If you were in the mortars, you carried a mortar and your number two had mortar bombs plus his M16 and every other thing. The same with all other platoon weapons. These marches were brutal experiences. If a guy fell out, he would have to make up a march at another time. They were not going to let you out of this. No excuses!!

Once back at Sanur after our time off, we had our jump physicals, and we all passed. Although we had in fact finished our first three months of basic training, there was no satisfaction, because we knew that whatever was up ahead was just as bad as what we had already experienced. There was to be no let-up.

We did some riot control at Nablus, Ramallah and Jenin, on the West Bank. We did this to keep the people from tearing things up and making a mess of their own towns, and it was always done on *Shabbat*. We could actually feel the hatred in these cities when we patrolled on foot. The hair on the back of my neck would stand up. Nablus, Ramallah and Jenin – these places were seedbeds of hatred. They wanted us out of there, which is understandable.

We worked a lot with the border police and they themselves are a mixed bag: they are for the most part Druse, some Christian Arabs, and some Jews.

After we finished the *Shabbat* riot control we got on open vehicles and drove to Tel Hashomare at night. I can remember standing up in the front of the truck bed and the wind was hitting me in the face, reminding me of being out at night, back home on my Harley Davidson. The cool night air in my face and the feel of the machine pounding away underneath me brought back some very, very nostalgic memories and also made me slightly homesick.

We arrived at Tel Hashomare on August 17, 1975, and were given a speech by the commanding officer, after a very long night on the road. No one paid much attention as we were all dog-tired. We all thought that it would be better here, as there were women. It was rumored that the troop handlers didn't punish as much because they wanted us in top condition for jump training. We all reasoned that we would have to sleep more to be in good shape for training.

We set up our little camp and then punishment began. Now we were going to be punished for everything that went wrong – on the riot control, all the goofing off, backchat and everything that we were sure to be guilty of. We were never without *sararote*, sin. These guys were the worst sinners I have ever seen. We were receiving punishment for making a mess of our tent area. That went on for the rest of the afternoon and right into the evening. At the end of the day we were almost at our wits' end. So much for the rumor! Welcome back to normality.

There were times when I felt I just could not go on any longer, and I am sure every one of us felt that way, most of us on a daily basis. Our hands were in pretty bad shape; they were still swollen from being in the field. My system was run down and I actually had to go to the sickbay for the first time. The doctor pumped me up with antibiotics. I had open sores on my elbows and arms. I was not the only one: there were a lot of us in this state. We had guard duty at night, after a long day's training. The day would start at about 5:00 a.m. with exercise, then we would clean up our living area, have morning inspection and then breakfast. After breakfast, we would start training for the rest of the day.

The training consisted of rolling in the sand in the heat, doing parachute-landing rolls. There was jumping out of the towers, which was a bit of a thrill. We were hooked to a harness, because you don' t just jump 50 feet out of a tower not hooked up. We never had spare time to do anything. If we did have free time, our heads would just fall over and we would sleep. In the early part of the training, we climbed into a CH-53 helicopter for a familiarization ride. It was thrilling for me, because it took me back to when I was in the marines where we also flew in 53s, and it brought back many special memories. The first helicopter I ever flew on was a 53, when we went and dropped napalm in Vietnam. I remember that day in particular, because when we got back we ran around the base at Tel Hashomare five times, which is about 10 miles in all. Not being a great runner, it was all I could do to keep up and finish.

I had my first anniversary in Israel on August 24, 1975. I had come a long way in that year. My Hebrew was starting to shape up, I was in the army, my goals at that point had all been attained and it was up to me to hold on to what I had attained.

We never got away from the old readiness inspection in the middle of the night. It was a famous form of punishment. If the troop handlers had not got you during the day for anything, they were going to get you at night. It always started with the words "Readiness inspection in another seven minutes, everybody *out*!" We would be standing outside in the dirt, then it would start, one on one. We had one small platoon sergeant, Sergeant Yosie. He had mean, close-set beady eyes, ever alert to whatever we were doing. He smiled through thin lips and crooked teeth whenever he greeted us, and he would say,

"*Shalom*, Platoon No 1, one on one." He never stopped running us around. It was rumored that he had shown himself to be a very aggressive soldier in the *Yom Kippur* War. Whether the wrongdoing was real or imagined, we deserved it. That is the one thing I'll say, we deserved it. No matter what we did, these guys would do it wrong. If we were told to be somewhere at a certain time, we would never be on time because somebody would always be late. I'd never seen mentality like this in the marines: everybody was early. Nobody was ever early here, they were always late. You'd think they would learn, but they never, ever did. As the Bible says, God's people were a very stiff-necked race. That is the *understatement* of the entire Bible.

We had readiness inspections throughout our time there. They would have us up for two to three hours, meaning a night's sleep might only consist of anything from three hours or less and the rest of the next day we would be going all the time. So much for more sleep! Perhaps the troop handlers hoped that we would all kill ourselves when we jumped, from not paying attention in the training.

We were in and out of mock-ups, jumping out of towers, rolling around in the sand, until finally we went to the parachute packing area and there they explained some of the nomenclature of the parachute itself. The personnel who pack the parachutes are female soldiers, called *mekapelet*. These girls are made to jump with the men every two weeks. It is actually a very prestigious thing for the girls to be parachute packers while doing their National Service. A male's National Service is three years and a female's National Service is two years.

On top of all this we had guard duty. We might finish our training day around 9:00 p.m., but sometime during the night we would catch anywhere between three to four hours' guard duty. There were not only platoon guards, but also guards for certain parts of the installation. One might be guarding the supply area, or the ammunition dump, or the mess hall – people steal food at night, mostly the guards. They always found something for us to guard, even our own living area. You just hoped that if there was to be punishment you were on guard duty, then you did not loose that little bit of sleep that was allowed.

All through this time we were waiting for the first big jump. At this time I had not jumped for well over a year. By the time I had left the States in 1974, I had made over 112 jumps as a civilian parachutist. Finally the day came when we made our first jump, and I remember the excitement everyone was experiencing, getting ready to go up and jump. I also remember being out on the tarmac. We would have just drawn the parachutes, all the boys would be getting geared up, and the arguments would start. One started arguing with the other, the other started arguing back and then the spectators put in their two cents as well. Before you knew it, the whole platoon was shouting at itself. About this time the *memcaf* got upset and we knew that tonight there would be shit in the land.

We made our first jump that day, and all the memories of free fall parachuting came flooding back to me, but this was nothing like it – this was my first military jump. The lights went on, we stood up, hooked up and shuffled to the door. The bell rang and out of the doors we went. It was nice to float underneath a parachute again, although I didn't feel the same apprehension that the rest of them did.

When they got down to the ground, instead of arguing, everyone was slapping each other on the back. They were big mates now, and hey, this was the greatest thing since sliced bread. It was amazing how their attitudes turned around.

We made one jump a day, then two jumps for the next few days, and then we made our first night jump. At this stage we were doing this with gear. I jumped with a machine gun and ammunition, all bundled up in bag that fit to the harness between my legs. There was a rope attached to the bag, and the harness. Once out of the plane I looked up make sure the parachute had blossomed, then released the bag on the rope. The next thing was to hit the ground two seconds after the bag hit the ground.

After this there was always backslapping and good old merriment. The trouble was that the *memcaf* and the *samal* did not see it in the same lighthearted manner that everybody else did. So of course, no matter what time we got back to the living area – this was normally 11:00 p.m.or 12.00 midnight – it was time to pay for the sins of the day. They would let us get to bed, get to sleep and then, "*Mizdar conenute* in seven minutes." Once again, everybody was outside waiting. "OK, Platoon Number One, one on one." Everybody up and we would start running around in circles with someone on our backs. It would either be Zockme or Heaflock on my back. We became very close to one another in those months of misery.

Through these times we started to lose people again. There was always the odd guy who could not take it any more and he would be dropped to the *mifcada*, which was the admin/rear echelon of the paratroopers. It did not often happen, but sometimes it did. Then there would be the odd guy who would not jump, and he was out, that was it. He would go to the infantry.

On September 4, 1975, we got our wings and had a movie that night as a reward. Well, wonders never cease. Tel Hashamare was a very nice base. We still lived in tents in the dirt, but the rest of the so-called humans on the base, the parachute jump instructors and all the girl soldiers, lived in concrete buildings. I have never seen so many girl soldiers in all my life. There was a good PX, which we didn't get to frequent, except very rarely.

The excitement was running high, and the arguments soon started. When we got back to our living area, some of these guys were just full of themselves because they had this pair of wings on their chest. They though that they were hard-assed soldiers now. That was a big sin: the *samals* and *mem-mems* were operational veterans from *Yom Kippur*, the last war. They didn't share the general sentiment that the rest of the lads did. We were going to be put into our place properly. We ran around in the fireman's carry, or they would get us with a cot. We would have to take our cots, with all our bedding on them, and run around, holding the cots over our heads. We would run into each other and end up cursing and screaming at one another. It was quite unbelievable, total madness. It always reminded me of my drill instructors when I was in the marines – the old "Hippity ho, mob go," and "Hippity hop, mob stop." If there was ever a mob, it was us.

We celebrated the Jewish New Year, *Rosh Hashanah*. I remember we were at a base called Beit Leit, right next to the Beit Leit bus stop where we shot the terrorist. There we had a nice meal and there were some songs. One thing they do together very well with no music to accompany them is singing. I remember some of the faces of the boys, they were very sad. Obviously these were the first holidays these kids had every spent away from their mom and dad. I've got to admit, for all their bullshit they were tough, they were stubborn: stubborn, miserable bastards to be around, but they also had a real soft side.

We soon left Beit Leit and moved to the desert for the first time, to a place near the Dead Sea in the Judean Desert, which is characterized by dryness and high temperatures during the day. There are years with no rain at all – years of drought. Strong solar radiation raises the soil temperature up to 70°F. On September 9, it was incredibly hot. It was still summer there. The Dead Sea is the lowest place in the world and you can just imagine what the heat would be like. From here we were going to start trench warfare, and upon completion of this training we would be fully operational, but this had no bearing on the 14 months basic training. It meant if a war started, we would be up front.

I also remember the apprehension of the boys every time we moved to a different part of the country. There would be a completely new set of rules for the new terrain. This was to be some of our hardest-ever training, because the hours were endless. We were lucky if we slept for two or three hours at night. Mealtimes, as with everything else, were rushed affairs as always – if you got them at all. It was the first time I had really been in the Israeli desert.

We would get up at 4:00 a.m. and train: we would come back and have breakfast and train again until late morning, early afternoon. Then we would come back for inspection and have a meal in the middle of inspection. Inevitably everybody would flunk it. Then we would go out and train again in the afternoon. We would be running in the trenches. We would have to run to the training area, which was over ¾ mile away – no laughing matter, as it was probably 115 degrees Fahrenheit, 42 or 43 degrees centigrade. We were at the lowest part of the world and the heat was staggering. We trained through the afternoon, came back, had a hurried dinner and went back out for training again in the evening. Late evening we'd have exercise, where we did push-ups, sit-ups, squat thrusts and then run for up to six miles, less if we were lucky. This was all uphill, downhill, over rocks, on sand roads. The terrain was very open, very much a desert and even at night, I dare say it was between 95 and 100 degrees Fahrenheit. We were constantly sweating. I cannot ever explain to somebody what the heat, coupled with the fatigue that we had, was like. In all this running and training we were doing dry exercises and live fire exercises, then at night we'd come back, and do it all again. The troop handlers would finally let us turn in, usually around 11:00 p.m.or 12:00 midnight. A guard was set up and inevitably there was going to be punishment for something we had done wrong during the day or night. At no time was I able to blame my *memcaf* or the *samal*, or the platoon lieutenant, because we deserved it. They were always at each other's throats.

I remember one night in particular. I was sitting on top of the hill, about 200 meters (around 650 feet) from the camp, at a listening post for any Bedouins that might want to come to our ammunition dump and steal. There was no electricity and so no lights, just the glow of the moon. It was ever so quiet, there was no wind, and I felt at peace with myself and God. I looked back over the three-year period that had passed since I had decided to go to the Middle East. I looked at where I had come from in civilian life. I had been on a steep downhill road when I got out of the Marine Corps. I was drinking a lot, I was a bum, I was out on the Harley Davidson all the time, drunk. It is a wonder I never got taken out by a car. I looked at how far I had come since I left my mom and dad on that early July morning to go to England and make my way to Israel. I remember sitting on a cliff on the Isle of Wight, looking over the English Channel and feeling I had grown up. I knew I was moving into a world of experience, of hardship that I had never quite known before, especially in the Middle East: so totally devoid of anything I had ever known as an American. It's true I had had plenty of hardship in Vietnam and plenty of hardship in the Marine Corps, but this was a different type. Though I wouldn't be shot at all the time there was a constant danger of accidental discharges. Live fire exercises were dangerous, and we were using live grenades and live ammunition. I was becoming a person with more experience in life than an average guy and looking back at my background in the States, I would say I had come a long way.

Moving into another sphere, loneliness was a factor I had to fight all the time. I was very lonely at times. I remember sitting on that hill in the dark that night and being so at peace with the world that I could feel the strength coming back into my weary bones.

The next few weeks we had continuous training in trench warfare. There were two weeks when we did not have a shower: we were wearing the same uniform when we arrived at the base. We lived in dirt and slept in dirt in little two-man shelter halves. Before we went to sleep we would check for scorpions, centipedes and snakes, which might have got into our gear. One guy had a ball of twine and when he pulled it out to use, it had a scorpion attached to it. How it never stung him, I don't know, because those scorpions were deadly. We went to Beit Leit over a *Shabbat* to do some guard duty, and there we had our first shower. Because of the normal plugged drain, we were wading in about four inches of swill on the shower floor just hoping there was no razor blade or something else that could cut our feet. But it was a shower nonetheless, and I am sure there were two inches more mud after we all got out. One thing the Israeli army was very good about: it would come around and give us nice clean new uniforms if we had been out in the field for a long time. Nice clean shorts and socks! We felt that we were on top of the world.

The *mem-mem* called me into his office to give me a bit of a talking to, and asked me if I wanted to go to one of the more elite organizations. Looking at this in retrospect, I was actually wrong in not having gone. I think I would have had a more enlightening time in the Israeli army than staying where I was.

I felt that if there was a war the paratroopers would be more involved in it than any single smaller unit. I was probably wrong, but at the time didn't know it.

The paratroopers, *golani,* (the infantry), and tanks are the units that are in the vanguard of the fighting in the Israeli Defense Force. Another reason, and it was the main reason that I declined, was that I was never a good runner. It used to take everything I had to keep up with these guys. One thing I have got to say about the Israelis, they can run and they do a lot of it! I felt it would be too much for me, because the elites and the scout groups run even more than the paratroopers. I felt I wouldn't shape up. Now, in retrospect, I was probably wrong in feeling that way. At the same time, I'd been a bit down in the dumps and the *mem-mem* put my mind at ease about a lot of things that had been bothering me.

Soon we were back in the field and I remember that I sprained my ankle quite badly on one of the training exercises. It was bad enough to take me out of the field, but as far as I was concerned it wasn't going to, so I wrapped it up and I kept going. This sprain was to bother me for years until one day it wouldn't matter at all.

After another week or so, we went back to Beit Leit and I was to have my first *Yom Kippur,* which is the Day of Atonement. It is a day of fasting, in the hope that one's names will be written in God's big Book of Life. I remember that they sang, beautiful songs. These things will always stick in my mind, because they were very peculiar. I supposed I looked at it in a very mushy, romantic sense. I also remember on the day of *Yom Kippur* we went to a room that was different to any other room in that shabby base. There were pictures in the room of all the dead Battalion 890 paratroopers from past wars, starting with the inception of 890 Battalion. I got a tingle down my spine for those that had gone before us, lest we forget them. After that, they took us out and punished the hell out of us. Even at times of rest there was time for *onesh.* I will say they respected the *Shabbat.* Even though they respected it, though, they would get us at night when *Shabbat* was over. They made sure that when that sun went down and there were three stars in the sky, we got the big *zion.* They got us back for everything: we paid for all our sins of the day, real or imagined.

Then we went back to the desert to finish our training in trench warfare. Upon completion, we had to march for our red berets. Getting these would signify that we were fully-fledged paratroopers.

The march got going after a long day's training. At the end of the day, we first broke down the tents. There were no shit house tents to break down, because there were no shit houses in the field, one crapped off in the wadis and toilet paper was nonexistent. We used newspaper. So our asses got as tough as the rest of us.

When the march started, I was carrying 700 rounds and the machine gun – just my luck. This march was known as *masaw pacal*, which means marching with what one would carry to war. The load was devastating. The weight of 230 rounds is 14 lb. I was carrying 700 rounds on my back, and the machine gun. The march was to be 35 miles. It was up and down hills through the night, in the tremendous heat, all the way to our final destination, Jerusalem.

Through the night I would tell boys to grab on to my pack and I would help pull them up the hill. I don't know where I got the strength to do this, as we were all run down. I don't want to sound like Superman or anything like that, because I certainly wasn't, but I wanted them to succeed so they wouldn't make us do it again. They had threatened us with that right from the beginning if the march went bad. I can see why it could go bad, because the boys were fatigued, we were strained, we were stuffed – all of us were, and it was just out of sheer determination on my part that I could do what I did. The ones that were a little stronger were trying to help the ones that were not as strong. Through the night we marched. I started to get cramps because I did not have enough salt. I managed to get some salt tablets at one of the stops.

Cramp is a pain that is beyond telling. I crushed my toenails again, which in the meantime I had proudly been growing. Going downhill was something out of hell. Finally at sunrise we made Jerusalem. Altogether the march took us 13 hours after a full day's training, and we had possibly had two hours' sleep the night before. We could see the buses in the distance. Oh, that wasn't good enough, because we still had time to run around in circles and do some other funny things because we didn't do very well. Always time to pay for *sarrote*, sins.

We arrived at the buses and in a way it was a sad affair because we were being awarded our berets by the *magod*, the battalion commander, who told us "Well done." It was obvious he had not been on the march with us! This march had been done in platoon singular formation. The battalion commander gave us our berets when all four platoons were assembled. We were now paratroopers, according to the battalion commander.

There was a boy with a very pockmarked complexion named Markovitch, a very genteel soul and my tent mate. He and I shared the same little shelter half when we did our first training in the field. I had a soft spot for Markovitch.

Save for the fact that he never shut up, he was a very sensitive lad. I remember when he was being handed his beret the tears were rolling down his cheeks. Later I asked him what was wrong and said he remembered when his brother was awarded his beret. His brother was killed in the *Yom Kippur* War. So it was a very touching moment for him – soon, all to be spoilt. Our company *mempay* took us off after the speech and the awarding of our little red berets, and addressed us: "Don't under any circumstances consider yourselves paratroopers. You are not paratroopers until you have done this march again. You people did such a piss poor job, I am ashamed." One consolation was that he did not take our red berets away from us. To have gone home without his beret would have finished Markovitch.

It was at this point that they gave us a week off, a five-day break. I made my way to the kibbutz, kind of heavy-hearted at what the *mempay* had said. I did not want to make that march again.

I arrived at the kibbutz in the late afternoon and rested for some hours. I was in one of my reflective moods and remember seeing all the couples on the kibbutz. I remember them holding hands and I remember seeing them at the dance that night. I was sitting there on my own, totally exhausted after the *Shabbat* meal.

Kibbutz Ramat Hashofet was a non-religious kibbutz. Before the *Shabbat* meal they would give us a little talk, but never a prayer. It was a Hashomer Hatzair kibbutz, (this means the Youth Guards), and its origin dates back to the early part of the twentieth century in Poland. In fact it was the head of the Hashomer Hatzair movement in Poland who was the leader of the Jewish resistance in the Warsaw ghetto during the Second World War.

(To backtrack a little: the Warsaw ghetto saw the raising of the flag bearing the Star of David for the first time. They held the Germans at bay in the ghetto for over three weeks. This was the first time that the Jews fought back against the Nazis.)

Anyway, getting back to the original theme here, I remember seeing all the people together and I felt very lonely. This was not only for lack of family and friends, I just felt very apart from other people, living in the same world that I lived in, especially after the long hard day and the night before that and the training before that.

Looking back on it now, I also remember that I made a trip during my short leave to a place called Dalyat El Carmel, which was a Druse village. I went to the shops in this village because I wanted to buy my mother something.

I had been paid a bonus because I was a "lonely soldier," meaning I had no family in the country. As it was the *Yom Kippur* holiday, I wanted to spend money on my mom and get her something very nice. I went up to that village as I knew somebody living there, a fellow named Sammy. He was an Israeli soldier and a Druse. He showed me around the shops, and we stopped in one old shop. A little history here: by the way, this village, Dalyat el-Carmel, hid a lot of the Jewish soldiers of the Ha'agana before the war of independence from the British, so they were very much on side with the Israelis. There were a lot of people from Dalyat el-Carmel that worked in the factories on our kibbutz.

Anyway, in this shop there was a samovar, with the stamp of the tsar of Russia on it – I believe it was Tsar Nicholas, the last tsar of Russia. There was also a woman on the kibbutz who could speak Russian and she said that there was a stamp from the king of Poland on it as well: something to do with an alliance between Russia and Poland, which I found very interesting. I bought the samovar and remember the Druse bringing out the arrack. Arrack is a very strong alcoholic drink – it will knock you flat if you don't watch it. Between Sammy, the shopkeeper and me, we sank about half a bottle. Then out came the apples. They cut the taste of the arrack, and we all drank super-strong coffee – we could almost chew it! After that it feels as if you'd had nothing to drink. Soon we were saying goodbye, with pledges of friendship, and eventually were on our way back to the kibbutz. I cleaned the samovar and sent it off to my mom. She has it to this day.

On October 5, we reported back for duty, and made our way to the Sinai desert for more training. The Sinai is funny. Though it is not far from the Dead Sea in miles when you look at it on a map, at this time of the year it was blazing hot during the day, but believe it or not, it froze at night. I mean froze, water would freeze solid. In the early morning we did dry runs, then live fire, and the same in the afternoon. Then we had our meal, and punishment. Training was into the night, as usual. When evening came, a lot of the time we were still a long way from the camp. We would run around all day with a big jacket rolled up with our gear because it would get cold and we would just freeze without it. The drawback was that one tended to sweat and soak the jacket during the day, but it was better than nothing.

One night in particular, the machine gun was dirty and we were punished all night. We did not sleep for 48 hours, just no sleep.

We did the next day's training like zombies. We were running in and out of the armored personal carriers called APC. These are American-made tracked vehicles. They look like a giant shoebox with a slanted front end. They were called in Hebrew *Zeldas*. The whole back of the vehicle opened up to take on or let off troops. It was also equipped with a heavy machine gun, two MAGs, a 60mm mortar, and held a squad of troops – nine men.

We had started our armored vehicle training. We had to exit the thing while it was moving. The ramp at the back would be lowered, we would have to get out while the vehicles were still in motion, then we would have to run full out to get back on. Of course, if your *memcaf* or *samal* or the *mem-mem* suddenly had a sense of humor he would tell the driver to go a little faster. You would then be trying to get on at superhuman speed. And of course there was the leering face of the troop handler to irritate and distract us from the ultimate goal of getting back on. In the meantime your heart was ready to explode and you'd be sweating profusely. It was common for this to go on for most of the day. As soon as we caught our breath we would be ordered out once again.

One of those nights the punishment period was unique. We had done something wrong – arguing, talking while standing in formation, late for inspection, or whatever it was, it did not matter because we always deserved it. They told us to take our tents and all our gear and moved it back 20 feet. We had to do it in a certain time, and of course these guys could never, ever be on time. These fellows were the most tardy and lax people when it comes to keeping time I have ever seen in my life. Anyway, up came the tents. Markovitch was still with me and we moved it back 20 feet, got all our gear and moved that as well. It all had to be set up just so, and because we did not keep to time we had to move it all back again to where it was. This went on all night long. I will never forget it!

It was another of those nights when we did not sleep at all. These nights were not exceptional: it happened all the time. The fact that we got at the most four hours' sleep a night was incredible. Some people complained that their teeth ached and would go to dentist just to find out that there was nothing actually wrong with their teeth. They were just so fatigued that it caused their teeth to ache. We were so run down the medics would pump us up with antibiotics. Open, running sores were quite common. We were at war, and our training was to bring the physical and mental strain of war. Every single day we were firing hundreds and hundreds of rounds of live ammunition and live grenades. The only difference was that we were not being shot at, and sometimes it seemed as if we were. There would be bullets zinging around us, as well as bits of shrapnel and bits of rock, which were flying around when we were shooting inside the trenches. We did wear goggles so it was fairly safe, if you wanted to call this safe. They put us under incredible stress so if you were going to crack, you were going to crack before you were ever in a real combat situation.

When we started, our company was about 90 men strong but by this time the original number had dropped to a lot less. We would pick people up regularly. The people we picked up were people who had dropped out from their original induction, for whatever reason, but who were now ready to go back into the system and continue their training.

One day we were running behind a *Zelda* and I tripped and sprained my ankle. I actually heard it crack and I hoped I had not broken it. If I had, I would have been out – for me that was the worse thing in the world that could happen. It would have meant failure, and also being put back. The guys carried me on a stretcher back to the camp, which was the tent area. I was put on a truck to the main base area in the Sinai. I was told I could possibly have a cracked ankle, the thing was swollen up to twice its size and I could not walk on it. The next day I was put on another truck, taken to the airport, flown up to Tel Aviv and taken to Tel Hashomare, which is also the main Defense Force hospital. They X-rayed my ankle and found out it was not broken, which was a great relief, but at the same time I was told it was very badly sprained. They managed to get the swelling down and I was sent home to the kibbutz for a week.

The doctor in fact, wanted to give me more than a week off, but I got word while resting on the kibbutz that we were to go the Golan Heights. When the doctor next saw me he wanted me to go back there, but I refused because I did not want to be dropped from the company. That ankle gave me hell for the rest of my service in Israel. It just painfully dangled on the end of my foot, and I used to tie it up with a sling bandage, which meant I could walk straight forward and the ankle would not bend to either side.

7
Basic Training Continued

On or around October 23, 1975, I made my way to the Golan Heights. I had a terrible limp. The company had taken up position on a mutsav, which is a trench position with bunkers in it, on top of a hill. We were to do guard duty and training in the cold of winter, and were now overlooking Syria. Some of the landmarks were pointed out to us. Looking out across a great valley there was a hill a little higher and more distinctive than the rest of the hills, some miles away.

The only Israeli trench was located behind the Syrian border and the kibbutzim Merom Golan and Ein Zivan. We were watching El Kuneitrah, a Syrian city, at an elevation of 3,313 feet above sea level The city, a short distance from the de facto border between the two countries, was almost completely destroyed before the Israeli withdrawal in June 1974,and is populated by only a handful of families. Syria refused to rebuild the city and actively discourages resettlement in the area.

The guard was set up around the mutsav. The hill where the trench was located was known as Tel Harah. Harah in Hebrew is shit and tel is hill, so it was the hill of shit. This is from where the Syrian Central Command looked back at us. The highest of all these mutzavs was known as "Hermoneat." It was on top of Mount Hermon, which was 9,200 feet high. It was the start of another three months of pure misery in the freezing cold.

The Israeli army, never being one for creature comforts, had certainly outdone itself this time. The days were as long as any other day. They started at around 5:00 a.m: of course it was still dark, and we would have to stand to attention in the trenches to watch the sun rise over Syria. It was quite beautiful in a bizarre and brutal way, because it was a cold bleak land. Some of the biggest tank battles in the world had been fought on the Golan Heights.

The worst battle was in the Valley of Tears. This is the name of an extensive valley between Mount Hermon and the town of Al Qunaytirah, through which the Syrian divisions attempted to break through the Israeli defenses during the Yom Kippur War. Tanks of the 7th Brigade and 188th Brigade, with the assistance of the 405th Battalion, halted the Syrian armored forces, a defense which lasted four bloody, difficult days. Israeli forces had 150 tanks and infantry, against 450 Syrian tanks. The commander of the 7th Brigade, General Kahalani, attacked the Syrian army and destroyed 260-300 Syrian tanks. Israel lost up to 89 tanks and established instead a monument to their memory.

Imagine what this place looked like. It was not yet late enough in the year for the snow to come, but it was cold – so cold that during summer, in the early morning and evening we still had to wear heavy foul-weather jackets.

When the sun had risen over Syria, and we knew we were not going to have an attack, we had morning inspection and breakfast. We would then clean up and work around the *mutzav*, going out to train and coming back in the afternoon for lunch. The food was a little better here – in fact it was quite a bit better. Somebody from the platoon did all the cooking, so there was a little more feeling for the people for whom you were cooking. It obviously also had to be because of the cold. After lunch we would do a live fire exercise in the open field, or whatever else we had been training in, and we would also get vehicles ready for a night patrol. Then the evening meal was served.

A night patrol was four hours long, in the cold. We were not allowed to keep mufflers around our necks and ears. We had to be able to hear because we were looking over the minefield that surrounded us. It was cold and it rained a lot and to stand there for four hours in the night meant you lost feeling in your limbs. It was very miserable and very lonely. The troops who did night patrol used a half-track vehicle. These are open tracked vehicles, with two front wheels for steering. They go back to the Second World War. All night long we would sit in the back in the rain, and it would be freezing. If we got an alert, we would drive from one place to the next. We also had morning patrol. A squad would walk six miles along a certain area with a *gashosh*, a tracker, who would usually be a Beduoin. He would look for the footprints of anyone who might have tried at night to come through the minefield and over the fence that separates Syria from the Israeli-occupied Golan Heights.

One particular time when some terrorists did get through, we were mobilized that morning to go out after the guys. We started following them and after about six miles the *gashosh* felt we were very close to them. I twisted my ankle again, badly. I had to be taken out. I could not have been more miserable, because half an hour after I twisted my ankle, we heard shooting. Two terrorists were killed, and a couple more wounded.

I missed that because of my ankle. I was depressed, lower than whale shit in the ocean. When the doctor saw me, he sent me back to the kibbutz for five days. I could not walk on the ankle and I was told to keep my leg up, which I did.

When I returned to the company, I was determined that this wouldn't happen again. I put a support bandage inside my boot, and tied a sling bandage tight around the outside of my boot. This immobilized the foot altogether. I seemed to get along reasonably well, but I twisted the ankle all the time, although it did not swell any longer. With it tied up I could just bear the pain and continue. The thing was bound so tightly that I could hardly move it. I was still carrying the MAG during the day. It was a lot of weight. The machine gun itself was heavy without the ammunition. When we went out on morning patrol, I went with the machine gun, and trained with it during the day. I twisted my ankle almost daily: the pain was excruciating but I would simply get up, tighten the sling around it and just carry on. I refused to give in to it. One time I actually spoke to one of my *memcaf* about it and asked to go to tanks, but he refused. He would not even consider it. So I just carried on this way.

I received a letter from my mom and dad, saying that my sister Mary Ellen and Rick were going to get married. I said a prayer for their marriage, but I felt very lonely and left out at the time. The letter went on to say that my life-long friend Cress and his wife Danine announced the arrival of their first son, James Michael David. Here again I had the same feeling of emptiness, because I was not sharing in anything. I was in a totally alien world, one they could not understand. Though I could understand it, the feeling of being apart from everything because I was not a Jew was very strong. Oh well – I had made my bed, and I would lie on it, no matter what.

The days went by in a kind of blur of fatigue and misery. Punishment was regular. Night patrols were also regular, with long hours on guard. There were times during the day when, if you did not go to training, you would be sent out to an intersection in the road and made to stand there for three or four hours in the freezing rain or hail. At times we also stood there in the snow. It was a totally bleak area of the world, but the sunrise over Syria always gave me a certain strength, power. I was alone and I can remember saying a prayer in the morning, for strength to get through the day, and to do well for those I served. At these times I felt very close to God.

One day we were working on the vehicles and somehow, somebody goofed up with the track. The track flew off the vehicle, which went out of control and almost ended up in the minefield with us in it. The *memcaf* and everybody else just went wild. The punishment started immediately. There was the usual hollering and bickering between the troops, and this continued for the rest of the afternoon.

Depending on the alert situation, we often slept with our boots on. We slept down in the cold bunker, or if we were the immediate relief to the guard, we slept in a little hole cut in the side of the trench, called *shefania*, rabbit's house, so the guard if need be could go and relieve himself. If it snowed you would have to push the snow out. This was another great way to get a night's sleep.

We had training in the field, and work around the *mutsav* all day. We would have four hours' guard duty at night, which is the easy part, and we would also be out on patrol at night. We'd come back and start all over again the next day. It was an endless cycle of fatigue.

Garby was a Yemenite: tall, thin and quite dark. He was also *a kaskeshan* (he talked too much), but far more seriously was that it was a constant stream of lies. He would never shut his mouth, and somehow he made the *mem-mem* mad. Peled told us to take him off and put him in one of the sleeping holes inside the trench. We put wire in front of it to keep him in. I remember taking him his food – he was there for a good 24 hours or more, to teach him to shut his fucking mouth, because every time his mouth was open the rest of us would get into trouble as well. It was funny how tolerant they were with one another when you got one of these guys running their lip and getting the rest of us into trouble.

When I took him his food, I felt like a prison warder when I gave it to him. He thanked me and ate the food.

There is an expression in the IDF: "If you will not be dependent on each other, you will be hanging next to each other." We developed a sense of responsibility and caring, despite the paradox of endless conflicts. [

Of course Garby had something negative to say about the whole situation, also "*Zion* to the army," and the *mem-mem*, and everyone else as far as he was concerned. I suppose I would also have a rather negative attitude after spending nearly 12 hours in a little slot in the side of a trench. All you had to do, Garby was to shut your mouth.

I did a lot of cooking while on *motsav*. I guess I have a bit of a flair for it, although anybody that has eaten in my house in the past might not agree with me. At the time I seemed to be a pretty good cook – either that or everybody was ravenous from the cold.

In December we started our house warfare training, entering buildings. We would start with one person, then go to a team of three, then to squad formation clearing houses. Trench warfare and house warfare have got to be two of the most dangerous types of training an infantryman can do. We could be hit by pieces of flying rock, we used live grenades, going everywhere in teams shooting in different directions. It is really very scary, stressful training, but also very good training and I could see why the Israelis were so successful at it.

Sometimes during training we would foul something up, and the *memcaf* would say something about what we did wrong. The arguments would start; the troops saying that we didn't do it wrong. Then the silence would come and we knew there would be trouble that night. One particular night we had a punishment period where they called us out at about one o'clock in the morning. It was cold, and there was snow on the ground. We put the guilty parties with the biggest mouths throughout the platoon. On a stretcher with them went a 20-liter (five and a quarter gallon) jerry can of water. Each of us also got a 20-liter jerry can to carry in a free hand.

With the chosen many we wandered down through the snow and slush, behind the *motsav*. I clearly remember wading into frozen water, frozen on top that is. The *samal* said: "You clowns want to argue, let's argue! All I could think was: "Just keep your mouths shut." The test of wills had started. We had the *memcaf*, Yoel Nitzani, the hardest of the lot of them, and *Samal* Yosie of the platoon sitting up on a rock, very nice and cozy in their ski suits while we were freezing our asses off. We were up to our knees in frozen water, holding on to a 20-liter jerry can in one hand and holding on to a stretcher with the other hand. Can you imagine how miserable this was? To crown it all, they all started arguing with each other.

When they had finished arguing, the troop leader would say, you guys did this: mentioning some sin that had been committed. They would deny it, which was an outright lie. Once again they would swear on their mothers that they didn't sin. They even denied breaking guard duty, (sleeping on guard), which they did all the time. I would be saying to myself: "Shut your fucking mouths, and agree with him, so that we can go back and get a little sleep." We were freezing. This went on for one and half to two hours.

You might look at this and say it was impossible. I look back in my diary after all these years and I say to myself it was impossible, but looking back, seeing us there at the time: it did happen and we did it. That night ended with us going back up the hill and feeling like killing the sons of bitches, because on top of all this the men on them had gone to sleep. So we dropped the stretchers instead of putting them down.

Something the officers liked doing was to call us out for a patrol, and then make us stand in the cold – often it would be snowing out. We would stand there in shirtsleeves, tired, holding on to our rifles, webbing and gear, all ready to go and shoot somebody, and they would say: "Go ahead, argue," or even worse, the *memcaf* would call us out and just disappear. We could not leave until he returned and we never knew when he would come back. I remember sometimes standing there for one and half hours, in the freezing cold, praying he would come back, almost sleeping on my feet and shivering. Then the son of a bitch came out and said we could go, or he would say, "You people like to argue, now argue about something." No problem! They'd argue, instead of shutting their mouths and saying: "No, sir, we were wrong and we don't want to argue.. *Princip* was a word in Hebrew meaning principles, and they would argue over any principle, whether they were wrong or not. But the main principle was to argue.

One day we were called out on an alert, and all of a sudden the FN rifle was thrown at me. This rifle carried a rifle-propelled grenade on the end and I remember grabbing my webbing. I do not know who had the rifle before me, but all the ammunition was wrong. There was no blank cartridge to fire a grenade, only live ammunition. It was someone else's mess. I wasn't the one responsible for this weapon. The *mem-mem*, Peled – he was medium height, medium build, and had light brown hair with a Dennis the Menace cowlick, and a thin face. His eyes were beady when he was upset, and they were beady now. He got really mad at me and there was nothing I could really say about it. For the next two days he made me run around with my helmet on, and I even had to sleep wearing my big American tin-pot lid. I worked in the mess hall serving food with this fucking great helmet on. If I was doing guard duty I might be silhouetted against the moonlight with the helmet. I also had my webbing on and had to carry my rifle, and during all the little chores of the day I would have everything on me. I was truly "ready for war." That was how they punished someone who was wrong as an individual, when they chose not punish the whole platoon.

At other times, if the boys did get stuck into each other with a real fistfight, the classic punishment was to hook the two soldiers together after it was all over. This happened to me more than once. We would spend the rest of the day with our two helmets strapped together on our heads. So, everywhere we went, we went together. Imagine eating, or if one man had to go to the toilet! The toilet facilities were a little better now. There was a hole in the ground with a small wooden structure around it .You would straddle the steps and do your thing. Funny, the Israelis were never very accurate here either. It was a great way to teach us to love each other.

The training moved into deeper phases of house warfare on December 24. We had the morning exercises, the afternoon exercises and then we had night exercises. We had been relieved from doing the night patrols so that we could do this training. I received a package that had been sent to all lonely soldiers who were serving in the army. Little did I know that it was also *Hannukah*, so in fact I received a Christmas present. However nobody told me it was a Christmas present. I remember training for war on December 24, with Jews in a country that did not recognize the Christmas holiday, and feeling very lonely once again. To be home in a warm house with my mom and dad, having a turkey dinner on Christmas Eve or Christmas Day would have been fantastic.

It was the same on Christmas Day. We trained from early in the morning until late at night. We finished about noon or 1:00 p.m. The day was 20 hours long – longer if we got punishment – sleep broken, long hours of guard duty in the snow. It was a very difficult time for my morale, though we would sing at dinner.

At another time I also received another package, from Elli Showhat's mother. He was one of the troops who had befriended me. This lad was also an intellectual. He was a tall, slight boy, with a very long nose and deep-set eyes. Elli had lived in different parts of the world. He came from a very good family and he had a girlfriend he raved about all the time. It reminded me of how I raved about my girlfriend, Kris, when I was in the marines. In that sense he reminded me a lot of myself. I opened the package from his mother, and there was some of the nicest cake in there that I have ever eaten. That reminded me of the packages my mother would send me every other month. Only, lo and behold, when I opened this one there were no cockroaches running out of it, like the ones we got in Vietnam. It was always gratifying to receive packages from home. It really touched me to receive this one.

The training went on for the rest of December and into January. The high level of fatigue was constantly with us and nothing healed properly. In late January we started to get ready to make a move to the desert, but before we went we loaded everything up on the trucks, and were given some time off.

I made my way to the kibbutz for *Shabbat*, and then to Beit Leit, where we got a briefing that we were to go to Tel Noff. We had to get our parachute gear and make a jump in the desert. We were issued with our jump gear, and sat on the end of the runway waiting. Sure enough, the *magod* –it was Nahamia at the time – showed up. We loaded on to the C-130, flew down to the Judean desert and made a jump at night. I had the MAG machine gun plus 600 rounds, then the parachute – I had to pick it up and put into the bag – and put all this on my back. then go back to the assembly area to get ready for the exercise. It was about three miles, back to the assembly area, and it was grueling carrying all that gear, especially when the sand was very soft and deep.

Once we all got back to the assembly area the exercise started. We had a long night march, and at the end of it there was a shooting exercise. They just wanted to see how fast we could move from one part of the country into a situation where we jumped into what would be a potential battle. I guess we did OK, because we did not hear much about it afterwards. We loaded into buses and trucks, sand in every pore, our boots, our underwear – all this combined with sweat. What a wonderful way to live! We left for Misday Boker in the Judaean desert, to a training area to start desert warfare on a larger scale.

We were going to do open hill fighting, trench warfare and anything else that pertained to desert warfare. We once again started as singles, then threes, then in squads, platoons, and company level. This was the first time we actually did exercises at company level. From there we would do battalion level: the whole of 890 would do an exercise, and we would get support from real tanks. These exercises were very exciting. We were no longer just a platoon or company on our own: we were starting to be part of the whole.

Nonetheless, it was bloody cold and we were up in the high part of the desert. Sometimes it would even snow lightly. The snow obviously does not stay on the ground, but it was bitterly cold with the wind blowing. The training would go as usual, long morning, more in the afternoon after inspection, into the evening and late at night. Towards the end of the day, if we did not do well, they would make us go back and do it all over again.

We were in a place called Nabi Musa. This godforsaken place is in the middle of the desert about 10 miles south of Jericho and 12 miles east of Jerusalem. Nabi Musa is the Arabic name for the biblical figure Moses, who by tradition is buried in Nabi Musa, Only a single structure was intact, a shrine built by the Mamluk Sultan Baybars in 1269. There is a dedication in Arabic that hangs on one wall of the mosque.

One day in particular, we had *Shabbat* out in the desert. That afternoon we had our shower (while out in the field we showered once a week). Even in the *mutsavs* we would only shower once a week. We would have to heat the water to melt it so that we could shower. Showers were done by numbers: 30 seconds of water and you soaped up, and then 30 seconds to rinse off. A navy shower on the *Shabbat*, when we were lying around. These guys, even in their most fatigued state, just could not leave well alone. They would argue and shout, and eventually bring the *memcaf*, who would put a stop to it all. That evening we went out for a good six-mile, run, coming back sweaty and hot, and I thought we would go to bed. Like hell, now it was time to pay for sins. This time we were in big tents, one platoon to each tent. Now we had beds and were no longer on the ground. They were metal frame beds and they were not much more comfortable than the ground, I can assure you.

We had a problem with the *rasap*, the company first sergeant. He was upset because someone had left dirty dishes in the mess tent. The people who were supposed to wash the dishes hadn't, and when he was upset the whole company got it in the backside. *Zion* all the way! Here, on a beautiful moonlit desert night, he had us running around with our beds over our heads. We were all running into each other, cursing one another, and one another's mothers, and family. We banged our fingers while holding the beds, and this went on for at least two hours. Finally they let us go.

That evening we had a readiness inspection as well. We moved into the center of the *maal*, the tent area we lived in. There we had one on one, so everybody up, one on one. This time I had Zockme, a short tough Yemeni with curly hair on my shoulders. He was my No 2 on the MAG. We ran round and round in circles, and when I put him down he was crying and holding his balls. My shoulders were killing me and my back hurt. It was rare, funnily enough, that I ever dropped anybody, even with my ankle, but by this time I was wearing a double sling wrapped around my ankle and I had two ace bandages inside my boot. This totally immobilized my ankle.

During another punishment period we were told that anybody who dropped the person off his back would not go home that particular weekend. If ever I wanted to go home to the kibbutz, I wanted to go home that weekend. I had Zockme on my shoulders and by the end of it, Zockme and I were the only guys who went home, but it took Zockme half an hour to get back on his feet afterwards. He was on my back for over two hours – I am not exaggerating. I cannot tell you how my feet, knees, back and shoulders felt, let alone Zockme's stomach and bollocks. He was hollering – they always holler – *betzim, betzim,* which means eggs, which mean balls. The long and the short of it was that Zockme and I went home that weekend while the rest of the platoon stayed right where they were. We deserved it!

One particular time in our training was a day when it was freezing. There was a very light snow and we were out on the hilltops. We were running a lot in this particular exercise and sweating, so when you stopped, it really froze you up so it hurt. We'd be shivering and shaking, our muscles were tightening up. Stopping was agony. I remember that our *samal*, Yoel Nitzani (he had been promoted), said, "Right, everybody in a big *horrah* circle." (The *horrah* is a circular dance.) So there we were in the middle of the night out in the Judaean desert, in a big circle, arms over each other's shoulders, doing the *horrah* and other Israeli dances and singing stupid songs, just trying to keep warm. I could just see it on camera! This is something that ought to be in a comedy of some kind, in fractured flickers perhaps.

I would not speak in English. If people spoke to me in English I would not answer in English and I would tell them to shut their mouths. A couple of times I actually came to blows over this. There were a couple of people that could speak English. Elli Showhot was one of them: his English was good, even better than mine. Yoel Nitzani was another one, but I would only use English in private, not in front of everyone else. I only spoke Hebrew to these people and I only spoke Hebrew at any other time. By this time my Hebrew was really improving I was able to carry on conversations. To me this was a great accomplishment.

Another great form of punishment at the end of the day was what they called *goozenikim*. A goozenik was a little tin can, cut open and filled with dirt and diesel fuel. We'd be told, "Go up the *jabal*." This was a hill that just went straight up – I don't know how high, but it was very high and very steep. They would say, "Go and spell out 'We will not break guard duty' on the side of the hill and light the goozenikim. We want to be able to see it in the next two hours."

So we had to run one kilometer (over half a mile) to get there, we had to carry two 20-liter (five and a quarter gallon) jerry cans of fuel – somebody had to carry it on their back. We had to climb the hill with all these cans, cut them open, fill them up with dirt and then spell out on the mountain side, "I will not break guard," all at night. We were always breaking guard. One of the *memcafs* would walk around at night and find somebody sleeping – and of course they would always deny sleeping and breaking guard. If they found someone breaking guard, the whole platoon was called out, and it would be time to fuck around for a while. Running around, one on one or just running round in circles making our lives miserable, when we should be sleeping instead of having a readiness inspection. There were a couple of times that I did nod off, but I wasn't caught.

The *goozeniks* up on the side of the hill must have looked very good from a distance to the *samal*, or the troop handlers. By the time we got down and looked up at the hill, half of them were burnt out. *Samal* Nitzani would say, "Go back up and light them again. We can't read what it says. Go back up and do it again." Sometimes the whole night was spent doing this and we had absolutely no sleep.

When it was time, they'd finally say: "We give up on you people. You are m*etumtam*, idiots, useless." By now, it would be time for morning inspection. The training day had started. We were now no longer having inspection in the afternoon because there was no heat. It was very cold.

I can remember when we were given some time off. The buses would only take us to Jerusalem. Depending on where we were going, they would put us down in a popular area. We would have to hitchhike – it was called tramping. I used to find it very interesting because I used to struggle with my Hebrew in different conversations, other than ones dealing with military subjects. The Israeli drivers were frightening. They compare with the worst drivers anywhere in the world, although years later I would take those words back. When you ride with these people you are always on the edge of your seat, although it was always good when they pulled over and picked you up because you wore a red beret. If you were standing in a queue, they would say: "The paratrooper there, get in the car." They didn't care for the fact that others were in line before the paratrooper. Israelis didn't care too much for being polite.

It's noteworthy that Israelis are returning lost property. There is a newspaper called *Bamahane* (*In the Base Camp*) – it is a Hebrew-language weekly, published by the Israel Defense Forces, which describes this.

One story, for example, told of two paratroopers who took a ride from Beersheba (southern Israel) to Tel Aviv, sleeping all the way. When they reached the central station they quickly thanked the driver, jumped out the car as they had a strong desire to return home – and forgot something on the back seat.

The good citizens of Israel kept the personal belongings of the soldiers, and advertised in *Bamahane* messages of the following type: "bag with underwear, a towel, socks," and "My brother was flying on Friday at a hitchhiking station ..." "About a month ago at Ashdod, in the direction of Tel Aviv. The soldier who lost his bag is welcome to contact..."

It would come out quite often that the person giving a lift had been in the paratroopers, or had a son in the paratroopers. It was always a nice feeling, and people always wanted an armed soldier. Not all soldiers were allowed to take their weapons home with them, but the paratroopers did. When I set out on the road I carried my M16 and two magazines. As I related earlier in this book, it can be useful!

At times I would walk through cities like Jerusalem and Tel Aviv to get to a bus stop where I could get a ride back to the kibbutz, and I would pass tourists eating sandwiches and drinking beer, having high times out on the sidewalk. I would think to myself that I was proud of what I was doing and why I was doing it, but I did not have enough money for a pack of cigarettes and a beer. The pay I received was only $50.00 a month. I could have joined the regular army after six months, because I only had a six-month obligation, having served three years already in the marines, but out of idealism I waived that, and the extension of a year and a half extra after the six months. So the whole two years I was in the army, I received National Serviceman's pay, which is virtually nothing. The other boys were subsidised by their families but I did it because it was my gesture, a silent one, to these people, and this great country. I was not there for money; I was there to serve my ideals in the State of Israel. I always had a proud feeling thinking of what I was doing and then watching other people with money in their pockets on holiday. I often wondered what it would be like to have a holiday with money in my pocket. On any trip I have ever done there has barely been enough money to buy a tin of beans at the end of the day – and sometimes I had to worry about that cost. That was not to change in years to come.

I've been asked whether I did a lot of sightseeing. Well, the Israeli army is not a very good place for sightseeing, but at the same time they were very good, when we had map and compass marches, especially while out in the desert. Generally, they were about 12 to 15 miles at night. We would march during the day, or night, in groups of two, from one historical point to another. For example, one of the points on the map we found our way to was Joseph's Tomb, which was out in the middle of nowhere. This was a place of vast history.

We were now in a place out in the Negev Desert called "Sde Boker," a kibbutz well-known as the place where David Ben-Gurion retired when he left politics in 1970. He spent his last years living in a modest home on the kibbutz. The army could do anything they wanted to us as I've already demonstrated. If we failed inspection, it was up in the middle of the night, and they would start running us around. Breaking guard was another crime. These guys would break guard all the time: they just could not be kept awake. Looking back, you can't really blame them, because we didn't get more than four hours' sleep a night. There was always some excuse to get us out of bed in the middle of the night, as well as the fact that we sometimes had to get up to do guard duty for an hour or more. Then of course there was *mizdar conenute*, readiness inspection: everybody out. We would get out with all our stuff and they would start running us around in the fireman's carry.

One day in particular, the *magad* gave us a speech. He actually asked me, in front of the others, what I thought of the level of people in the paratroopers, and I said, "When you start with shit, you end with shit." I was just pissed off with the whole lot of them. He was quite astonished – as everyone else was. Everybody looked at me, and believe me: if looks could kill I would have been dead. I was given the cold shoulder for some time after that. The guys' attitude was: "So we are a bunch of shit, are we?" I would say, "Yes, you are." The *magad* did not pursue the matter after I told him what I thought that time. Another time, we had just been punished and the whole platoon was throwing things at me after the *samal* caught us doing something wrong. He asked me if we were out of line. I said, "Yes." I would just pick it up and throw it back. They were throwing anything from kitbags to uniforms. I was very much at odds with them at times, actually many times. I had a measure of discipline instilled in me in the marines, which they did not have. We chafed each other quite a lot.

If I was asked: "Well, were you the only foreigner there, then?" I'd say, "No, I wasn't." There were a few South Americans, but they were just as bad as the Israelis. Maybe it was just simply the mentality of the bunch of men in the May induction – to make as much trouble as they could. The South Americans and other foreigners were all Jews, I was the only non-Jew there and nobody knew it. I had done very well up to that point keeping my secret to myself. Had they ever found out that I wasn't a Jew, I could have been in a lot of trouble.

Our training progressed to armored vehicles. We had done a little of this training in the Sinai, but we were now doing more and more of it. We had *Zelda*s assigned to us, American armored personnel carriers. Our breakfast consisted of hard-boiled eggs, bread and tomatoes, and quite often, when we were out in the field at lunchtime, the food would be the same thing. The *Zeldas* were incredible because when you are running around in them, inevitably somebody would fart. It was disgusting, to say the least, but it was all part of being in the *Zelda*. If it was a hot day, it was even worse. The poor driver could not even stick his head out of the top unless he opened up the hatch. We would hear him holler something very foul back at us. When thinking about it, however, he must have been just as guilty as everybody else. Every dog smells its own hole first!

A fellow named Naomony and I were constant offenders to see who could be worse, and other people would join in the chorus. There would be nobody with his head out of the top of the vehicle, and suddenly heads would pop out of every opening. Most of the time we were standing on a bench inside the vehicle and the top part of our chests and heads were outside. If we made someone mad, such as the platoon sergeant, he would command us to close the vehicle. All the hatches would then be pulled down, everybody would be inside, and then inevitably somebody would fart. It was a miserable experience, but it was also something that seemed to amuse everyone for a while.

One day I had to see the doctor because I had a cold. I can still remember this doctor, who had very gentle hands. I would get these moods when I was very thoughtful. I remember him cleaning his rifle and I was appreciating the doctor's hands. He was doing such a nice job on his rifle and I thought: "The hands of the man who saves a life, cleaning an instrument of death." Somehow it just struck me as odd. Even in war one thinks about a doctor there in the operating theatre saving lives, never cleaning his rifle. But then Israel has a different way of doing everything.

One evening, after a very long day at Mizdar Boker we were told to get ready for a live fire exercise. It was after dinner, and dark. Now on a live fire exercise, I would carry anywhere from 400 to 800 rounds of ammunition and then there would be the number two, also carrying ammunition. We started out on a fast march and we had not been told our destination before we began. The march then progressed to a trot and all of a sudden we were running downhill, all the way down to the Dead Sea. I remember thinking my heart would explode, and my knees were buckling. When we got to the bottom of the hill we had run for five miles. Although it was cold, we were soaking wet and panting. We had a few minutes' break at the Dead Sea, and started back up another route. It was incredibly steep going back up, as we had to run or march back up the side of a canyon. A few times I thought I would actually pass out because I was under such strain. Looking around at the other boys one could see they were experiencing the same thing.

You might ask: "What would they do if a guy fell out of a march?" If someone was falling back other guys would help, because if they didn't, the whole platoon would be punished. They would run us in circles, get us on top and tell us to go and get the son-of-a-bitch – the whole platoon, that is. They would really make us miserable. The men would help each other: and it was not because they loved each other, that was for sure. The guys would always pull together if something was directly against them as a whole, such as the troop leader or the platoon sergeant, but amongst themselves they would always argue and carry on. It was incredible. They would just curse each other and their families, the other guy's father, his grandparents all the way back to creation, yet they would not come to blows. Another very funny thing – and it was not uncommon – after one of these heated arguments one would walk up to the other and ask him for a cigarette. The other guy would promptly give him one. The attitude was one of, "The argument is over and this has no bearing on what is happening in the future." There was never bitterness towards each other. A wonderful saying of theirs was, "Don't take it to heart."

We got to the top of the hill and were sent down again to fetch somebody who had not made it. From there we had another six-mile run on flat land. I was carrying 400 rounds and a MAG. This number of rounds would be about between 27 lb to 29 lb, plus water bottles, which by this time were empty, grenades and anything else we would need. We were carrying a lot of weight and to run with it all that distance was incredible. When I say I thought my heart would burst (I thought that quite often), I can only thank God for the strength I was given and that I didn't fall out.

The whole time was in the Israeli army I only fell out of one march (but that was still to come). It was something I was very proud of, but at times I had to pray for the strength to continue. The things they used to put us through were horrendous at times. Mind you, these marches were never done during the day. They started after dinner, and many times we would have been on the go for 16 or 20 hours before we began them. All day we would have had weight on our backs, climbing hills, shooting, been under tremendous mental and physical pressure. Then we would start the march and it would usually be a long march. In the end this particular march was 16 miles.

Our training was becoming very complicated. We started out in ones, then threes, then squads, then a platoon, then a company. By now our training had progressed to company level, and in one case we were using helicopters. CH-53s came in one night to pick us up and took us a few miles away to a potential battle site, and into a live-fire exercise. Of course we made a mess of it all. The long and the short of that was that we had a good punishment period. We had to run the six miles back. At least I was light, being low on ammo.

We got back at 2:30 a.m. Then we had more punishment. We had a little something to eat, which was cold by this time. No cook would stay up and wait for a bunch of yoyos like us to come back, because there was no telling when we would arrive.

We eventually got to bed at 4:00 a.m. and were up again at 6:00 a.m. for another day of the same. I remember when everything would go wrong. The *memcaf* would be sitting telling us something and somebody would nod off. The *memcaf* would say, "You're asleep!" and the man would open his eyes and say, "No, I don't sleep." The *memcaf* would accuse him again and he would still deny it. The *memcaf* would say, "I saw you, you had your eyes closed!" and he would still deny it. It would usually begin right there. We knew we would get it that night for lying, or breaking guard. The *memcaf*, or whoever was duty NCO of the company, would come to check the guard and find the guard sleeping. Mind you, there was a guard for every platoon, so there were three guards, plus a *memcaf* walking around checking them. There had to be three guards, because one of them would be sleeping and the *memcaf* always caught one asleep. He would say, "You're sleeping, you broke guard." The guard would reply: "No, I didn't break guard." "I saw you, you were sleeping. You were snoring." The guard would actually deny snoring and would swear on his mother. (Mothers carried a heavy burden). They sounded, and looked so truthful – yet they were lying through their teeth. I have never met liars like this in my life before. You would catch a guy doing something red-handed and my mentality would be to admit it, but not these guys! They would deny it.

We had a lot of problems with live fire exercises and dry fire exercises. The problem was with the repeating of orders. For example, "Go to the right". Everybody was supposed to holler back. "Go to the right". The order would be passed from the Squad Leader to the men on the ground, or from the Platoon Sergeant to the Squad Leader to the men on the ground. It was very important that the order was repeated and of course the troops would not repeat it. Whatever the order was: "Fire on the right flank," "Fire on the right flank" or "Charge" – they were not repeating it.

One night they made us go up the *jabal* and start screaming, "We will repeat orders." A whole company of idiots out there, in the middle of the night, pitch dark, hollering: "We will repeat orders, we will repeat orders." They were supposed to hear this. We were, however, well over a mile away at the top of the hill. I dare say, out in the middle of the Judean desert, in the middle of the night they could hear this, though the troop handlers only replied, "We can't hear you." Reflecting back on this I think to myself we must have sounded like a bunch of morons, screaming, "We will repeat orders, we will repeat orders." All this did not help, because we were up there again on many nights screaming: "We will repeat orders, we will repeat orders," and then fail to do it the next day – nothing unusual.

There were other types of training. They took us down to the Mediterranean Sea once for water training. The whole *pluga*, which is a company, had a total lack of motivation. I was sick, so they put me in the mess hall. A day in the mess hall involved 16 to 18 hours washing dishes, peeling potatoes, helping the cook – you name it. The rest of the company was doing water training. After the training they were punished for different things. One day I managed to get away in the afternoon, and took a walk down by the ocean. I remember looking west across the Mediterranean, thinking about being back home with my mom and dad, what was happening back home, my Harley Davidson – I was actually quite homesick. I did not often get homesick, because we did not have time to think about home, so it was not a persistent problem.

There was total lack of motivation. Reflecting on it now, I can see why that was. The hours were incredible. A lot of it was due to plain fatigue. Even though the guys were being punished in cold water, they would still fall asleep in class. I have never seen such a bunch of sleepers in my life. Even though I was tired, I rarely fell asleep I suppose my motivation level was much higher. I am not saying that it is due to me being an incredible or special person. I was a volunteer. They were conscripts – they would volunteer for the paratroopers but they would still be conscript soldiers, and that is a different mentality, besides peer pressure. They did not want to be different from one another, so they were all involved in mischief or fiascos or lying to the troop leaders, and one would follow the other.

I think it would be good at this point if I read a diary entry of a typical day's training:

> March 11, 1976, Entry No 632. We rose at 05:00 to start a long day. We had our morning inspection as usual and a couple of other little inspections. At

> the end of the morning we had a briefing on the exercise that is to take place tonight, we will be flown down to El Arish, in the Sinai desert. Afterwards we collected all our gear and prepared to move out. I put the machine gun, ammo belt and pack, full of ammo, in my jump bag and so did the others. We then boarded the bus, which took us to Lod airport. We arrived at about 17:00, had a briefing from the battalion commander, the *Magad* Nhaimia, at the end of which we received our parachutes and got geared up. Our dinner, jam sandwiches and hard-boiled eggs, which we could smell in the plane afterwards. We ate on the flight line with the parachutes and all our equipment on us. Finally, at about 19:30 we boarded the big, powerful C-130 transport aircraft and soon afterwards we were airborne and on our merry way south, to the El Arish area.

When the lights went on, everybody stood up, and hooked up, shuffled to the door, the bell rang, out we went. I was third out of the plane and could not see the ground underneath me from 800 feet. I released the bag with my machine gun and everything else on it.

The purpose of the exercise was to raid the enemy's military base. The drop was not far from the base in El Arish, where we would make a combined attack with the strength of our paratroopers and other armored forces. While we were in the air, though, it became clear that the wind speed was three times faster that it should have been for a safe jump. Letting us jump was wrong but it was a complex exercise, so the decision was made not to cancel it and continue to the end. With the *Magad* Nhaimai it was always go.

The bag was on a 3-meter-long (10 feet) rope, which hung underneath me. The wind was howling and I could feel I was really moving through the air, but did not know which way because of the sand that was blowing and the darkness. I heard the bag hitting the ground. Two seconds later, wham, into the ground I went. I was dragged along in the sand for at least a quarter of a mile. I could not cut away from the parachute because there is a screw through the cape well, the coupling that connects the risers to the parachute harness. As I was being dragged through the sand, my parachute by chance caught the edge of the fence around a Bedouin family's living area. Like most Bedouin, they had a camel, and the camel started going mad. It was running around and making a funny grunting noise, then spitting. The object of the exercise here was not to get to within 15 feet of this thing. The penalty for failure was to be hit by a big wad of spit. I very cautiously got my parachute off, and deflated it.

Now I had to get it in the pack and get my machine gun and everything else together.

In the meantime this camel was making the rounds and every time it came round it went *hunnnnn* and spat a big goober. On the next pass, Lieutenant Gual from another platoon went right into the Bedouin's tent. This time the camel went berserk, and started bellowing while on the run. The family was adding to the confusion by running in all directions, and increasing the anger of the camel by screaming at each other. It was the middle of the night, there was sand flying and the camel going *hunnnn* and spitting. The lieutenant didn't know that he was in range of the camel. It spat at him and hit him right in the back of his neck. He danced around like a banshee, and his hand went into the goober. He was hollering and cursing. He just carried on and on while this big wad of spit was rolling down the back of his neck and in his hand, collecting sand all the while. There was sand all over his uniform. Oh my gosh, but it was disgusting!

So much for camaraderie. By this time I was all packed up and I thought to myself as I was sneaking off into the desert to the assembly point, "Well, lieutenant, you pays your money, and you takes your chances." I left him there to take care of himself. I didn't want to get involved with that fucking camel.

One guy from my platoon, Joselevich, jumped directly into the part of the Bedouin tent where the women were living. As soon as they felt that someone had fallen from the sky they were sure it was Allah himself, and started shouting, "*Ya Allah*!" They just kept yelling "*Ya Allah*!!" A big mess ensued. The parachute had covered all the tent. Staying in the tent was not the thing to do. An unhealthy situation was sure to follow when it was discovered that Joselevich was not Allah. I immediately started to remove the parachute and pulled out the tent pegs. When the Bedouins saw this, they joined us in fear, as they thought, "What Allah is doing we have to do," without asking any questions. However, by taking the tent pegs out we left the family without a home.

Once we were actually at the assembly point, we started a long march to the El Arish area. This was very soft sand. It was almost one step forward and two steps back, plus we were carrying a lot of weight. Then, believe it or not, the rain came, but at least that settled the sand. Sand was everywhere, including inside our uniforms, our backsides, our boots. We did our exercise, I won't say we did it very well, but we did it nonetheless, at the end of which we were very cold and hungry. We were given a tidbit to eat – more hard-boiled eggs.

At the end of the exercise we got on to buses, drove back to Tel Noff, and turned in all the parachutes. They told us to get into good uniforms, which we had sent down on another truck, because we were going home for the weekend. What was to happen next was very typical of the Israeli paratroopers. We got into our good uniforms – sand was coming off us everywhere – and then we sat on the buses for four hours, just to be told that was it, we were not going home over the weekend. Right, what do we do for dinner now? They brought out some tinned meatballs and bread and that was our Sabbath dinner. No knives or forks. We were finally told we could go and shower at the main base, which we did, to get the sand off. *Shabbat shalom*, as they say.

The *mempay* gave us a speech on the *Shabbat* holiday. He said there was trouble in Lebanon and we were to go in ourselves. So everybody geared up to go and then we were told we were no longer going. The reason given was that there would be problems with the Americans telling us we could not go in. Syria had invaded Lebanon. We could not do the same thing. Anyway, there was a very anti-American feeling at that time because of the way the Americans treated the Israelis. The Arabs could do whatever they want but not the Israelis, even though America was our main supplier of arms. We just had to listen and take the intimidation. It was of course the weak-minded liberal Carter administration.

They then sent us off to Jerusalem to do riot control. We walked around the Old City in threes and I remember an Arab motioning us over and offered us a cup of coffee. He was very pleasant and I was shocked. After all, we were on the West Bank of Jerusalem and there were many foreigners in the street.

In the early 1970s, the Old City of Jerusalem, beloved of the archaeologists, began a process of rehabilitation and reconstruction, while attempting to preserve the ancient alleys and roads as much as possible. Synagogues were restored and cleaned of the cattle manure and dirt that had accumulated in them. The authorities were able to put all the electricity and telephone cables underground. We were at that time keeping things quiet so normal life in the city would continue.

Being an English-speaker I spoke to people from all over the world. The boys could not speak English very well, so I translated for them. I was actually quite proud of myself. My Hebrew was at a level at which I could translate conversations from English to Hebrew and they would understand me quite clearly. Being able to do it made me feel very good. Learning to speak Hebrew was one of the greater accomplishments of my time in Israel.

At one time we were guarding the West Bank as well, in a place called Nablus. An Arab bus came around a corner and there were a couple of Arab boys out in the road. The two guys had to move fast to get out of the way. Their fear, the way they ran and the look on their faces made everybody laugh. The bus driver had a big bus and he did not feel like slowing down when the bus came around the corner. I did not see it as openly malicious, though another person might. They treat each other very harshly at times. When you are walking around and faced with things like this, you can feel the hatred of the people: it is electric and it is not a pleasant place to be. I never saw an Israeli openly mistreat an Arab that didn't deserve it to start with, and yet the boys I served with had lost loved ones and friends. Everybody knew somebody who had been lost in the war, let alone a loved one or a relative, and that itself is a seed of hatred. They would start throwing things, and then we would go for them. It did not happen that often, but obviously it has changed over the years.

I remember coming back from the West Bank one afternoon. The bus had a flat tire, so I went prowling around and came across an amphitheater. It would have seated about 800 to 1,000 people and it was at least 1,000 years old. Back then, that was a lot of people who could have fitted in there. There was also the old ruin of a village off in the distance, so this was obviously their entertainment area. I stood up on a big rock slab in the middle of the arena and gave my first public address to an audience that had passed from the world 1,000 years ago, a millennium before my birth. I stood there in front of these imaginary people and gave a speech. I told them of my life, how things were going with the training, how incredible it was to be here in the land of Zion, how with God's grace, I would do well and serve the Israeli people and the country to the best of my ability. I can remember a funny feeling at the end of the speech and I said: "Thank you very much," and I bowed. There was total silence. I could feel the spirits that had passed away so long ago. It was amazing. It was as if the ghosts of the past were there, looking upon me, and I wonder to this day whether they were applauding me or throwing rotten vegetables. You might ask, "Did you speak to them in English or Hebrew?" I spoke to them in both English and Hebrew. I just hope I didn't put them back to sleep.

Finally, on April 19, 1976, we moved from the desert to our NCO course, at a base just above the city of Tiberias and near the northern city of Karmiel, in the Galilee Mountains. Upper Galilee is a mountainous region, and therefore movement and living is more difficult. Because of the nature of the land most of the settlement is in the Upper Galilee communities – they are working settlements of *kibbutzim*, *moshavim* and villages. There are also many villages of minorities, such as Bedouin, Druse and Circassians. This was to be another two months of very grim, hard training, but we would be using our initiative more. We would be doing more leadership, because this is what the NCO course is all about. We arrived there at the start of Passover, and the *matzo* (thin pieces of unleavened bread) was out. In the Israeli army we had no bread during Passover. We had no choice: everybody was eating *matzo*, tinned beans and meatballs. I thought to myself, "Another week of eating *matzo* and we will all be farting dust."

One of the first things we did after establishing ourselves in the barracks was a 15-mile forced march. I was carrying about 55 lbs, and the MAG. I didn't take enough salt tablets, and I remember this to be one of the most painful marches I was to have. It was just a 15-mile march, almost at a run all the time. It was downhill, uphill, over rocky, thorny areas. There were no roads at all, except the last portion where the road led back into the base. It was either downhill or uphill: we would be climbing over things, jumping and running and trying to keep up. I was getting cramps in the back of my legs. It was tremendously painful. I was pushing water out as quickly as I put it in and I remember saying to myself, "This is incredible." We finished the march in four hours, 55 minutes, from start to finish. Some might say, "That is only four miles an hour, not very fast!" Remember the terrain we were on: it was rocky, it was at night, we were in columns of one or two a lot of the time, running, stumbling, falling down, bashing ourselves, scraping our elbows and hands. We also had to stop for two minutes every hour and drink as much water as possible or we just would not make it. On top of this I was having tremendous cramps. We were then told to get ready to go home over the *Shabbat* holiday. By this time the night had passed and we had morning inspection, got our dress uniforms on and went home. We'd had no shower, so we stank.

Now, after a day's training, live fire exercise, this, that, whatever, inspection, meals – it was a very long day, and then we would have *maddas*, or exercise again. They had basketball, stretcher runs – great fun, but nobody really gave a fuck because they were all too tired. Our guys, that is.

In the meantime two groups of people had arrived. One was the *Hon*, who were the parachute regiment's demolition team. They were a very motivated bunch of troops. Then there was another outfit called the Desert Scouts, the *Sirat Sheked*. They were also very highly motivated. They were all from the kibbutz or *mishav* and all very different from the rest of us. All of a sudden we had these elite groups with the *Mayniks*, the guys from the May induction. Our reputation had preceded us as being a bunch of shitbirds. The day was already 16 hours long and our guys did not give a flying fuck about basketball or anything else. All they wanted to do was go and break guard, sleep and lie about it. The *Hon* and the *Sheked* thought that exercise was great after the long day.

A lot of this was affecting me personally. I found myself taking on some of these guys' habits. I really could not care about going out and playing basketball after a long day.

I remember the Independence Day holiday when I got away to go to the kibbutz. The look the Israelis got on their faces when they sang certain songs fascinated me and always will. We all gathered outside the big cafeteria and had a talk about the War of Independence and the *kibbutzniks* that were lost during that war. There was a very different feeling about the day. There were some songs sung such as the National Anthem. The Israeli National Anthem is incredible: it is so romantic and heartrending and I will always remember the faraway look the people would get on their faces. It was almost hypnotic. I would look around me and study their very Semitic features and the look in their eyes. We had the big noisy party afterwards.

Kibbutzniks did not drink much but I did. I was getting stuck in: there was free beer and everything else I find hard to afford in normal times, as well as all the other little goodies, like salami and cheese. I was known to really tear the ass out of it sometimes.

Once back at the base, we were going to have a 35-mile forced march. We were having classes during the day while we were on the base, and we were supposed to go home for the weekend after the march. I was carrying the MAG and about 400 rounds when the march started, and I had trouble right from the start. My hay fever was acting up, I was sneezing a lot and I am sure I was dehydrated even before we started. I also twisted my ankle.

The march was from the base course in Karmiel to Gamla at the Golan Heights. This was a Biblical city, which stood bravely before the Roman legions in A.D. 67. Our march symbolized the steadfastness and determination we showed through all those 14 months of basic training. Against all odds, and with difficulties, the ones that were still there had made the decision not to give up and wanted to continue to the end, with the belief that what we did was good for us and especially good for the country.

On the way I started getting cramps, and all the time we marched I was drinking water. It was just going out of me as fast as I drank it. About 20 miles into the march I blacked out. I could feel it coming: it was as if my whole world was coming to an end. The worst thing in the world for me was to fail a forced march. For me that was showing a weakness, and it was something that I just would not do. The next thing I knew, the *mem-mem*, a new one now, named Gual, was slapping me and throwing water in my face to wake me up, and they put a drip in.

They said I had dried out and I had to be put on the drip. I was taken to an ambulance that was following the company and taken back to the base, where I was given another drip. I had not urinated for hours. After a while I started to feel a little better, but I still spent the night and the rest of the next day in hospital and I was determined to complete the march. A few other guys had fallen out as well, and they urged me to just leave it alone. They said I should not bother to go back and say that I wanted to do another march.

There were two companies doing the NCO course. One company would do the march one week and the other company would do the march the following week. The other company was 202 Battalion of the Para Brigade. At this time the other company was getting ready to do the march. I requested to march with them. This meant that the others that had fallen out were to do a second march with me. I was, to say the least, very unpopular once again!

8
NCO

The guys in my company said that if I asked to do the return march they would have to do it as well, and they were certainly not interested in that! There were six guys, including myself, who had fallen out. I said, "To hell with you guys! We all failed the march: we have to go and do it again. If you don't want to do it, that's fine with me, but I'm going to try it again."

Up till that time, I had not fallen out of any of the marches, and I was determined to do this one as well. I was very embarrassed and my pride was hurt, so I went and spoke to the *mempay*. He agreed that I could do the march. He also said that the other guys who fell out for whatever reason, sprained ankles, bleeding blisters, should do the march with me.

I went back and broke the happy news to the guys, and once again I was an outcast, a prick, a dog, a *ben zona* (son of a whore), and everything else that they despised. That Thursday finally rolled around after a long day's training, and our company went home. The six of us who had to do the return march went over to meet up with the other company.

They were going to do a stretcher march and we all left the base, going downhill, across country, around the top part of the Sea of Galilee. This is the place were Jesus was supposed to have walked on water and our march took us right by the area, but to say the least there was no time to dwell on such things. We went up and up, on to the Golan Heights and marched right to the very end. The march went on, hour after hour and sometimes we had as many as four people relieving, though most of the time it was just two. We were carrying a stretcher with a person on it. He had a rifle and a radio as well as all his gear. We tried to find a small guy to carry on our stretcher, but we ended up with someone with a medium build and height, which meant we were carrying a lot more weight. We had our own rifles, our American tinpot lid and all the rest of our gear to carry, as well. Thankfully I wasn't carrying a machine gun at the time. To say that we were sweating profusely was quite an understatement.

We were now in a company formation and once again the lead platoon was marching fast. The next platoon was marching a little faster, with periods of running mixed in. The platoon at the back was running all the time in order to keep up, sometimes even flat out. At the same time we were carrying the stretcher with the guy on it, and it was bashing our necks and shoulders unmercifully.

It was pitch dark as there was no moon out, and the roads were very rough, which made it even worse. Over and over you would hear the command, "*Ovlef, ovlef*!" being shouted out. This was the order for us to relieve someone. It meant that we would have to go and find the guy who needed to be relieved. It was a good time to have an accident and drop the stretcher. We had to hoist it up in order to put the relief person in position and get the tired person out: all this while either marching fast or running. After about six hours of this, both shoulders would be rubbed raw, and were more than likely bleeding. The stretcher itself was nothing to write home about. It was rugged and heavy, made of two wooden poles shoved through some hard canvas with metal braces going from pole to pole. It must have weighed about 14 to 16 lb on its own, and then of course you added to it the weight of the "wounded" man and all of his equipment. It was a rough march.

The pain was terrible. Our feet were on fire and our legs ached. I can remember that sometimes we would be coming downhill and one of the guys at the back would be pushing harder than the guys in the front. Or it could be the complete reverse, with the guys in front going faster than those in the rear. Either way, it was total misery. Once again I had crushed toenails, which was incredibly painful. The pain was made even worse when we had to go downhill. Halfway through the march they stopped us, made us get on our backs, put our feet up in the air and start to bicycle with our legs. This was to get the blood out of our feet. By this time we would have sores on the inside of our thighs, which were made even worse by this added exercise. After a few minutes of this, it was time to get back on our feet and have a drink of water, pick up the stretcher again and get going. If we dropped the stretcher, we were in trouble and the guy who was lying on it would get nailed. We would catch it big time from the troop leader if he saw what happened.

Up and up we went, with the occasional small downhill turn to relieve the monotony. After hours of climbing we finally made it to the top of the Golan Heights, to a location that had some historical significance. This was supposed to be part of the motivation. Dawn had not yet broken when we came across a table laid out with bread, hard-boiled eggs and cheese. I came to learn that no meal in the Israeli Army was complete without eggs. We were just glad that hadn't had hard-boiled eggs the night before, or else the entire march would have been punctuated with the sounds of egg-induced farting. There was also a big steaming pot of tea set in the middle of it all. Just as we were all psyched up to sit and relax and have a meal, they kept us marching past the table. No one could believe it. To see the table all laden with food was like seeing manna from heaven and we just went right on past it. You can imagine the mood we were all in by that time!

They then had us start running around in circles. After that, they told us to run just one more kilometer (three fifths of a mile) in a particular direction, just one more kilometer in another direction, then we could go back. When we finally did get back to the table, the feast had lost some of its appeal. The tea was stone cold and the food looked wilted. We were all shattered. When they finally told us that we could put the stretcher down, the relief was incredible because we knew that we wouldn't have to pick it up again and run. Everyone gathered around the edge of the cliff and the rabbi came forward and started chanting. The *mempay* gave a talk about the historical significance of the area: something to do with the 1973 war. Only after that were we finally allowed to go back to our cold tea and hard-boiled egg sandwich. Wonderful, what a reward!

In the end, when we put down the stretcher for the last time, I told myself that it was worth it. It was a great feeling to be on top of that mountain, knowing that we had overcome all the hardships and had finally made it. Looking out over the edge of the cliff at the great valley down below the Golan Heights truly was a magnificent sight. It had all definitely been worth it.

In the end the march totaled 53 kilometers (33 miles), and we completed it in under 12 hours. We started the march after we had already completed a full day's training. We had been on the go continuously for over 24 hours.

On these marches I always managed to sprain my ankle, so it was permanently bandaged. I used to have it tied up so solid that I could hardly move it at all. Yet as soon as the march began and I had to put all that weight on it I would inevitably sprain it again. Somehow I would manage to keep going. I began to get really concerned when it felt like my ankle was just hanging there, it could propel me forward but it had no real strength of its own. I started thinking that maybe surgery was the only thing that would be able to correct it.

We were having a lot of map and compass exercises and I remember not being able do them quite as well as I should have liked. Maybe it was due to the fact that I just couldn't navigate on my own. On the other hand I didn't know how well the other guys were doing, because they were always so busy arguing about everything. We were always in a three-man team and no matter what it was we were supposed to do, we had to argue about it first. One guy would say: "I think we need to go over that way," then the other would say, "No, we have to go over here!" In the end we would have a huge argument, and the winner would be the one who could shout the loudest. Away we would go, following the guy with biggest mouth: usually only to discover that we were going in the wrong direction. I never did learn what I was supposed to on these training exercises, and would have liked to have done a better job than I did: if for nothing else than the fact that I really did love being out in the country, climbing the hills, looking for some historical monuments or old graves that had been out there for centuries. I always found our treks out in the wilderness to be very interesting.

We had another stretcher march and just as an example of how much we were improving by that time, we went 13 miles in two hours and 26 minutes. At that pace, we were running almost all the way. I wouldn't say that we were getting physically stronger as much as we were getting mentally tougher. We were able to tolerate pain and fatigue far more easily. We were learning to overcome it and just keep pushing ourselves further and further beyond the limit. All this was making us more and more ready for the reality of war. They weren't so much concerned about how many push-ups we could do as with our being able to run a certain distance in a certain time – this with a full load and perhaps with a stretcher. Overall, they were trying to making us as tough as we could possibly be. They wanted us to be able to endure tremendous hardship for prolonged periods and I would have to say that they made a smashing success of it, especially given the caliber of the people they started out with. The guys from the parachute demolition teams and the Desert Scouts had an even better level of training than we did, but then they also had a better level of motivation to begin with, and they were also a different type of people. They probably lived a healthier lifestyle when growing up, having come from the kibbutz and the *motshav*. This was generally not the case with the individuals who had come from the city. The demolition men and the scouts generally had a better level of education than the boys from the lower parts of Israeli society. It was apparent in they way they spoke and thought, even though the 890 guys (that's us), were really shaping up. I figured by now they could hold their own in a real knockdown drag-out fight.

To get back to map and compass marching, I remember one time in particular, when we marched to the top of Mount Tabor. From there, we could look down on the Sea of Galilee in its entirety. The view was beyond description, it was so beautiful. We could see the area where Jesus had walked. Further on we could see the town of Tiberius, which was right along the shore of the lake. It was almost heartrending in its beauty. At times like that, I would say a prayer of thanks for the strength I had been given to be able to accomplish the things I was doing, and for the sights that I was seeing. To be able to look down on something so old and so much a part of our own living Bible, always stirred something inside of me. At times like that, it was very easy for me to communicate with God.

We were still bringing punishment upon ourselves. We had been out to a West Bank city, and in between our guard duties we were given a map with exercises to do around the city perimeter. This time in particular we really messed up, and Platoon Sergeant Yoel was so upset with us that the officers made our company grab seabags. We tried to tell them that they actually belonged to another company, but they just wouldn't listen. I can't really say that I blamed them for not believing us, as so many of our company were habitual liars. So there we were, running around with all these seabags that didn't belong to us – and of course after the exercise they were all mixed up and nobody could figure out what belonged to whom. Everybody started shouting and throwing bags at one another. Eventually we discovered that our bags were in fact somewhere else, and we ended up leaving the other company's bags more organized than they were to begin with. We eventually got our stuff and were finally on our way again.

On June 7, 1976, we moved to the Negev Desert for a short period of training. We were doing trench warfare, and I can't begin to describe how hot it was out there. We were supposed to rest during the heat of the afternoon, so they decided that was when we would actually do our "morning" inspection. Doesn't make much sense, does it – but apparently it did to the Israeli army. I would clean the machine gun and the rest of the guys would clean their rifles. It was always interesting doing this, because every day just before 3:30 p.m. – about the time we would get finished cleaning our weapons, we'd look out on the eastern horizon and see a big yellow ball coming straight at us. We were still in the little two-man half-shelters we'd set up and we would have to take the poles out, lying them down flat on the ground and then lying on top of them. Almost like clockwork, when 3:30 p.m. rolled around, a sandstorm would hit us. The storm would be so vicious that we couldn't see further than five feet in front of us. The sand would be whipping around us and we put rags up to our faces in hopes protecting ourselves while breathing. After about 15 minutes it would all be over, and the howling winds would be replaced by silence and heat. We would all get up, dust ourselves off and carry on. We would then have our inspection and of course we would all fail miserably, because of the sand that now coated our "clean" weapons.

Our food out in the field was something else entirely, and I would say that the term "unique" pretty much described it. I can remember one time in particular when the food was so bad that it really did stand out. The meal set in front of us was half-cooked, and to make it even worse, it was stone cold. The troop leaders wouldn't let us get our hands on the cook, because they knew that we would probably have killed him, given half a chance. This particular meal was so bad that rather than eat it, we had a serious food fight. It started off with some of the guys throwing peas at one another and then it progressed to hard-boiled eggs. Eventually everyone got in on the act and stood up, hurling food at one another. It was no surprise that all of our carrying on led to yet another punishment session in the middle of the night. Unbeknownst to us, the troop handlers had been over on the other side of the tent when the food had begun to fly. They had caught some of the food backlash and apparently didn't find it as amusing as we did. I thought it was very poor humor on their part. There was an upside to it though. This was one time when there was good camaraderie on our part.

Another thing stands out in my mind from our time in the Negev Desert. One particularly peaceful night, everyone was resting in their two-man shelters. I was on guard duty and was standing on top of one of the *Zeldas*, our armored vehicles. I remember that there was a brilliant quarter moon up above. The quiet was so intense that it was almost felt heavy. I was filled with a sense of complete solitude. I'd been on guard for about an hour and my mind had been reflecting over things in the past; my old girlfriend, my parents, home. I was off in another world. I suddenly became aware of a low rumbling off in the distance, in the direction of Jordan. From what I could tell, the sound was still quite a few miles away. My first thought was that we were about to be attacked by tanks. It's amazing how your imagination runs wild at a time like that. Then the noise changed slightly, and I detected that it was a pounding noise rather than the rumble of tanks. It was a weird droning sound. All of a sudden a herd of 40 camels came roaring through our camp. As they raced in between the tents, their hooves kicked up sand and they made the camel sounds of "hunnnnn, hunnnnn." The whole time they were spitting, in the disgusting way that only camels do. As the sleeping men woke up and realized what was happening around them, their small two-man tents went flying up in the air. The guys started running in every direction, trying to avoid the flying hooves, cursing Allah the whole time (using this word means they are not taking God's name in vain). Having seen the whole thing from my safe perch, it was almost as though we had been attacked by a tribe of Bedouins, just as might have happened a century ago, only there were no Bedouins on the camels. In the end it was quite funny, at least for me. Nobody had been hurt, but everyone was milling around, pissed off that the night's rest had been so abruptly interrupted. The whole session was subsequently scrapped after that. We were told to break the camp down, and then we moved out for training a few hours earlier than usual.

We were in that area for another one and half weeks and then we moved back up to our NCOs' course base in Galilee near the town of Tiberius. I was put in charge of the mess hall, something that was very frustrating for me. Every time I turned around the messman would be sick and having to go see the doctor. He would disappear, and I would find him sleeping in the barracks or just generally trying to hide out in one place or another around the base. There was never any shortage of creative excuses; "My foot hurts," "My back hurts," "My face hurts." You name it: he had it. After a while I just got sick and tired of hearing all the excuses. It was the same with the other messmen. Every time I needed someone, they'd be gone. In the end, it was so frustrating, that I ended up doing a lot of the work myself. I just hoped that I would find a way to get even with the bastards for all the bullshit that they were putting me through.

One event stands out. I remember that we had a live fire exercise. We were using different types of weapons, and at one time I was carrying an RPG, which is an anti-tank weapon. There was a lot of cactus around the base and while we were running around, I somehow fell off of a ledge right into a bed of it. Holy mackerel! I came up out of that thing dancing like a banshee. I was running around hollering, with cactus thorns sticking out of my backside and pretty much everywhere else. The guys came running with a stretcher and carried me back to the camp. It was so embarrassing. You couldn't believe how much my pride had been hurt. I lost track of how many cactus needles they plucked out of my backside and legs. There were too many to count.

On another occasion, we had a house warfare exercise. We were going through some houses and came across a bunch of Arabs living in one of them.

Of course we hadn't expected to see them there, so there were all kinds of things flying through the air, and grenades exploding. They were Bedouins, but we didn't stop the excerise because of them. We just kept on the move, shooting the place up. They just kept their heads down, and out of our way. I guess the moral of the story is that you just never know where or when the Israeli army is going to show up.

On July 1, I made an entry in my diary, specifically mentioning the fact that I had been away from home for two years. This was the longest period that I'd ever been away. That night, while on guard duty, I reflected about my family and how they were doing and how I just couldn't see myself getting home to visit them for at least another year. I had certainly found all of the adventure that I had been seeking originally, and my ideals had been put to the test, that was for sure. I won't say that I had got everything out of the Israeli army that I had hoped for, but at that point for the most part I was certainly satisfied.

On July 3, we were told to stand down and to congregate at the base theater. We were also told to get our weapons and equipment, ready for war. By this we knew that something big was in the air. At that time, we had heard about the Air France jet that had been used for a terrorist attack at Ben-Gurion Airport. We didn't know exactly what was going on, but we knew something was up. Later that evening we were told about the Entebbe raid. I nearly crawled up the wall, thinking that I had missed out on participating in something like that. It would have been the ultimate high to have partaken in the raid. We later found out that our *mempay* had been one of the men involved in the raid, as well as some the officers and NCOs that I had known from basic training, guys that had been our *memcafs* and *samal*. I was sick to my stomach that I had missed it. At the same time I was also very happy that the mission had been pulled off with such success and professionalism and, of course, with such a small loss of life – only one Israeli casualty. It was certainly a shining example of what an army can accomplish through training and dedication to attaining perfection in the military arts.

July 7 was to be the last day of our 14 months' basic training. For the last couple of days, they had been doing a lot of troop and stomp, marching left, right, left. We were practicing for the parade, which would signal the end of all those months of basic training. I put out my uniform all nicely cleaned and pressed, a condition that it had not been in often. I then had some other duty that I had to take care of, so I was away from the rest of the guys. One of them came to the barracks I was in, and said, "Hey Dave, you're going to be the honor man for Battalion 890." I was shocked. He told me to get out on the parade ground and I hustled out there as fast as I could. When I got there, I practiced in front of the base commander, who would later present me with my stripes as a]corporal. After that I would be given a "Well done!" by Mr. Big, who had the rank of colonel.

Later in the afternoon, I went back to barracks and someone had stolen my nice clean uniform. The one I was wearing was covered in grease and dirt, and it stank to high heaven. It would have to do.

We were to graduate that afternoon and I stood to attention in formation, waiting for my name to be called. When they did call you, you were supposed to say "Here, sir." I was so nervous about the uniform I was wearing as it was filthy, wrinkled and smelled to high heaven. When they finally called my name, my voice caught and all I could manage was "Ah, sir," in quite a high-pitched tone. I then had to run forward and get into line in front, where the base commander would hand me my stripes. There were guys there from parachute demolitions, from the *Sirret Sheced*, and guys from each of the two parachute battalions, 890 and 202. I was there as Honor Man for Battalion 890. Finally he came over to me and his eyes went all over me as if to say: "What the hell is this?" I stood in front of him looking like some grubby ragamuffin. I tried to look proud and composed, but I don't know that I carried it off. Of course, I had made matters worse already by my rather pitiful "Ah, Sir." I stood there wondering what he was going to do – whether he was going to make me go back and start over again, or make me put someone over my shoulders in the fireman's carry. He caught me off guard by asking me what I thought of the course. I said, "Very good, sir. Very good!" He then went on to ask me a few more questions that I can no longer remember. I was in a daze at the time. But I do remember as he handed me my stripes and shook my hand, he took one final look at my uniform, shook his head and then went on to the next fellow. I can imagine what he was thinking, "*Maynik, Maynik. Mau mau*!" ("The May induction. All a bunch of shitbirds!"). Even so, it was quite a moment for me.

After we had all received our stripes, we were told to get back into formation. Then the colonel addressed all of us, congratulating us for having completed our 14 months of basic training. All of the guys threw their berets up in the air and started dancing around and hugging each other. It was finally all over and we were now actually NCOs. Some of the guys would go on to be troop leaders and others were going on to what was called the *pluga rabatim*, or the Company of Corporals. The latter was where I was heading. It was the spearhead of the parachute regiment. Some of the others went on to be squad leaders, and they would be sent to Sanour, to a new bunch of recruits. It was quite a moment to look around and see all their faces, especially with their families there with them. The best part of all was knowing that finally we were going to be treated like soldiers.

We had a little time to ourselves in the barracks and later we were called to one of the big auditoriums and given a talk by the base commander. He himself had been in on the Entebbe Raid. He told us exactly what had happened and who had played what role. He also told us about the casualty, and how they had managed to get the civilians out. It was a very interesting talk and it lasted almost an hour. We went back to the barracks afterwards and prepared for the evening meal and the party that was to follow.

My appetite disappeared as soon as we sat down at the table. The 14 months of hardship was actually over and I guess all at once the finality of it hit me. I managed to get my meal down but it was certainly without my usual gusto. The rest of the guys were carrying on and throwing food like nothing had changed. I got up and excused myself, and went back to the empty barracks. I got my mattress and sleeping bag and dragged them up to the roof. I lit up a cigarette and just gazed out over the edge of the building, down into the valley below. I just remember feeling very empty. I said a prayer and thanked God for the strength he had given me to get through those many months of training, and obviously to do it well. I had been chosen as Honor Man. I then lay back and looked up at the stars above and eventually drifted off to sleep. I had climbed to the top of the hill and there really was nothing there after all. That's how I ended my day, and my 14 months of basic training.

At the end of the training we were given our written orders to where we were going, even though unofficially each of us knew already. We were then given 30 days leave, which of course was our first really long break since we had started 14 months ago. I headed back to the kibbutz, and after a few days started working in the citrus orchard again. I helped with the irrigation and anything else that needed doing. It was very beautiful down there in the valley of Israel, right below Tel Meggdo. The area is also better known as the Valley of Armageddon, the place that the Bible says will be the site of Armageddon, the final battle between the armies of the east and west. It really is an incredible place, with the orchards running off for two or three miles in any direction. It is also a very significant place historically, as it was there that the armies laid siege to Meggdo centuries ago.

There were three cute girls from Canada who were living in the room next to where I was staying. As we only had one alarm clock between the four of us, we shared it. I would keep it at night and then every morning after it went off, I would go next door and put it in their room all set to wake them up later on. They worked in a different area, so they got to sleep in a bit. I used to call them the Three Sleeping Beauties because they looked so cute and young lying there asleep. I was often struck by their innocence, especially when I compared it with everything I had gone through in the last 14 months. I hadn't been able to visit the kibbutz often during my training as we were in one state of readiness or another the entire time. It felt good to be back finally, and to relax.

It wasn't long before my leave was over and I had to report back to my unit once again. I spent the first couple of days just working around the camp, doing odd jobs. I remember the dust was terrible at the time. Everywhere you went there was a thick coating of dust. The main company returned to camp after completing a two-day exercise and everything was starting to settle in again just like before.

The next morning, we did a navigation exercise that took us to a location in the Negev that we had not been to before: followed up with another one that night. There was another fellow on the exercise named Ernesto, a South American. We eventually went on to become very good friends. We were sent out on our own and we had a march of about 20-kilometers (12 ½ miles) to complete. Somewhere along the route we heard a great hissing sound. It was one of the most evil sounds I had ever heard, and it was coming at us out from the bush in the middle of a very black night. I hadn't had any practice catching snakes since I was a kid running around in the Mojave Desert. I remembered that back then I used to actually think it was fun catching hold of the things whenever I saw them. Now when I heard that noise and realized that it was a viper, I didn't even give a thought to catching it. I simply fired a few rounds into the bush, hoping to stun it. I knew that snakes didn't have eyelids, and from all of the dust and other debris flying around, I knew there was a pretty good chance that I had blinded the thing as well, if not killed it. Then I heard a low hiss and immediately grabbed my flashlight and turned the beam in the direction of the noise. I saw the snake and I could also see that I hadn't killed it, as I'd hoped. I took my rifle and just pushed it down into the bush and pinned the snake's head down. I reached down into the bush and pulled it out. It was a black viper, a very deadly snake. I cut its head off. I guess I hadn't changed that much from when I was a kid, because I carried the thing back to camp and hid it down in the bottom of the sleeping bag of a fellow named Alteea. He obviously wasn't a very good navigator and the fellow he was partnered with evidently wasn't either, because they didn't get back from their march for another few hours. In the meantime, I had told Yoel and a couple of the other guys what I had done and we were all dying to see what would happen when the two came back.

It was always customary to shake all your gear out whenever you came in at night just in case anything had crawled in to keep you company, namely scorpions and centipedes and anything else that could be detrimental to your health. Alteea finally got back and he was obviously not only tired, but also stupid, because he didn't shake any of his stuff out. He just rolled out his sleeping bag, took off his boots and socks and climbed inside. He must have immediately felt the cold, bloody snake as soon as his feet hit the bottom of the bag. Then all of a sudden we heard this screaming "Arrh . . . arrh, snake, snake, snake!!!" and the sleeping bag with shelter half raised up off the ground like a missile launcher. He came shooting out like a rocket, hopping around and hollering: "Snake, snake! It bit me! There's a snake in my sleeping bag!" at the top of his lungs. He carried on running around, and of course by this time we were all in hysterics. Thankfully nobody ever told him who put the thing in there in the first place.

On September 3, we had a full day of training, including live firing exercises and everything else that normally went with it. It was still very much like we were in basic training, only without *mizdar conenute*. We were getting more sleep. We had to get up at 6:30 a.m. and prepare for morning inspection. Then we'd have breakfast, go out into the field and train for the rest of the morning. We would come back in the afternoon, have a bit of a break and go back out to train again, then finish it all off with more live fire exercises. In the evening it would be the same thing all over again; the same type of exercises, a dry run and more live fire training. We went through all of that and then they told us to saddle up and get ready to go out on a forced march. Now what the hell was going on here? We thought that the forced marches of our basic training were all behind us.

Anyway, I was told to march carrying the MAG machine gun, and I also had to carry about 500 rounds of ammunition. Everybody was carrying a full load. We were told that the march was to be about 15 miles, and it was already pretty late at night. In fact it was most likely early morning before we actually set out. The *mempay* really pushed us hard that night as we trekked across the desert. It was quite cool, as the summer was starting to wane. We ending up at the base of Masada and I had been twisting my ankle over and over again throughout the march. I was really in a great deal of pain, yet even in that state, I could still appreciate the immense history of the place that we had reached. Masada had a great deal to do with the mysticism of the Hebrew warrior. As dawn was just breaking, they told us that we were going to climb up the old Roman road. This ramp up to Masada had been built by the Roman soldiers in A.D. 73, centuries ago, as part of their plan to defeat the rebels who held it. The rebels in Masada rolled boulders or boiling oil down on the soldiers as they were constructing it. This had been the last great stronghold of the Hebrew warriors. Up and up we went, and when we finally got to the top, the rabbis were there, waiting to greet us. They led us to the far eastern side, where we looked down at part of the Dead Sea and the outline of what we were told were the Roman army camps that surrounded Masada. They were still very definitely visible off in the distance, so many centuries later. Rabbis started to chant a prayer. As we listened to them, the sun came rising up over Jordan, and the sight was so incredible that it sent a shiver up my spine. To be witnessing such a beautiful, yet powerful sight in this place of such history – the spiritual feeling that I experienced was overwhelming. When the sun had fully risen, the rabbis stopped chanting and we all looked out at the awesome view. Now in the full light of day, we could clearly see the Dead Sea. The experience had been so powerful that if we'd been asked to jump off the cliff, just as those ancient Hebrew warriors had done at the end of their last battle, rather than be taken alive, we probably would have done it.

We were then given a bit of a tour of the rest of the place, and eventually we were taken back down to where they had buses waiting to carry us back to the base. Once we got back and settled in, we were allowed to go home for the weekend, which for me meant returning to the kibbutz. Generally, by the time we were given leave for the weekend, we'd all be physically and mentally done in and weren't able to do much more than go home and collapse.

On September 5, we had a week of what they called *nofes*, which loosely translated meant "rest and recuperation." That was after the Masada experience. We spent the week of R & R at a very nice camp which was right on the seaside, near Tel Aviv. The food that was served there was quite good, and we were actually given something other than hard-boiled eggs for breakfast. The accommodations were pretty good as well, with only four guys to a room. The block that we were in was right on the sea. I didn't get much out of the week myself, as I was most interested in going out and boozing it up. This of course somewhat defeated the purpose, as the whole week was supposed to be some sort of team building, company endeavor exercise. I spent quite a bit of my time out on the beach on my own, both during in the day and in the evening. I would get myself a six-pack of beer or maybe even two, and go and find some real secluded spot on the beach. I'd sit there and stare out at the ocean and drink my beer. My thoughts would always wander back to home and how my mom and dad were doing. Of course I'd get more and more sentimental with every beer that I guzzled down. I also used to think about all the times I'd ridden my motorcycle along the beaches back in California. Newport Beach, Huntington, and Balboa Beach all used to be my old stomping grounds. I had a whole string of favorite watering holes up and down that stretch of coast. I'd ride down there and hit every one of them. When it was time to head home, I'd climb on the back of the Harley and take off, half-pissed. Sitting there on that beach, I realized how far away it all seemed now and how different the world was that I was in now. I thought about the unique path that I had taken in life and the choices that I'd made so far. There was no conformity to what I was doing, and my lifestyle was far removed from the average, middle-class citizen in America.

We completed our week there, and then headed back to the desert to continue with our training. Only now we were all taking turns at being the *Zelda* commander, even if it was only for a couple of hours at a time. The *Zelda* commander would sit up above the rest of the troops in the armored vehicle, behind the 50 caliber machine gun. It was his job to give the commands to the rest of the troops as we were racing around in the vehicle.

One day, it was finally my turn to be the commander. My Hebrew was pretty good by this time and I was able to converse with just about anybody about just about anything. Some might think that it was about bloody time that I could, but I'm a slow learner at the best of times. Learning had never come easy for me and this was the first time that I had been faced with learning a new language. I was wearing the radio helmet that was mandatory for the commander of the vehicle. There were several other guys in the *Zelda* with me. One of them was Yoel, our normal vehicle commander. They all had a pretty good sense of humor and were having a great time heckling me every time I gave a command. It got to the point that every time I would say something, they would prod me in the back, mimicking what I was saying. At one stage they were so busy laughing and carrying on that they almost put the vehicle in a ditch. The driver started yelling at me that it was my fault. He said that he couldn't see where we were going and that it was my responsibility to give decent commands, which he obviously thought I was not doing. The situation was made even more comical when someone would fart and the driver, who was stuck up front in a confined area, got the worst of it. Keep in mind that our diet still had a lot of hard-boiled eggs and you can appreciate the situation more fully!

Our antics must have been noticed by the others, because it wasn't long before the *mempay* was on the radio, wanting to know what the heck was going on in our *Zelda*. Everyone knew that I would catch it if we didn't straighten out our act quickly. Not surprisingly, this made them even more intent on their clowning around. They kept prodding me in the back and carrying on, while I was trying my best to straighten everything out over the radio. Eventually we made it back to the base but we didn't hear the end of it for quite a while.

One evening, we were out on another live fire exercise and I ended up falling twice because of my weak left ankle. My ankle had been giving me pain for months, and unfortunately it really didn't seem to be getting better, only worse. There really wasn't any strength left in it at all. I had no other choice but go and ask Platoon Lieutenant Eitzcovitch if I could step down as the MAG gunner. He agreed, but who should he pass the job on to but Alteeas, the "snake man." After that, I became a plain old rifleman, which seemed extremely easy after battling with the MAG gun for over a year and half. At least now when I fell, and I still did that quite frequently, it didn't hurt anywhere near as much when I was carrying only 30 lb of ammunition and a rifle as opposed to the 70 to 80 lb I used to have to carry.

One *Shabbat*, we went out to guard a kibbutz, instead of going home. David Ben-Gurion, one of Israel's most important figures, and his wife were buried right at the edge of this particular kibbutz. The location was stunningly beautiful. I've always had a great affection for the desert and the peace and solitude that I found there. I spent some time sitting beside the graves of those two people and as I watched the sun go down a very strong spiritual feeling flooded over me. I watched as the sun's last rays moved across the valley down below me. I remember that I said a prayer of thanks for being in such a beautiful pace and also for the well-being of my family, so far away.

On September 22, I had just returned from visiting the doctor, who wanted to take a look at my ankle. When I got back I was told that one of the guys in our basic training platoon, Heaflock, had been killed when there had been an accidental discharge. He was one of the fellows that I used to carry on my shoulders in the fireman's carry during our basic training. We had shared 14 months of pure pain, misery and hardship together. Apparently they had been out at Sanour, the basic training camp, when the accidental discharge occurred. He had been shot, and the bullet had hit the main artery that runs down along the spine. He had died before they could get him any proper medical attention. It was quite a shock. I had never known anybody personally in the military who had been killed as the result of an accident. Perhaps I had just been lucky that I'd never experienced anything like it before. The incident made a really big impact on me.

Often, when I was back visiting the kibbutz, I would take the volunteers out to a valley that was about three or four miles away. I'd let them shoot my M16 whenever I happened to have some extra ammunition with me. I did this because so many of them were anti-military, anti-war and anti-firearms, even though they'd never had any military experience at all. I'd set them up with the M16 and watch their eyes closely as they began to shoot. I could see a change come over them almost immediately, as they realized the enormous power they had when they held that weapon in their arms. Afterwards, they wouldn't be able to stop talking about what a wild experience it was, and how much they enjoyed it – so much for peace and love! That rhetoric went out of the window as soon they started shooting and the adrenaline began pumping through their veins. Some of them had never fired a weapon before in their entire lives, and they would walk away from the experience with a different attitude to firearms. On our way out of the valley, we would always stop off at the tent of one of my Bedouin friends, named Eli. He would always have some arrack and apples waiting for us. Everyone would take a shot of the arrack, and the strength of the stuff always shocked us. I don't know what proof of alcohol it was, but it was downright strong – it would knock your block off, if you weren't careful. After throwing back a shot of the stuff, we would immediately eat a slice of apple, which helped to cut the strong licorice taste of the alcohol. The volunteers thought the whole experience was great because they got to meet a "real" Bedouin Arab – and of course they also got to stumble back to kibbutz in an alcohol-induced haze. It was a bit of a break for them from the regular *Shabbat* routine, which usually entailed just sitting around drinking, or spending some quiet time talking or reading. In my case the choice was obvious. I'd be sitting around drinking. I would always have a case of beer and a bottle of vodka stashed away, and it wouldn't take me long to get stuck into it. It was party time and I usually had a good time just goofing off. Unfortunately, more often than not I also made quite an ass of myself.

Once we had all just returned to camp when we were told about a mission we'd be going on. It involved a mock break-in into some prison and busting someone out. The prison in question – if my memory serves me correctly – was a maximum-security facility, used to house convicted Arab terrorists in Ramallah. We were briefed on how we were to gain entry to the facility. Yoel and I formed a two-man team. We managed to sneak up on the prison that night, and got into the guard tower. We actually managed to get into the prison itself, and at that point we were to consider our mission was accomplished.

The individuals in charge of the prison gave us a tour of the place and it truly was grim, almost like something out of *Night of the Living Dead*. They were housing a lot of mean, nasty-looking characters. I don't even know why they even bothered to keep these guys alive. Most of them had been tried and convicted of planting bombs that had killed innocent people. These men would be incarcerated in the facility for the remainder of their lives, and I dare say they deserved to be there.

Getting back to the kibbutz again brings to mind a memory of a young woman I met one weekend. She was named Patty, a rather buxom redhead, with pale freckled skin. I was carrying on in my normal fashion, slowly getting tanked but having a good old time in the process. Patty was matching me step by step, all the way. I remember suggesting that we go up and look at the stars from the top of the water tower. She looked at me as though I was nuts, and I told her I would take up a mattress to lie down on so that it would be more comfortable for stargazing. I couldn't believe that she went along with my idea. Soon I was giving her a lift up on my shoulders so she could reach the first rung, which was six feet above the ground. She climbed up the tower with me clambering up behind her, with the mattress on my back. She was waiting for me when I reached the top, and it wasn't long before one thing led to another and we were making passionate love to one another and having a great good old time. Of course in this case, it was up on top of the water tower but nonetheless, we were still ready, willing and able. So that's how that rather enjoyable evening was spent, indulging in flagrant delight under the stars, 100 feet above ground.

At about this time, I started carrying the MAG again. It wasn't that I really wanted to carry the thing, but it still interested me as a weapon. Alteeas wasn't doing very well as the MAG gunner and none of the other guys seemed to have any interest in it, so it just naturally fell on my shoulders again (no pun intended). I just resigned myself to the inevitable pain in my ankle that I would undoubtedly experience from then on.

One day I was picked to do a live fire exercise, along with my number two gunner, Naomany. We were to do the exercises in front of a group of civilians, in this particular case people from the United Jewish Appeal, who were over visiting from the US. My number two gunner and I did dry runs all morning. It was his job to carry my extra ammunition, about 700 rounds over and above my 600. The afternoon finally came, and it was time to do our live fire exercise. The MAG that I had been issued for the exercise wouldn't work properly, and I had to keep cocking it. After a few rounds it would jam and I would have to cock it yet again. I thought my arm was going to fall off from working it so hard. I managed to get another MAG machine gun to use, but when I tried to fire it, it also wasn't right. There was no turning back by that point. We were committed, and there was no time to try another gun.

The time finally came for the live exercise to start, and we were picked up by helicopter. When we arrived at the specified area we were lowered down, and we all jumped out on to the ground. It reminded me of the mighty Israeli paratroopers on a roll as we came flying in with the big CH-53. There was dust and debris flying around everywhere as the helicopter hovered above the ground, and all of sudden it just belched out all of these paratroopers. We hit the ground running and quickly got into formation, laying down a base of fire with the machine gun. All of a sudden, the MAG went bad – and I mean bad! It just started to run away. In other words, when I pulled the trigger to fire it, it just started shooting and it wouldn't stop. It was like it had a life of its own. The only way I could get it to stop was to twist the belt, and then I would have to cock it again.

We managed to get through it somehow and then it was time to move on to the next exercise. We started moving up a hill, shooting as we went up. All of a sudden, the buckle on my belt came loose and my pants came down and tripped me. Naomany kept trying to help me get up while I was trying to pull my pants up. As this was happening, I could here a voice over a loudspeaker saying, "Where is the fire from the machine gun? Where is the machine gun?" Little did the voice know that the machine gunner was trying to get his pants up! I finally got them secured again and off we went to try it again. The exercise had been in progress for about half an hour when I ripped the whole backside out of my pants and my underwear was pretty much ripped to shreds as well. Anyway, we had the entire United Jewish Appeal entourage there watching the whole thing. To make matters worse, my indignity was captured in all its glory on film. I kept going up the hill though, with the MAG running away with itself the whole time. Imagine what it was like – constant bursts of 40 or 50 shots that only stopped whenever I could mange to twist the belt. I was just lucky that I had enough ammunition to last throughout the exercise. It must have appeared that I was shooting a moon as I went up the hill bent over and with my ass hanging out of my pants!

Throughout the exercise Naomany was a great help to me. The Yemenite fellow and I had got on like a house on fire ever since we met. He was the only Israeli I knew who drank beer. When we had leave, we would go off to one of the nearby towns and the two of us would get stuck in good. We had a lot in common, and I really enjoyed his company. He had been my number two man in basic training as well, so we worked well together. He was quite a character.

After the exercise was finished, the United Jewish Appeal people got back on their buses and off they went. We had a speech given to us by an Israeli general. I don't know where they found the guy, but I tell you I would have been really worried if he was actually in charge of an operation. He was talking such a lot of bullshit that the guys were actually snickering under their breath and whenever they could manage it, one would fart as loud as he could. At once many people joined in with the farting: it was as if an orchestra was in session. I know that these guys were farting loud enough for the general to have been able to hear it from where he was standing. He must have been an actor in his former life though, because the look on his face never changed once. He never even batted an eyelid. This was yet more evidence of the unique Israeli sense of humor.

Back at the kibbutz, I would do a lot of drinking. I started when I arrived there for *Shabbat* and I wouldn't stop until the night before I left. After these binges, I would go back to camp very hung over. For some reason, at that time there was quite a lengthy period when I fell into a deep depression that I just couldn't seem to shake, no matter what I did. I have no doubt, though, that the booze had a great deal to do with it.

One time, we were hitchhiking back from the desert. It was getting very late. Yoel told me I should come with him to his house and spend the night with him and his family. His mom and dad didn't mind that we turned up late, and right away set about making us a big dinner. The whole family sat around and talked in Hebrew. It reminded me of my home, only Yoel's family didn't seem to argue as near as much as we had done. I got a very warm feeling inside being around those people. They were very friendly to me and I went on to have a close friendship with them for the next several years.

Our next move was to go up to the Golan Heights once again, to take up positions in the *motsav*, the hilltop trenches. We made the move up there one afternoon in late October, 1976. This was to be much easier on us than the time we had gone up there during our basic training, months before. We still had to stand guard for three hours a night, and we still went out for training. I remember that it snowed while we were up there, and it was bitterly cold. It was rough going, to say the least. Our day would start early in the morning with a seven-mile foot patrol along the fenced perimeter. We were looking for evidence of terrorists having climbed over the barbed wire and making it into Israel. Then we would go out for some kind of training exercise before breakfast, come back to eat, and then head out again to train for the next few hours. We would head back again for a midday meal and then back out for more training. The day would wind down in the late afternoon and we would spend some time cleaning our weapons. If there was to be a night patrol, we would prepare for it: if not, we would just take our turn at standing guard. There was no punishment being doled out us any more. Those days, thankfully, had fallen by the wayside when we finished our basic training. That doesn't mean that we weren't subject to frequent verbal ass-chewing, though. But all in all, we had graduated from our former lowly status of shitbirds. We were now soldiers of the Israeli Parachute Brigade.

There were many times that I froze my ass off doing guard duty in a trench looking out over the Golan Heights into Syria. I think the most memorable part of that time was the mornings. I used to watch the sun rise over Syria, and it was a truly beautiful sight. I used to be able to see Tel Hara, the "hill of shit." That was where the Syrian Central Command was located, hence the name. At sunrise everybody would be in the trenches, ready for the morning patrol, and then we would move into the daily training routine.

In November, arrangements were made for me to go on what was called a "Hebrew" course. Supposedly, the six-week-long course would help me to appreciate Hebrew more fully, and I would be able to read and write the language at a higher level. I guess I was able to brush up on my Hebrew a little bit, and maybe there was some slight improvement, but I don't think they were as successful as they had hoped. There was a South American fellow taking the same course that I was and when we arrived, we discovered that the accommodations were certainly not as beautiful as the language we were supposed to be studying. The room we were staying in was pretty basic – there weren't even any blankets on the beds. We managed to scrounge one between us, and ended up sharing it our first night there.

The course we were taking was held in the city of Jaffa, just outside the large metropolis of Tel Aviv. While I was there, I decided to get my mom a nice gift. I hadn't sent her anything since I had bought her the samovar and I figured it was about time. The only way I could make some extra money was to do some security work at night. Through the grapevine I found a job doing guard work for a butane storage plant just outside Tel Aviv. School would finish around 4:00 p.m. I would get something to eat and then catch a bus downtown. Someone would pick me up at the bus station and give me a ride out to the storage plant. My first night there, they gave me this old horse to ride around the property. It was obvious right from the start that this horse hated me just about as much as I came to hate him. To make the situation even worse, it was near the end of November, so it was raining and cold and just generally miserable. So here I was facing a ten-hour shift of riding that horse back and forth in the cold rain and he didn't want to cooperate. I couldn't get him to go when I wanted, and then when he finally got moving – when he wanted to – I couldn't get him to stop. It reminded me of what my old drill instructors in the marines would shout at us whenever our marching was getting screwed up: "Hippity ho, mob go. Hippity hop, mob stop." Later on, I started saying that to the horse, only I would change the words to: "Hippity ho, horse go. Hippity hop, horse stop." Oddly enough, he seemed to respond to this. I was to spend many a night on the back of old Trigger, the rest of the time I was up in the watchtowers surrounding the plant, keeping an eye on things from a high vantage point.

I can't even try to convey how tired I was. I would spend the whole day in school trying to learn something, and then go directly to work. Then I would do my 10-hour shift there, get a ride back to the bus station, catch a bus and make it back in time to eat breakfast and grab an hour's sleep. I felt like I was done in all the time.

There were numerous Russian students taking the same course. They were recent immigrants from the Georgia area of Russia, and generally they acted like pigs most of the time. They used to just laugh and carry on the whole time, with absolutely no regard for the female soldiers who were trying to teach us

Hebrew. In all my experience with teachers, I have never seen any who were as patient and persistent as these two women were. The fact that they were both real lookers as well certainly didn't hurt. They were both so incredibly calm in the way they dealt with all the shenanigans that were going on around them. I was trying in my own way to learn something, but the Russian idiots were making it almost impossible, with all their hollering and throwing things around. At least they managed to keep me awake most of the time.

Our school day started about 8:00 a.m. and went through right until 4:00 p.m., and it was a real challenge for me to stay awake the whole time. After the classes were over for the day, I'd just about have enough time to grab a shower, and then it would be time to leave for the butane plant. I dreaded my nights almost as much as my days. At least during the day I knew what was going to happen, but at night I knew I'd be dealing with the horse from hell. His mood would determine how the night would go. He would look at me as I was coming towards him as if he was thinking to himself, "Oh no, there's that son of a bitch again!" I stuck out my nightly ritual for about a month and then I finally had enough money to buy my mom her present. I took a while to find the right gift, but I finally settled on a beautiful Star of David diamond pendant. I'm pleased to say that she still has it today. It was really gratifying being able to give her something nice, especially considering all of the worry I'd put her through. I remember haggling with a guy in Jaffa over a two-day period to get him down finally to a decent price. The fellow owned a shop that looked like it must have been 1,000 years old. I think he finally relented and gave in to my incessant badgering because he knew I would not go away until he did. As he wrapped it up he told me to give it to my mom with his compliments.

After I'd earned enough for the gift I happily quit my night job, but I still had two weeks of the course left. I had a little bit of spare time, and I decided to go and visit Anat, our old *pikeyda* (girl soldier). During our basic training, she had been the equivalent of a military Girl Friday for our unit. I remember her telling us that she had lost a brother in the 1973 War. She had invited me to her home on previous occasions, and I had always been warmly received by her family. They would always put out a really nice spread for us, and her father was not averse to having a drink either, so I always got a glass of Scotch as well. I visited them a couple of times over that six-week period, and I always ended up walking back quite drunk. I would take the scenic route back to the barracks and would wander down along the ocean. I always managed to find my way back, despite my intoxicated state. At least now I was getting a little more sleep at night!

With only two weeks of the course left, the decision was made to throw the Russians out. I guess the teachers had finally reached the end of their rope with them. If it had been my decision, they would have been sent back to their units long before. I guess it's not surprising that I did most of my learning during that final two weeks.

I remember spending that New Year's Eve in the barracks. I was feeling pretty homesick, and decided to give the folks at home a call. It was only the second call I had made to them in the two years that I had been away. I guess it was probably the time of year, but I was feeling rather depressed and couldn't shake it off. Perhaps I felt I was wasting time, or that I wasn't getting out of the army experience what I thought I would? I wouldn't be at all surprised if the booze didn't have a lot to do with it as well. I know that whenever I had the opportunity to drink myself stupid I'd end up partying like crazy, usually whenever I was back at the kibbutz. For the next few days, I would feel terribly miserable and would have a really hard time shaking it off. I still managed to get through the day's activities all right, doing all of the training exercises, but by evening I'd still feel I had this dark cloud hovering over me.

On January 2, I packed up my bags and headed back to my company in the Golan Heights. My Hebrew had NOT improved, probably because of my constant fatigue and all the problems with the Russian students. Anyway, I was just glad to be back, serving with my regular unit. I reported back to the company headquarters and I was sent out to the *motsav* where my platoon was stationed. I was back on guard duty for three hours every night and was doing about the same amount during the day as well. At that time of year, there was plenty of snow on the ground. So our training continued, only now we were freezing our asses off while we did it.

I'd like to provide a bit of a description of the area that we were operating in. For the most part, it was very bleak. It was so desolate and rocky, it was almost like being on another planet. No one in his right mind would ever claim that the Golan Heights was a hospitable place to be, but it did have a strange – almost bizarre – beauty of its own. It was very flat and open across the valley and there were no trees to be seen anywhere, just short, scrubby bushes full of thorns. This was probably why it had seen some of the greatest tank battles of all time. All over the area there are deep trenches that are up to 10 feet wide and 20 feet deep. These ditches are commonly known as "tank traps." We had even spotted some tank traps that were bordered by huge mounds of dirt. These ramps were designed so that a tank could come up behind the mound and get its barrel over the top, pointed down at the tanks in the trap. Any tank caught in the trap wouldn't stand a chance, because the crew couldn't see who was shooting at it, let alone try and shoot back. Then there were also the minefields that littered the entire area, and were especially concentrated where the cut-line was between Syria and Israel. A fence separated the two nations and went the length of the border. The fence had built-in sensors to warn if anyone tried to get in by climbing over from the Syrian side. Now that the area was totally covered with snow it was a brilliant white, with only the odd scraggy rock showing through here and there. We also had to contend with a bitterly cold wind that blew incessantly through the valley. At times, we even wore ski-suits because the conditions were so severe.

Even the harshest weather would find us out training, running across the snow-covered fields. We would go on for hours, until we were all literally soaked with sweat, despite the bitter cold. We would make our way back to the camp in the afternoon, when the next section would go out for their training exercises and we would stand guard. Luckily the number of nighttime training exercises had been cut way down, but we still had the occasional one to go out on. Every night we would all have to take our turn standing guard for the three-hour period. There were positions throughout the *motsav* that had to be manned, so there was more than enough work to keep us all busy. The cold at night was so fierce that we had to wear mufflers around our heads to protect our ears. As a result, we couldn't hear anything. Our positions were surrounded by minefields, so we had to keep a lookout for saboteurs putting down bangalore torpedos so that they could clear the mines. We also had to watch out for enemy troops who might be reconnoitering our positions.

The time on guard duty always dragged by miserably, and I would find my mind wandering back in time to other places. I'd think about my childhood, and then the time that I had spent in Vietnam. If you weren't the type of person who could turn your thoughts inward, you would find those three hours interminably long and lonely. Doing guard duty every night, week in, week out, nearly drove some of the guys nuts. If you were caught breaking guard by the *mem-mem* or *samal*, you would be in a lot of trouble. Falling asleep was not an uncommon occurrence, but it wasn't happening as often, now that they were allowing us to get more sleep at night, than when we were in basic training. The other hazard was falling asleep and dying from hypothermia.

I can clearly remember the first *Shabbat* meal I had when I returned from taking the Hebrew course. The other guys would always sing nice Hebrew songs around the dinner table. Now I stress the word nice, which of course translates as "clean" songs. They would always be after me to contribute a musical offering of my own, and of course being American I guess they thought they'd get something culturally reflective of life in the USA. My offerings usually amounted to dirty limericks and poems, sung very off-key. My renditions of risqué songs such as "Airborne Daddy" usually went over like a lead balloon, especially as it was in honor of the Sabbath meal. Music was not my forte.

Later in January, we were told to get our gear together and get on a truck. We were going to Hermoneat, which was the company headquarters for the *rabotim*. We were going there to get a briefing before we headed into Syria. I quickly got all my stuff together and made sure that my machine gun and ammunition were all ready for action. It was freezing bloody cold when we all clambered on to the truck and settled in for the 15-kilometer (nine mile) ride. When we arrived, we were briefed on an incursion that would take us about one kilometer (three-fifths of a mile) inside the Syrian border. We were to make our way to a specific tank trap, hide and wait until some shepherds turned up. Every morning, they would come close to the fence and have a look around. The idea was that we were supposed to capture these guys. The temperature was well below zero and the wind was just howling, which of course made it even colder. That first morning we got ready, and after inspection, the battalion commander grabbed for my dog tag and it wasn't there. I got a serious ass-chewing for that one. I was really embarrassed by it, but more than that, my pride was hurt because I always tried to keep myself squared away when it came to stuff like that.

Around 3:00 a.m. the next morning, we got geared up and moved out of the position we had taken the night before. I couldn't really say where we were, as it looked like just another hilltop to me. In the freezing wind we moved down towards the fence and went through. The area that we went through had already been tarred, so we knew that we didn't have to worry about mines. We made our way over to a tank ramp and hid behind it in the snow. I hadn't had any feeling in my hands and feet for a couple of hours, because it was so cold. We sat there waiting for hours. With the cold beyond belief, we just continued sitting there. As far as I was concerned the timing was just way off. How could they expect us to do anything right when we couldn't even feel our hands? Dawn finally came and with it came an even more intense cold. By now, we were all stamping our feet and rubbing our hands together to try and get some circulation in them again. We were making a lot of noise in the process, as well. The long and short of it was that we must have been making a little too much noise, because when the shepherds finally turned up they had dogs with them, and they immediately started barking. All of a sudden, we had this Fido running around our position, which of course alerted them to our whereabouts. They were too far away for us to go and nab them, so they just herded their little flock and walked back away from us, in the opposite direction – to Syria. Why were we so interested in what some shepherds were doing? What they were doing was setting up a routine by coming to that particular area every day, so we could safely assume that they were actually reconnoitering it. Ultimately, at some point in the future, they would have been able to slip some terrorists through. Terrorists usually made their way into Israel to plant bombs, commit murder or whatever other terrorist activity they happened to be doing at the time.

As our position had now been compromised, we marched back through the snow and through the gap in the fence, into Israel. We waited for a truck to come and pick us up and then we returned to the Headquarters for debriefing. Of course we received a royal ass-chewing when we got there for making so much noise and making general idiots of ourselves. Our actions had compromised the whole mission without a doubt, but in all fairness it had been bloody cold and what else could we have done? We just hadn't been well prepared. If we were, we would have been wearing snow boots and heavy jackets instead of the clothes that were supposed to enable us to move fast and capture these guys. All in all, it was our own fault and I guess there was no way around that.

January 17, 1977, was a day that I remembered quite well, though it started out normal enough. We got up at 5:00 a.m. as usual. Dawn was starting to make itself visible. As the sun began to rise, there was just enough light to make out the silhouettes of the burned-out villages miles away inside the Syrian border. As usual, the fellows standing guard had to keep a very close look-out for any enemy movement. They could really only relax a little when the full light of day had arrived and everything was clearly visible. At that time we set out on a foot patrol to cover the seven miles of fencing that was our responsibility. The foot patrol was fairly easy as we were walking on a tarred road. When we got to the end of our stretch of fencing we would hop into a half-track and drive back to the *motsav*. We would usually have a *gahosh*, usually an Arab: Bedouin, Christian or Druse. The Bedouins were by far the better trackers, probably because of their nomadic heritage. I have met trackers on two continents but I would bet the Bedouins could give them all a run for their money. Generally the tracker would be on the lookout for any signs of terrorists making their way into Israel.

9

Returning Home

On that particular day, I had been told to return to the camp and get my machine gun and ammunition ready. There was a truck waiting, and we were soon on our way once again to the battalion headquarters at Hermoneat. When we arrived, we were given a very sketchy briefing about something that was going to happen. We knew that it involved some kind of incursion into Syria, but where we were going exactly, or what we were supposed to do when we got there, was a mystery. We were told that it could possibly take place that night, and to be ready to go. We waited around most of the day and into the evening and then had a gear inspection, which of course someone or other failed. So we ended up doing it all over again. Finally an order came to stand down and we were told to get into a truck that took us back to our *motsav*.

After we got back it was only a couple of hours until it was time for our 5:00 a.m. start to the day. It was a very bleak, cold morning as we got ready to head out on our 11-kilometer (seven-mile) fence patrol. We discovered that some asshole had put kerosene in the diesel tank of the half-track. So before we could patrol, we had to drain out the half-track fuel tank and clean the system out. It was a great start, and everyone was in a foul mood by the time we actually began the patrol. Needless to say, the Platoon Lieutenant, Yetzcovicz, was pissed off. Everybody else was pissed off too, and it wasn't long before the incessant arguing started.

When we got back, I was told once again to get my machine gun and ammunition ready, and once again we made the journey to the battalion headquarters. We had yet another briefing and then, instead of letting us just hang about like the day before, they had us do training exercises. We were running around most of the day and finally let up just as it was getting dark, about 5:00 p.m. The whole time I had been lugging around about 400 rounds of extra ammunition, which weighed about 34 lb, as well as the gun. I was also carrying some grenades and water bottles as well. The fact that we were training in snow halfway up to our knees had not made the exercises any easier. It wasn't surprising when once again I tripped and sprained my ankle. After that, I kept twisting it and it was extremely painful. One of the times when I had wrenched it I fell down, and ended up cutting open my knee. As far as I was concerned, the day had just been getting worse and worse. As we stopped the training, I started to get worried. The last thing I wanted was for us to head into Syria and have to make an emergency run out. How was I going to keep up with my ankle and knee in their current condition? By the time it was midnight, they finally told us to pack up our gear once again and to head back to our camp. We were not going to go out again! After all of the training we had done that day and the tension of knowing that we might be going into Syria, it was a big letdown to all of us. We were psyched up and again nothing came of it. Of course there was nothing to be done but to head back and try and get a couple of hours sleep before it was time for patrol. Later that morning, we were told that operation had been completely called off. It was a great disappointment to everybody.

On January 20, 1977, we were told that mission was back on once again. By now, when anyone referred to the operation, our joint reaction was "Bullshit!" You couldn't say that our motivation level was exactly what it should have been. We set off for the battalion headquarters, not really believing that anything would happen. We had another briefing and another inspection, and then were told once again that the operation was off. "Surprise, surprise!" was all we could say. We got back in the trucks and headed back to our *motsav*. We did our fence patrol that afternoon and then headed back to get our evening meal. Apart from guard duty, we were able to catch a decent night's sleep.

The next morning, we did our patrol as usual after our stand-to in the trenches, and then were told again that the operation was back on. By now, everybody was hollering at one another in the typical Israeli fashion. No one believed a word of it, but of course we had no say in the matter. We just had to get ready and hustle ourselves on to the truck. We arrived at the headquarters and went in to receive our usual briefing, only this time it was more thorough. We found out that we were indeed going into Syria, and we were going to either kidnap or shoot someone who had apparently been involved in some spying activity. Don't ask me how we knew that the guy had been spying on us, but I know they had a lot of sophisticated and sensitive equipment up on the Golan Heights, so I guess they had their ways of finding this type of stuff out. The briefing finished up late in the afternoon and soon after, we loaded into a truck and went down to the base of Mount Hermon. We got off the truck with all of our gear. I had the machine gun and all the extra ammunition. I was not looking forward to carrying all of my gear, which weighed in excess of 65 lb, up the side of Mount Hermon. It was quite dark by the time we actually got started and made our way to the base of the mountain. To get there, we had to cross a stream which was frozen over. That entailed breaking the ice and wading through, up to our hips in freezing cold water. It was about 15 meters (50 feet) across the stream, and by the time we reached the other side we were not only drenched but frozen as well. We began our climb with water coming out of our boots and our wet clothes clinging to our legs. The clothes that we were wearing were designed for easy movement. It was the standard military issue of a field uniform, with a sweater, a thin pair of gloves and regular leather boots. We hadn't been given any heavy jackets to wear.

As we began our ascent I looked up, but could not see the top, as the clouds were covering it. Mount Hermon's size was staggering – it is 9,232 feet high. We were walking up a winding road that just went up and up. Snow was falling as we walked, and soon it was up to knee level. I just kept putting one foot in front of the other, praying that I wouldn't twist my ankle and trip. It got to the point where it was even difficult to see the fellow in front of me, and he was only six feet away. My prayers didn't help too much because I did twist my ankle a couple of times on the way up and fell down as well. I was really starting to get worried as to whether I was physically up to making the rest of the climb. We just kept going up and up and my heart felt like it was going to explode on more than one occasion. I was soaked with perspiration – so much so that I felt like I had been running all day long on the hottest day of the summer.

If I were asked what my thoughts were as we made our way up, I'd say that in addition to worrying about my physical condition, I was worried about failing my comrades, my fellow soldiers, by not being able to carry out my duties to the best of my ability. By that point, my knee was giving me terrible pain and it was made worse by the fact that it was swollen from the training exercise a couple of days before. We did stop for a few moments while the *mempay* was figuring out our position in relation to a nearby minefield, but it would have been better not to, because all of the perspiration just turned to ice. We had ice in our hair, on our faces and our wet clothes froze on our bodies. The worse part was that our short break just made all the harder to get going once again. At least the exertion of our movement helped keep us warm.

We were coming up to the minefield and the plan was to skirt around the outside of it. We started moving level along the mountain as we approached the field and could see the markers. The *mempay* skirted the field as we watched him. It was an Israeli minefield but that didn't make it any easier. He knew that if he slipped up, he would be walking us right into the mines. He was wearing night-vision goggles and without them, he would never have made it, because the snowfall was so dense. The rest of us were literally walking blind. We had to keep the formation really close so we could keep sight of the guy in front of us. It took us about 45 minutes to get around the field and then we came to a stop as we prepared to make our descent into Syria. Almost immediately, the ice began to form on us again. Most of us were starting to get cramps in our legs, and we kept shuffling around in the snow hoping to get rid of them. I hadn't had any feeling in my own legs from the knees down for the last couple of hours. That was really frightening because I had no idea where I was stepping and if my ankle was going to go over again.

The descent into Syria was to be a nightmare of a different nature. There was no road or pathway to follow, as we had had when we went up the other side. We were now walking on ledges that we could walk on for about 50 meters (55 yards). Then we would have to drop down to the next one, which was about a meter (three and a quarter feet) below. To jump down would have been dangerous because of the shape my ankle was in. I was concerned about making it worse, or even breaking my leg because all of the extra weight that I was carrying. When I reached the edge of a ledge, I would get down on my backside and slide down to the level below. I lost track of how many times I had to do it, but I know it was a lot. The reason there were so many ledges was that we were in area where the farmers were strip farming, though obviously they were inactive at that time. We continued to go down for what seemed an eternity, all the while having rocks falling around us when we dislodged them. I wasn't the only one that was falling down either. Everyone was in the same predicament: not being able to see where their feet were landing. Although I had twisted my ankle about four times by then, the pain wasn't really a problem because of the intense cold. I couldn't feel anything any more. I can honestly say that I think that night was the coldest that I had experienced since I had come to Israel. Finally we got down to the bottom of the mountain – by then we were in Syria – and had to face going through the same frozen stream. After we made our way across that, we headed off in the direction of the village. The *mempay* told us to stop when we were about 15 meters (fifty feet) away. He set us up in the positions that he wanted, and pointed out the stone house that was our target. He then told us our arc of fire and said to shoot if we heard any sound, or saw tracers or muzzle flashes. He went on to the house without us while the rest of us held our positions. It was nerve-wracking to say the least, not knowing what was going on. We were all lying down in the snow and our clothes, which were soaking wet from sweating so much, froze on our bodies. We knew that his submachine gun was silenced, so we were straining to hear anything we could. We never did hear anything at all, and we never did find out if he found the person he was after. It was probably just as well that we didn't have to start shooting, because we couldn't see anything and we would have been relying solely on where we thought the noise was coming from. In a situation like that, it is very easy to take out your own people.

After about 15 minutes, the *mempay* made his way back to where we were waiting, and told us to gather around. It was incredibly hard to get moving again after we'd been lying on the snow-covered ground. He told us to get back into marching formation and we started back towards the mountain. We were covering exactly the same route that we had come down on, only now we had to walk along the ledges and drag ourselves up to the one above. It was even more tiring than the trip down. There was even more snow on the ground now and it made marching along the ledges treacherous. The people at the end of the formation couldn't see the *mempay* up at the front because of all the snow that was still coming down.

We continued our laborious climb back up towards the top of Mount Hermon, our progress being slowed down by the never-ending series of ledges. It seemed to go on for hour after bloody hour. My knee was killing me by now and I still didn't have any feeling in my frozen hands or lower legs and feet. It was at least a couple of hours before Moti the *mempay* halted us. He had seen the markers for the minefield and took the next few minutes to make sure of our position in relation to the field. He started skirting the outside of the perimeter and we followed closely behind him in formation. It took us about 45 minutes to clear the minefield, and then we continued with our descent back down into the Israeli-occupied Golan Heights. Once again, we all started stumbling and falling over ourselves because we couldn't see where we were putting our feet. Of course, I was stumbling more often than anyone else but I always managed to protect the machine gun trigger guard so that I didn't have an accidental discharge. Obviously that could have resulted in wounding or killing a fellow soldier, but in addition would have compromised our position. The machine gun was cocked, and had an open bolt, which was quite dangerous. By now, my whole left side was in absolute agony as a result of the pain from both my knee and ankle.

About 2:30 a.m. we reached the bottom of the mountain and broke through the ice of the stream one final time. We waded across to where the truck was waiting for us on the other side. I don't think I had ever seen such a welcome sight as that truck. At that point, I realized it was over and that I had made it. We had all made it. I remember throwing my gear up into the truck and then clambering in after it. Although we were in a truck, we were all freezing and our teeth were chattering from the cold. We all bunched together as close as we could, trying to find some warmth – we were soaking wet again from our perspiration and our most recent wade through the stream. It only made the ride back to the headquarters *motzav* all the more intolerable. When we got back, there was some steaming hot coffee waiting for us, as well as the proverbial hard-boiled egg and bread, but boy, did it ever taste good! We all gulped down gallons of the scalding brew and smoked a few cigarettes, and only then did we start to feel warm again. The *magod* and the *mempay* came in to do the debriefing and told us that the mission had been accomplished, congratulating all of us. No word was ever said, though, as to whether or not Moti, the *mempay*, had shot anyone.

All the guys started patting each other on the back and congratulating one another. I just sat back in the anticlimax and thanked the Lord for giving me the strength to climb that mountain twice in one night. It had been 10 of the most grueling hours, and thankfully it was finally over.

The next day, we were back in the *motsav* and things were back to normal. We did our normal stand-to and fence patrol. Yoel, Amsolan and myself were sent to an abandoned *motsav*. Obviously we were supposed to make it look like the *motsav* was occupied, just in case anyone was looking. We were given a good pair of binoculars to check out the surrounding areas that weren't visible from our usual *motsav*. We were supposed to look out for troop movement, or anything else that was interesting. When I wasn't on watch duty, I sat back with a book and read. I looked up and saw a little bird hopping around in the snow in front of me. Behind it I could see the wide, open valley. It was so peaceful at that moment, it seemed such a contradiction that the Golan Heights had seen so much war and catastrophe and yet at a moment like this, it was completely tranquil.

I'd like to say a little bit about our *mempay*, the company commander at this time. He was the one who had been on the Entebbe raid. He really was a great man. You could definitely describe him as a leader's leader and a soldier's soldier. Physically, he was man of slight build, with thinning dark hair, and very delicate facial features. He was very mildly spoken. His manner and his actions all clearly spoke of his sense of duty and conviction to his ideals and to Israel herself. He was a man that I was very proud to serve under.

It wasn't long after all this that I received orders to go on an explosives course. Naomany was to join me on the course. Like me, he enjoyed a good joke and one of our favorite pranks was to sneak up behind some poor unsuspecting fellow, reach between his legs, grab his balls and squeeze them. At the same time we would shout, "Your mother is a whore. Repeat after me, your mother is a whore." Inevitably the guy would scream out: "My mother is a whore!" and then we'd shout: "You're the son of a whore," and the guy would scream out loud once again, saying, "Yes, I'm the son of a whore." Then we would let go and laugh ourselves stupid. It was quite common on the base to hear guys screaming out obscenities about their entire family trees. It really was funny, but I guess you had to be there to appreciate it. Now, I have to admit that this prank was certainly not original. Everyone used to do it and expected to get it done back to them in turn. It certainly was not indicative of anyone's sexual tendencies, it was just something that we all did for fun. Naomany was also a great one for farting after eating hard-boiled eggs. This too, was a habit that the whole company indulged in frequently.

I never did really cotton on very well to the explosives course we were sent on. I tended to be an absent-minded person and you really can't have that characteristic when you work with explosives. Naomany, on the other hand, did very well on the course. On any of the exercises we had, he'd end up carrying the bangalore torpedo, which looked like a rocket, on his back. This held a long rope with about 50 grenades tied along it. This was why I nicknamed him "rocket man," just like the Elton John song of the same name. He'd put it down on the ground when he was ready to fire and shoot it over an area where there was a suspected minefield. The rope would come flying out and spread out over the minefield. About four seconds later, the grenades would detonate, clearing a path through the field.

The course continued, and it became apparent that discipline was quite a problem. We would go out on a lot of dry runs into the Negev Desert and would find something to blow up. After a while doing this, it got to be rather boring, that is if blowing things up can actually be boring. When we got back from these runs, we'd head over to the so-called mess hall and sit down to a really lousy meal. The food was really bad, and it wasn't surprising that everyone seemed to enjoy throwing their food more than they did eating it. Now I really don't think there can ever be anything that is more fun than a good food fight, even though I really hate to see food wasted. Maybe I should clarify that. I hate to see good food wasted. It usually started off simply enough. One guy would throw something small at someone, and then that person would throw something back. It wouldn't be long before everyone was getting in on the act, and hooting and hollering as well. We thought it was great fun, but of course the people in charge didn't share our opinion. I guess their sense of humor wasn't exactly what ours was.

At some point, we were moved out into the desert into small two-man tents. I think the real reason they moved us out of the camp was to prevent any more food fights in the mess hall, and to keep us away from more civilized people – as they surely considered themselves. After doing exercises for days, blowing up everything in sight, and cleaning up all of our weapons, we were given a weekend off to go and have the Sabbath.

I hitchhiked back to the kibbutz and spent the weekend there. On my return to the camp, I missed my bus. So I started walking and managed to hitch a few rides on the road into the desert. After I'd walked some distance, I decided to take a short cut across the desert in the direction I thought I'd find our little camp. Well, I didn't find anything out there except a bunch of Bedouins, but I had my M16 with me and a couple of magazines of ammunition, so I was confident they wouldn't bother me. I started walking and I knew it had to be about 12 miles to my destination. About an hour after I'd started, I heard the rumbling of tanks. I looked around and saw three M60 main battle tanks. They almost had the appearance of dinosaurs roaring across the desert.

I waved my rifle in the air to attract their attention, and they turned toward me, with their giant muzzles pointing in my direction. I thought to myself, "Don't shoot. There won't be anything left!" One of the leviathans stopped next to me. The commander looked down at me and said, "What in hell are you doing out here alone?" I told him about missing the bus that was supposed to bring me back to our camp. He motioned for me to climb up and I lowered myself halfway down into the turret. It was a really great experience to be riding on a tank. Finally, I was getting a taste of what I had originally joined the Israeli Army for. I guess all good things come to them who wait. The commander told me to "Hold on!" and the mighty machine took off *RRRRRoaring* through the desert.

The Negev Desert, as I've mentioned before, is a very bleak place, and the area that we were in had lots of canyons and washes. The tanks went through these washes at incredible speeds – anywhere from 20 to 30 miles an hour. They just roared and bashed their way through them as though they were nothing. I was amazed at how sturdy they were, and that they never fell apart. We finally arrived back at the camp. Of course, by then I was several hours late. Everyone was doing inspection when I showed up in the M60 battle tank, and you can imagine how inflated my ego was. I thanked the commander and they headed back out into the desert to continue with their training exercise. It was an absolutely amazing experience to have had the opportunity to roar across the desert in one of those huge metal beasts. It really did make you feel like you had incredible power and were somehow invincible.

As soon as the tank left, it was back to the same old grind. That afternoon, we had some more dry run exercises, live fire and then on to dinner. After it got dark, we continued our training exercises. I guess it wouldn't be unreasonable to ask, "Why so many training exercises when you'd already completed your basic training?" Well, in the Israeli Army, at least in the paratroopers, we were on a war footing the whole time, so we needed to stay in trim. In reality, the ongoing training we were receiving now was nowhere near as difficult as what we had done in the 14 months when we were new recruits. Things were a little different now, and the pressure was nowhere near as intense. We could get into trouble for screwing up, but they wouldn't run us around ragged for punishment as they had done before when we were still *teronim* – new recruits. The days of being rousted out in the middle of the night for readiness inspections and punishment sessions were, thankfully, now over. They assumed that we were now trained soldiers and as such, we should know what the hell we were doing!

By now, we were not really physically fit any longer because we had been worn down. When it came to being fighting fit and mentally hard, though, we were right on the mark. We could all take any kind of punishment, and we could dish it out amongst ourselves as well. By this I mean that everyone was always ready to argue, no matter how tired or miserable we were. This love of confrontation was something that I never really got used to during my whole time in the Israeli Army. It galled me back then, and still does today.

I had been sent on the explosives course in the middle of winter, and as a result, we often had to sleep out in the rain. At times it was so cold the rain turned to hail, and that wasn't a fun experience, I can assure you. We were cold pretty much most of the time and as it rained so often, the normally powder-dry dirt turned into mud. We spent a lot of the time wallowing through it on our training exercises. The conditions in general were nothing to write home about, the food was lousy, and what there was of it was never enough. One night in particular the camp was quiet, and I was on guard duty. I remember hearing a rumbling off in the distance and looked out over the canyon above which our camp was situated. I couldn't see anything down in the canyon itself, and I then I realized that I couldn't really tell what direction the sound was coming from. I looked back towards the camp and all of a sudden, I saw a herd of howling camels running right through the middle of it. Tents were flying up in the air as the sleeping inhabitants woke up and realized what was happening. By now, I'd hightailed it up on to a rock and was out of harm's way. Meanwhile, the camels were continuing to wreak havoc in the camp as they ran around this way and that, spitting the whole time. People were yelling and cursing and I guess from my perch it did all look rather funny. At the same time, it scared the hell out of me. The noise had been so loud that at first I actually thought we were being attacked by the Jordanians in half-tracks! The long and short of it was we nearly got taken out by a herd of camels! This was the second time that those disgusting creatures had ambushed us and I was really starting to despise them. But what great luck to be out of the way and observe it all happening.

Finally the course was over, and for some reason or another they passed us all. I never did anything with explosives because I was color-blind, and I am sure I'd have killed the lot of us by mixing up colored wires. I'm sure it had more to do with the instructors wanting to get rid of us, rather than us actually doing well. I can't say that we were very good students to begin with and things were made even worse by the fact that we were away from our own command and were generally acting like a bunch of jerks.

When we were ready to leave, we put all of our gear on to the waiting bus. We no sooner got that done than they told us to take it all off so that they could inspect it. We put all the gear back on – and then of course they told us to take it all off again so that someone else could inspect it. They wanted to make sure that nothing was being stolen. We finally got back on the bus in the evening, and we traveled all through the night. The bus ran out of fuel in the early morning, when we were only a short distance from the Golan Heights. Someone hitchhiked, or more likely he walked, the 10 miles to the nearest Israeli army establishment. There were absolutely no vehicles on the road, so it must have been quite a journey for the guy who made it. A few hours later, a vehicle arrived carrying some diesel fuel. We fueled up the bus and bled off the system, and then we were on our way once again. We finally arrived back at the *motsav*, but by then it was already late afternoon. All my old friends were there, and it was great to see them again, especially Yoel and Amsolan. It wasn't long until we were back into the old familiar routine; up at 5:00 a.m., see in the dawn, walk the fence patrol, and then do live fire exercises, morning, afternoon and night.

The only thing that broke the momentum during that time was that the Israeli basketball team beat the Russians. There was a big celebration that night at the *Shabbat* meal. Everyone was in high spirits because of the Israeli triumph.

Shortly after that, in the middle of February, we packed up and left the camp to go and spend some time out in the desert. At that point, we moved back into an all too familiar routine of getting an order, which was followed by a counterorder, which was then followed by disorder. It was something that I had grown to expect all too often.

I remember cooking our last meal on the *motsav* before we left for our desert training. At that time, I was cooking the meals quite regularly, and I have to say that I did a good job of it, which would surprise anyone who has sampled my cooking in recent years. I guess because I wasn't just cooking for myself I took a little more pride in what I was doing. It was quite a big deal to cook meals for 30 men in our little kitchen. On average, I was responsible for all of the meals two days of the week. I didn't really mind it too much because one of the benefits was that you got to eat more food when you were doing the cooking. Another thing that happened was that the kitchen in our *motsav* had to be scrubbed regularly. When I cooked I didn't care about what pot or pan was kosher. I would just use it. By kosher standards my kitchen was probably the dirtiest kitchen in the army! One day the top rabbi came to inspect the kitchen, and when he was done he said that it was the cleanest kitchen in the brigade. He just gushed at how clean he found it. Little did he know how unkosher it really was. When he finished everyone was happy.

We set ourselves up in the desert on a steppe just outside Jericho. We were briefed on some guard duty that we would be responsible for back at the *motsavim*. I was then in the final stages of my time in the army and I was told to stay at the camp and help Moreal, the company sergeant major, get everything set up. Moreal was an immigrant like myself, only he was originally from Russia. Quite often, the two of us would take the command car out at night and drive around the base area, or rather our camp in the desert. The area was quite beautiful, as it was dotted with canyons and high plateaus, but it was also a very tough area for training. This was the area where the Dead Sea Scrolls were found inside a cave. It was a bit of a disappointment that I was never able to get out there and explore any of the caves. I know that whole caverns of dead Arabs had been discovered and also that the Bedouins had themselves used the caves to bury their dead in for centuries. It was a very interesting area, full of history. A great deal of it had been documented in Leon Uris' book *The Haj*. Now the real reason that we were out driving at night was to see what we could steal from other camps and bring back to our own. We were always missing something that we needed and we thought nothing of going and taking it from someone else. We didn't really think of it as stealing, but rather as just going and getting what we needed from another unit. We generally "borrowed" these items from some unit that was involved in basic training. We knew that anyway they really didn't have as much use for the stuff as we did.

When we were building up the camp, we had to drive in some stakes with a huge stake-driver that took two men to use. We would work from early morning right through to the night, and it wasn't long before the insides of my hands were all covered with blisters. Then night after night, as soon as the sun went down, we'd head back out into the desert on our covert borrowing operations. Along the way, the sergeant major and I would stop off at an Arab café that was down the road, and have a beer. Then we would sit outside and look at the moon and listen to the radio wailing some Arab song, or just chat amongst ourselves. The sergeant, Alberto, the South American fellow and myself would discuss what was going in the rest of the world and what we thought the future held for us. We also talked about what we wanted to do when we got out of the army. Alberto had already decided that he would remain on the Kibbutz En Gev, of which he was a member. As for myself, I knew that I would go back to the USA to be with my family, but as for what the hell I was going to do when I got there, I didn't have a clue. I was starting to feel exactly the same way I had when I got out of the marines. The long and short of it was that my time in the Israeli Army was coming to an end, and I was starting to get a little nervous.

During the day, we worked at various odd jobs around the camp and then got ready for the all-too-frequent afternoon sandstorms. These storms would be big, and had enough force to blow down the large tents that we'd set up. We would wait until everything settled down again, and then as night fell, we'd set the tents back up again. Now at that time of year it wasn't uncommon to have severe rain or hail storms. A fierce wind would accompany them – and would also cause the tents to come down. As a result, we seemed to spend as much of our time putting the tents back up as we did building the camp.

This was all happening around the time of *Purim*, which is the Israeli version of Halloween. Although the holiday doesn't have anything to do with ghouls and goblins, people still dress up in all kinds of costumes and have a good time. We had a good *Purim* celebration there in the main camp where we were staying, and afterwards I had to leave to go back to the kibbutz. When I got there, another *Purim* celebration was under way and this one was a little more enjoyable, because on the kibbutz there were women and lots of booze.

I boozed it up and remained drunk the entire time I was on the kibbutz. My regular beverages of choice were beer and vodka – usually the cheapest I could get. The beer I drank was the Israeli brand called *Nesher*, which means eagle. *Nesher*'s logo was an eagle flying off holding a glass of beer in his talons. It made me think of an eagle pissing in a glass and then flying away with it, because the stuff really did taste like piss. This wasn't really surprising as it only cost $2.00 a case, and that was for pint-size bottles! The vodka was almost as cheap, at $1.00 for a 750 ml (one and a third pints) bottle. The vodka was really rotten stuff, and it tasted just like kerosene. One of our favorite ways to choke the stuff down was to drink a little beer out of the bottle and then to fill it up with vodka. Believe me, the next morning your head felt like it was a boiler, and it was ready to explode. After the *Purim* festivities were over, I headed back to camp and ended spending a lot of my time there getting drunk as well, even during the day. The camp was nearly built by that point, and I was able to take some time to walk out to the surrounding canyons. I spent hours there enjoying the all-encompassing silence. I guess it was also a time of winding down. I was looking within and asking myself: "Now what?"

I was due to receive the 30 days' leave every soldier was given when they had completed their time in the army. They gave us that time to go and find some work, and to prepare for a return to civilian life in general. In my case, I had to find a job somewhere so that I could make enough money to get back home to the United States. My salary in the army was only $55.00 a month and when the holiday period rolled around there would be a little extra money for any soldier that didn't have any family in the country. It was never anything to write home about, though.

March 17, 1977, came around. It was my last working day in the Israeli parachute brigade. The *mempay*, Moti, gave me a bit of a talking to and said it was a job well done and wished me luck for the future. He said he would see me within a month, when I had to turn in the balance of my gear. I thanked him and left for the kibbutz. When I arrived, I was assigned to work in the orchards and it gave me some time to wind down and try and get my head together. I also tried to find a job, though on a very casual basis. I went into Tel Aviv to see a doctor about my left foot: not about my ankle, but about some type of fungus I'd picked up. I thought maybe it was athlete's foot, but all of my toes had swollen up, split open and were bleeding. This wasn't the first time this had happened, either. The doctor examined me and then gave me some antibiotics to take and told me to come back and see him again in another few days. After my appointment, I went over to Yoel and Michael's apartment. They had both separated from the army a few months before and had a place down by the ocean. It was a little basement apartment, but it was nice and suited two single guys pretty well. One night we all got drunk and went out to Dizengoff Street, which was an equivalent of our Sunset Boulevard. We stopped at a few sidewalk cafés to drink beer and goofed around and make general asses of ourselves. We had a dummy with us, which we were carrying around on our backs, pretending it was real to psyche out all of the tourists. We finally put each other on our backs and ran up and down the streets. I remember I had Michael on my back and I twisted my ankle. Both of us went ass over tit on to the pavement. It was a good laugh, but as usual, I was in terrible pain.

During this time I was also looking for work: for anything that would make me enough money to get back home. My job search efforts were thwarted though when my foot kept swelling up even more over the next few days. I went and saw the doctor again at the military hospital in Tehashomare. This time he put me in hospital so they could try and bring the swelling down. They also wanted to treat my ankle and try and figure out once and for all what the problem was. I still thought that maybe it was just a bad case of athlete's foot, like the one I had picked up in Vietnam.

Yoel came to visit me and brought me some chocolate and a can of beans, which of course was a joke because I used to like beans, and would eat them whenever I got the chance. I can also remember my birthday, April 12, 1977, when I turned 25. I was discharged that day from the hospital and went back to Yoel and Michael's apartment. I felt very depressed that I'd just had another birthday, and yet I still had no idea what I was going to do with my life. I had no feeling for my future whatsoever, other than just getting back to the USA and being with my family. The only other things that I was really looking forward to was being able to ride my Harley-Davidson and resuming my skydiving. I just couldn't help thinking about what I would do with the rest of my life. It really was a big worry, and my depression showed no signs of lifting. I felt like I was heading back into a life with no meaning and no positive direction. I hadn't been making much progress with my search for work, until I made a connection with someone who knew someone and was looking for men to work on an offshore exploratory drill, run by Global Marine and located out of Ashdod, one of Israel's main seaports.

I was actually very lucky and did indeed manage to get a job on the drilling rig. My month of leave was nearly up by that time but I couldn't go back to the camp in the desert to do my final separation from the army until it was all used up. As a result, I went directly out to sea, flying out to the rig in a small helicopter. It was the first small helicopter ride I'd taken since leaving the marines, and it really brought back some old memories. I was reminded of flying over Da Nang and the South Pacific Ocean. My job on the offshore rig was to wash dishes in the pantry, which I did in 12-hour shifts, seven days a week, two weeks at a time. I felt like I was washing dishes morning, noon and night, which in fact I was. I'd never seen so many dishes in my entire life but I wasn't complaining, because along with all those dishes to wash came a clean room that I had all to myself. I also had as much food to eat as I wanted, and it was good food for a change, the likes of which I hadn't seen since I arrived in Israel. We regularly had steak, chicken, mushrooms and everything else I could desire. I could have as much as I wanted, and I was just beside myself after all those months of food deprivation. Looking back, I don't think I stopped eating the whole time I was on that job. The food was definitely the highlight of my offshore experience.

We were given half an hour a day to do whatever we wanted and I used to go back to the fantail where it was cool and shaded. This was part of the rig that actually hung out over the stern. We were quite a few miles out to sea, and I can remember looking out over the ocean and thinking, "North is the direction of Greece, west is the direction of home. My route home will take me through Greece, to England and then on to home." Yoel had also got a job working on the same rig, only he was what they called a roustabout. As pantry steward, I was the lowest of the low, but nonetheless it definitely had its advantages, as I've explained. I usually spent my half hour of free time under the fantail smoking my cigarettes, relaxing and daydreaming about my return to the States.

The rig I was on was called the *Wingate* and it was an exploratory drilling ship. It was actually a Norwegian ore cargo ship that had been converted to a stationary drilling rig. It now had 28 7,000-kilogram (7-ton) anchors holding it down in place. It was really quite a big ship, with a 120-foot-high derrick that went straight up from the deck. During my time on the rig, we experienced a period of bad weather and really rough seas. The waves were about 10 feet high and were smacking the side of the ship. As a result, the ship was really rolling from side to side. Up on the drill floor, they continued to do drilling work, despite the less than ideal conditions. One evening during this period of rough weather, I was washing dishes when the tool pusher, who was second in command after the captain, came looking for me. He asked me if I wanted to change over to a roustabout, as everyone had moved up one position because someone had got hurt up on the drilling floor. It was a known fact that the drill floor was the most dangerous place to work on the whole rig. I jumped at the chance. It turned out that it really didn't mean that much of an increase in pay after all, because as subcontractors our pay was only a fraction of what someone hired directly by Global Marine would be making.

I only worked as a roustabout for one night, and when they came around asking for roughnecks, I quickly volunteered. Once again, this meant more money, but this time it really was a substantial increase in pay. It meant that I had moved up on to the drill floor permanently, and it really was quite an interesting place to work. There was a driller sitting in a box-type apparatus. He would be sitting across from you on the drilling floor, watching every move you made. The whole time he would be hollering at you through a loudspeaker, barking out instructions. There was certainly nothing nice about these guys and the way they shouted at you: "Thongs, slips, hammer. Get off the fucking drill floor!" Their language left nothing to question and they sure didn't care about your feelings. To them, time was money. You cost them time, you cost them money: that was the only concept they understood. I can't say that it was surprising, because at that time it cost about $20,000 a day to operate the rig. They needed to be up and running as much as possible just to get their money's worth out of it.

One driller in particular was a Norwegian fellow, who was always shouting out the same old thing: "Thongs, slips, hammer, chain." We'd hear this one line in an endless repetition that would go on for the entire 12 hours of every shift you worked, seven days a week. By the time you'd finished your shift, you'd have been listening to this silly shit screaming the same old thing for hours, and you'd be just about ready to pull your hair out, let alone kill this guy.

Another trying aspect of the job was the actual work we had to do. We had to feed 30-meter-long lengths of pipe, nine inches in diameter into the seabed below the rig. At one time, we even had as much 4,000 meters (over 13,000 feet) of pipe beneath the seabed. The easy part of the job was feeding the extra lengths of pipe on to the existing one. The hard part was to bring the pipe up in sections to undo it and wipe off all the mud that accumulated with each new section we drilled through. Whenever we had to break the joints of another section of pipe, we would use big thongs to grip it, and in the process we would get covered in hot mud from head to toe. The thongs themselves were 300-kilogram (660 lb) wrenches, controlled by cables. These were in turn controlled by the driller in the drilling booth, in other words the guy that was always screaming at us. More often than not, the wind would be howling and as we were working in wet mud and soaked clothes, we would be freezing our asses off. I can honestly say I've never had any other job where I worked so hard physically as I did on that rig. We would all be sore and tired after the first hour of the shift and by the time we'd finished the 12 hours, we'd be like a bunch of whipped dogs. It was wonderful, though, to be able to go and take a hot shower, sit down to a huge dinner and then head off to the bunk to read and relax for a while.

There was a Korean fellow on board named Chung who was quite an unusual guy. At the end of a backbreaking 12-hour shift, this guy would go and do push-ups and other exercises for an hour. To him, this was a way of relaxing. We thought he was out of his mind. Another guy named Nick was originally from England. The only way to describe him was as a flaming romantic. One of the derrick-men was an Australian fellow named Pat, a really rough character. It was the derrick-man's job to catch the elevator as it came up through the derrick. The elevator was the name for the clamps that grabbed the stand off pipe at the top. If he missed it then you had a 30-meter (98-foot) stand off pipe starting to wobble and bounce around inside the derrick. This meant that the three rats, or roughnecks, had to run around to get out of its way. We would all be falling over each other trying to avoid this pipe that was just whipping all around. If the pipe hit you, it could kill you flat out, so there was a good reason to be running away. I have to say that as dangerous as it sounds, it was also quite exciting to be on the derrick. The derrick-man would be about ninety feet up in the air, with his feet on a plank the width of a diving board. For safety, he was tied on with a rope around his waist. His job was to lean out over the platform, and with the safety rope stretched to the limit he would hang on to a stand-of pipe with a type of rope harness. He would then have to drop the pipe into the open jaws of the elevator as it came up towards him. At a certain point, he would reach over and grab the elevator handles and close them and then push himself back up on the platform. As he was ninety feet up in the air and his platform had no rail around it, he had to be a fearless type of person. If he missed the elevator as it was coming up, and they came up at a good speed, he would fall off the platform and dangle at the end of the rope until he could pull himself back up. In the meantime, the stand-of pipe would be whipping around inside the derrick in every conceivable direction. Pretty exciting! To add to the confusion, the driller would be yelling and cursing at one and all.

Every once in a while, we would get on to a tugger, which is a pneumatic or air-operated winch. We would position a belt harness around our waists which would enable us to lean back in it, then hook the other end of the harness to the cable, which would then pull us to the top of the derrick, about 120 feet above us. Once we got up there, our job was to lubricate all of the pulleys. It was a big joke amongst everyone to send the most recent newcomer up to do this job and let him get about 60 feet above the drill floor. At that point we would yank on the tugger speed control. This would snap the new man up about 10 feet into the air and then he'd drop like a yo-yo with a backlash on it. The unfortunate victim would have a grease gun in his hand, and he'd start waving it around frantically as he tried to grab on to the cable for dear life. He'd be up there just about ready to shit his pants because he thought he was about to die. Of course everyone down below thought it was great fun. When it happened to me I was on the verge of a catatonic breakdown, because the little coupling that is only thing preventing you from crashing to the floor below doesn't look strong at all. In reality, though, it's supposed to be able to hold up to four tons. It's terrifying, nonetheless, because you really have nothing to hold onto when you're suspended 60 feet up in the air swinging like a monkey on a chain.

Eventually they brought me down to get another grease gun because the one that I had been holding on to was now firmly implanted in the drill deck. When they took me back up again, with guarantees of no more shenanigans, I was able to settle down and enjoy the view, which really was magnificent. I saw a beautiful sunrise over the Mediterranean and thought to myself yet again, "North is the direction of Greece and west is the direction of home." This was something that I was writing in my diary on an almost daily basis. I was full of anticipation and excitement about the thought of starting a long journey back to the United States.

I remember another time on the drill when we were experiencing some very rough seas. Chung and I were told by Pat, the derrick-man, to go up on to the derrick above the derrick-man's platform. Now his platform was about 90 feet off the deck, and the ladder we were using to climb up there was on the outside of the derrick. There was no back to the ladder and we were in rough seas, so the derrick was whipping back and forth. It hadn't felt that bad down on the deck, but when we were up there, over 100 feet high, we had to hold on for dear life. The situation was made even worse by the fact that we had to carry all the necessary tools up with us. When we finally arrived at the top, we had to walk along a steel girder, which had no sides. I was terrified at the sight of it, but Chung just walked out on it like he was going out for a Sunday stroll. I got down on all fours and struggled to stay within the width of the girder, which was only about nine inches across with little tiny sides to it. I hung on for all I was worth but I still nearly managed to fall off. I couldn't believe that they had sent us up there without any kind of safety device, but I knew that if we didn't manage to get the job done they would put us off of the rig. The moral of the story is that if you want to stick around, you better do whatever they tell you to. I remember clinging to that girder saying a prayer, asking God to please spare me. I guess He must have heard me because we made it to our destination and tightened the bolts that had got loose, as well as some other minor repairs. Getting back to the ladder was just as harrowing, but obviously I made it or I wouldn't be telling the story to you now.

I managed to make it through my first two weeks' shift without any major mishap, and then I arranged to get back to shore so that I could go back to camp and officially separate from the army. We waited for the helicopter to come after our shift ended and it took us to Tel Aviv. I headed straight for the black market to change some money. I was making about $500 a month on the rig, which seemed like pretty good money at the time, but looking back on it I worked bloody hard for it. When I'd changed my money, I went to Yoel and Michael's apartment. I had a week off from the drill, and wanted to get back to camp as soon as possible. In reality I was actually AWOL by this time, because I should have signed out of the army on May 1. Yoel and I got caught up on what happened since we last saw each other, and had a few drinks. Then it was time to change back into uniform and get on my way to Jerusalem. I arrived in the city and stopped at a few bars on the way to have a beer. It was nice actually to have some money in my pocket for a change, and be able to act like the tourists. I was feeling a little uncomfortable, though, because I didn't have my M16. I'd had to turn it in before I went off on my month's leave. I walked across Jerusalem and then started hitchhiking towards the desert and the West Bank. By then, the evening had set in and it was pitch black. I got a ride that dropped me off about 20 kilometers (12 miles) outside Jerusalem, on the way to Jericho in the West Bank area. After that I was on my own, out there at night and unarmed. By now I had sobered up and realized that being in uniform put me at some risk. If I'd been in civilian clothing, I could have passed myself off as an American tourist, but not now. I ended up standing out in the desert.

It was about two hours before I saw some car headlights approaching. I said to myself, "Well, here goes!" and stuck my thumb out to hitch a ride. A Mercedes taxi pulled over and as it did I could see that it had West Bank license plates, which meant that it was owned by a Palestinian. It was too late to do anything by that point and when the door opened, I climbed in. I had a fisherman's clasp knife, and as I was getting in the vehicle I opened the blade on one side and a marlinspike on the other side and then managed to hide it inside my sleeve. It was still about another 40 kilometers (25 miles) to get to the Jericho area, where the battalion headquarters were located. One of the occupants sitting in the back of the taxi was a Jordanian, and as we were riding along he kept asking me: "What if we wanted to kill you or do you harm? What could you do about it?" I just kept playing it cool, and kept saying, "I don't know." There really wasn't much that I could do anyway. The ride passed very slowly, and this guy was chirping away the whole time about what he'd like to do to me. I guess it was actually kind of funny looking back on it. They ended up going out of their way to drop me off pretty close to the headquarters. I didn't have much money on me, and happily gave what I had to the driver. As I gave it to him, the guy in the back was still carrying on so I took the knife and stuck it up to his throat and said, "This is what I'd do if you tried anything. I'd slit your throat!" Then it was his turn to be a little shaky and turn white. I backed out of the car, closed the door and that was the last I ever saw of them. I walked the last remaining mile to the battalion headquarters very much a sober young man.

When I arrived, I immediately looked for an empty bed and went to sleep for the rest of the night. In the morning, I signed over the balance of my gear to the army, and got a final talking to from the *mempay*. He told me once again that I had done a great job and that he respected me very much, as I respected him. This made me feel really proud, especially coming from a man of his stature. He said that he hoped he would meet me again at some time in the future, but this was not to be.

When it was time to leave the camp I caught a military transport back to Israeli territory on the other side of the West Bank. From there I hitchhiked back to the kibbutz and with that, on May 4, my time in the Israeli Army was finished.

I made good time getting back to the kibbutz and spent the rest of the afternoon getting cleaned up and relaxing. For a change, I didn't get stuck into the booze, but instead turned in early and had a good night's sleep. When I woke up the next morning, I remember thinking: "On this day two years ago I joined the Israeli Army, and now here I am on May 5, 1977, my first day back in civilian life." A sense of sadness and emptiness settled over me as I lay there in my bed, thinking about the last two years. I thought about all the sweat and toil I'd endured, the arguments I'd been involved in, and how I had come to know the Israeli people. When I arrived in the country, I couldn't speak the language and I didn't know a soul, but now I was speaking Hebrew and I had made friends that I would have for a lifetime. I said a prayer of thanks for the strength that had been given to me to survive the ordeal of basic training, and also for keeping me safe throughout it all. Shortly after that I got out of bed, put my uniform on for the last time, and went to the cafeteria to get something to eat. Then it was on to Bokum, where it had all started two years ago.

I arrived in Bokum in the latter part of the morning and saw the appropriate people to get my final clearing-out papers. I had to determine my reserve status and tell them what I planned on doing. I still had a lot of running around to do before I could legally leave the country. Now that I was an Israeli citizen, I had to get a passport. It seemed that everyone I went to see needed me to have a form from someone else, and the end result was that I ended up running back and forth across Bokum several times. It shouldn't have surprised me, considering how the army used to have us running around when there was really no reason for it. I wonder why I thought that separating from the army would be any different? The term G2 Intelligence always makes me laugh, as it seems to be a total contradiction. In any army, be it the Marine Corps or the Israeli Army, military intelligence as the name implies, never really seems to exist. I finally finished all my running around and went back to Tel Aviv, to Michael and Yoel's apartment, and settled in for the rest of the afternoon. Thus ended my two years' service in the Israeli Army.

On May 6, 1977, I was flown back to the rig, which was in total full-out mode of weighing anchors. It was in the process of being moved down to the El Arish area to start up another exploration area. All the pipe stands had been run up and all of the 28 anchors had been brought up from the ocean floor. It was an incredible operation to witness, with everybody doing their job and the whole thing going just like clockwork. When the operation was complete the huge ship/drilling rig made its way to El Arish, where they began to lay down all of the anchors. This was just as interesting as watching them being taken up. They would drop one down and then pull the ship up tight against it, using a smaller ship acting as a tugboat. The smaller ship also served as our tender and supply ship. The anchors were stored on the supply ship.

I was to start my first shift at 12:00 midnight, and it went on to 12:00 noon. I would work that shift for an entire week and then the following week would work the alternate shift. For me, those two weeks passed by in a state of semi-depression. Not only was I unsure what I was going to do now that I was out of the army, but I also knew that my time on the rig was coming to an end and I would have to make a move. I guess my frame of mind reflected in my work performance because I was constantly getting hollered at for screwing up one thing or another. Our rig foreman second in command was a really fierce Texan, who went by the name of Big Jess. He must have been one of the biggest human beings I have ever seen. If the size of his belly was any indicator, I'm sure he must have weighed well over three hundred and fifty pounds. He'd been a driller all over the world, and if he told you to do something, you did it quick. His word was law, and if you didn't do as he said, he wasn't opposed to giving you a smack to help you pay attention. To even consider smacking him back was unthinkable – there probably would have been nothing left of you. His pet name for me was "Catfish," which I certainly didn't appreciate very much. I remember him saying to me all too often in his Texan drawl, "Hey, Catfish! You better get your ass in gear, man!" I have to hand it to him, though: he told some incredible stories and I'd listen to him in the galley after our shift every chance I got. He would talk about drilling in different parts of the world and of course I thought it was all extremely exciting.

It wasn't long after I got back to the rig that Yoel also came back on to work, but he came bearing some awful news. A CH-53 helicopter, with a training company of paratroopers on board, had crashed while on a training exercise. Everyone on board had been killed, and the *mempay* who had been on the flight in charge of the company was our former *somech mempay.* He had been the adjutant commander of the training company that I was in as a recruit. I was very sad to hear the news about all of those lives lost, but especially about Cohavy. In him, the army had certainly lost a good soldier a good leader, and a good man.

The remainder of that month passed by in a blur of hard physical labor, but was in itself uneventful enough. I spent most of each working shift wallowing around in mud and being hollered at by the driller, or Big Jess, or the tool pusher. It seemed like every time I had to climb the derrick it was in rough seas, and it never got any less terrifying. I was also frequently sent down into what they called the "mud room." In that room the floor was covered with mud and as the ship lurched from side to side, we had to pick up any big chunks of mud and heave them over a wall so that they could be broken down. The mud was then circulated down through the pipe to keep the debris away from the hole that was being drilled. If the seas were rough, the mud would slide from one side to the other and carry us with it. It was not uncommon to be swept across the room by the waist-high sludge and be thrown against the bulkhead. The room itself was about 10 meters long by six meters wide (33 feet by 19 feet six inches). It was not a pleasant experience, I can guarantee you. Imagine how tired we were after being stuck down there for six to eight hours. Then we'd have to go back up on to the drilling floor and finish the remaining hours of our shift up there, with the wind blowing, freezing our asses off.

I remember one particular occasion when I was told to go up on the derrick. I had only managed to get up as far as the derrick man's platform when the driller started telling me to hurry up and get a move on putting a stand-of pipe in the elevators. We weren't doing a regular drilling job at the time, and for some reason they wanted us to put a stand-of pipe in. Anyway, I got the rope harness that the derrick man, Pat, usually used and tied it around my waist, as he was nowhere to be seen. I grabbed the stand-of pipe out of the rack, watched the elevators and leaned over the edge, holding on to the pipe for dear life; the whole time just shitting myself. I was on the verge of a nervous collapse, I was so scared. I could hear the droning noise of the elevators as they came up towards me. As they approached my position, I leaned out to push the stand-of pipe into the elevators, and as they came by, I grabbed the handles, closed it and pushed myself back on to the derrick man's platform. The stand-of pipe was picked up and everything was going just great – until I stepped over the edge of the platform and fell screaming about 10 feet. Next thing I knew, I was dangling at the end of the safety rope but while I'd been falling I thought: "This is it. I'm dead!" I'd forgotten that I was tied off. From where

I was hanging like a limp rag doll, I could hear the driller screaming up at me, "You stupid son of a bitch! Get back on that fucking platform!" So much for getting any sympathy from him! The other roughnecks were all smiling. I managed to haul myself up, using the rope, and by the time I clambered back on to the platform, I was like a gibbering idiot. As I got to my feet, the driller was already hollering: "Come on! Slips, thongs." This meant that the stand-of pipe was going into the ground and the elevators were coming back up for another stand-of pipe. I could hear the elevators coming back up at me and I got into position even though I was still incredibly jittery. The long and short of it was that at the exact moment I grabbed at the elevators, the ship must have rolled, or somehow my timing was off – and I ended up going over the edge once again. The elevators went racing up past the top of the stand-of pipe and while I was dangling there in the air, the pipe was whipping around inside the derrick. I remember looking down and seeing all the roughnecks running around in different directions, trying madly to get away from the stand-of pipe. Once again, I heard the driller screaming up in my direction, "You stupid son of a bitch! Get back up there and get on with it!" I managed to pull myself back up the platform again, warily got to my feet and thanked my lucky stars that I was still in relatively good shape. Pat, the derrick man, finally reappeared. I don't know where he'd got to: maybe to take a crap or go play with himself – it didn't make any difference to me I was just glad that he was back. He managed to get a rope on the loose pipe, settle it down and then get it on the tugger. We both pulled it back over and into the elevator, it was coupled into the waiting stand-of pipe that was at deck level, and they were then drilled into the ground. By this time, I was so nervous that even as I helped him, I nearly fell off the platform again. My self-confidence was shattered and all I could think about was getting back down the ladder on to the drill floor. Pat just snickered and said, "worm."

At the end of May, after a full month of backbreaking, nerve-shattering work with no time off, I told them that I was leaving the rig to make my way back home to the States. So I quit my job and returned to Tel Aviv. I spent the next few days running helter-skelter to get my passport done so that I could leave the country. I ended up going to Haifa, then Nazareth, then back to Tel Aviv, all to try and speed up the darn passport process. They asked me why I needed it so quickly, because usually it took them a few weeks to process everything. With a little bit of *chutzpah* I convinced them to help me out and finally got the thing way ahead of the normal waiting period. The truth of the matter was that I wanted to be home before the end of three years, it was just some fixation I'd developed. While I was in Tel Aviv, Michael and I would go out and get drunk every single night. Now that I had money in my pocket, I could afford to drink like a fish, and not *Nesher* beer either. On June 1, 1977, I went back to the kibbutz one final time, to clean out my room and to say goodbye to all of the friends that I'd made over the years. There were two persons in particular I wanted to see one last time, Goldie from the *ulpan* – my mother in Israel, as she referred to herself – and Eddie Goldberg. The two of us had been in the army at the same time, though he was in tanks and I'd been in paratroopers. Eddie was an American like myself and was originally from San Francisco. We had come to know each other pretty well during our time in Israel and I knew I would miss him. After I had said all my farewells I went back to Tel Aviv and on the morning of June 4, 1977, I remember waking up early and thinking to myself: "This is the day I am leaving Israel." It was a very sad thought indeed.

Although I knew that it was time for me to be going back home, it still didn't erase the sorrow I felt about leaving a country that I had come to think of as my second home. I felt an emptiness at the thought of leaving behind people like Yoel, who I cared about and had gone through so much with.

When I had all my gear packed, I called a taxi and took it to Tel Aviv airport. I went through customs without any incident and climbed on board the plane that was going to take me to Greece. As it took off and gained altitude, I could see the coastline so far below and I was filled with a feeling of absolute emptiness. When I had arrived in Israel, I had only $20.00 in my pocket, couldn't speak the language and didn't know a soul. Now almost three years later, I was leaving that same country with $900.00 in my pocket and the knowledge that I had made some solid friendships that would last a lifetime. I knew that my time in Israel had changed me. I had learned a great deal and had grown as a person. I was a very different Dave Barr now than when I had arrived, and I think the change was definitely for the better. Coming from a typical middle-class background, I knew that I had experienced things in the last few years that my contemporaries at home wouldn't understand, let alone appreciate. For all the problems I had with the *Mayniks* I have to say in final analysis that by the time they had finished with us, these boys would measure up to any challenge thrown at them. For all their hard ways, they would do in a real fight. In the end we had grown to respect each other.

The plane touched down in Greece later that morning and after I cleared customs, I made my way to a cheap fleabag hotel, where I managed to get a bed up on the rooftop of the building. I settled in for the afternoon, read, dozed and in the evening lay down to sleep. I remembered that the last time I had slept on a roof was at the end of my 14 months' basic training. I had the same empty feeling in my heart that I had experienced that night as well. As I drifted off, I thought entered my mind that I no longer had to try and act as a Jew, I could go back to being a gentile and a not-so-good Christian once again.

The next day, I purchased a ticket for a three-day ride on a magic bus, which would carry me across Europe, taking me through Yugoslavia, Italy, France and then finally into England. It was called the magic bus because it made the trip faster than any other bus line. When I arrived in London I remember riding around on all the subways and then making my way up to the Leeds/Bradford area to look up some old Australian friends I'd known on the kibbutz. We had all been good drinking buddies, and I knew that I could count on them to have a good time. I remember finding their small apartment building and I knew that they were on the second floor. Unfortunately the front door was locked, so I started throwing pebbles up at their window but nobody responded. It was raining like a cow peeing on a flat rock at the time and I knew I had to take shelter somewhere. I finally gave up trying to get their attention and took refuge in an open garage that was piled high with all kinds of junk. The guy that the garage belonged to came home and tried to park his car. When he saw me the first thing out of his mouth was, "Who the fuck are you?" I tried to explain that I was an American and that I was here to see the guys across the street. I knew they were home, because I could see the flickering light from a television. Anyway, the guy was decent and told me I could sleep in the garage for the night. So that's how I spent my first night in England – soaking wet and shivering on the cold stone floor of a stranger's garage.

I finally did get hold of my friends and stayed at their place for the next few days. Most of the time was spent boozing it up in the local pubs. It was just a rollicking, good old time, and it passed by pretty much in a drunken state. Ace and Plug, as they were known, could match me beer for beer all the way. I met another guy named Tony in one of the pubs and we immediately forged a friendship. We actually ended up spending quite a bit of time together during the week and a half I was in England. It was Tony who offered to drive me to Manchester Airport to catch my flight home to the States. It was a pleasant flight and I was definitely in high spirits. I was finally returning home! I landed in New York on June 21, 1977, feeling on top of the world and like nothing could go wrong. It felt great to be back, hearing American accents again as well as being surrounded by people and things that I was familiar with. I cleared customs, picked up my suitcase, which had shoulder straps on it that I had made from a bed sheet. I headed out of the airport. My first job was to hitchhike out of New York City, which was quite a feat in itself. Evidently it wasn't a very good idea, because nobody stopped to give me a lift. I had no choice but to use the subway and somehow managed to get off at the wrong stop. I found myself in the middle of a slum area. I didn't know where I was, so I was somewhat relieved when a washed-out looking, longhaired hippie guy came up to me and asked me where I was going. I told him I was going to try and hitchhike out to California, and he looked at me like I was some kind of idiot. He told me I wouldn't even manage to get out of the area before I'd be mugged, and suggested that I come and crash at his place for the night. I agreed and went back to a dirty little apartment that he shared with his girlfriend. It wasn't exactly Paradise Lost, but it served the purpose well enough. We ate a meager meal and then everyone turned in for the night. I woke up early the next morning and was careful to get my stuff together and leave them a note of thanks without waking them up. I slipped out undetected and made my way down to the subway station where I'd got off the day before. Someone gave me information about how I could get to the bus station. I figured that regrettably, that was the only way I was going to get out of town. I took the subway once again and made my way to the bus station. All I could see in every direction was graffiti-covered buildings. In fact, there was so much of the stuff it looked like camouflage. I bought a ticket that would take me as far as Hazelton, Pennsylvania, which was just outside the New York state line. Within an hour I was on board the bus and California-bound once again. Although it wasn't quite like I'd envisioned, it still felt good to be on the move again. I remembered that old saying: "Don't go ape, go Greyhound. It stops at every tree!" For the time being, it seemed like my dream of hitchhiking all the way across America was not to be.

The bus driver was an old Second World War veteran, and we got talking. I told him that I was coming home from Israel and what I had done over there. He had sympathy with me and dropped me off at a freeway off-ramp just outside Hazelton, instead of taking me right to the bus station in town. At least that way I didn't have to hitch a ride out of a city again! The driver had told me that Hazelton was the hometown of Jim Thorpe, an Indian who was one of

America's greatest athletes of the twenties, and incidentally one of my heroes when I was a kid. He had also been one of the greatest all-round sportsmen that the country had ever produced.

After the driver let me off the bus, I made my way to a nearby truck stop called The Buckhorn. I made up a little sign that said: "LA or bust. I'll buy you dinner for 500 miles." What I meant was, that if a driver gave me a lift, I'd buy him a big meal. I figured my new angle just might work. At least they wouldn't think that I was a typical hitchhiker looking for a free ride. I can't say that my sign helped any, because eight hours later I was still standing there with my crummy little "LA or bust" sign held in front of me. It was just about dark when some guy in a big white freightliner pulled up alongside me and asked me where I was headed. I said, "It's LA or bust, just like the sign says." The driver said, "Listen. I'm really tired. Just get in the truck and keep talking. That's all I want you to do. Just talk and keep me awake. OK?" I can't say this request inspired any real confidence on my part in his driving abilities, but I figured it was better than standing there with swollen feet outside the "Bullhorn," as I was now calling the truck stop.

We got on our way and I did exactly as I had been asked. I talked and I talked and I talked some more. I told practically every joke I'd ever heard, though I can't say he laughed very much. That was the first time that I actually got to listen to how truck drivers talked on their CBs. My ride's call sign was "Rocket Man" and his eyes did in fact look like rockets, he was so wired. Apparently he'd been taking truck driver's whites, which were Benzedrine pills, for quite some time in order to stay awake. I really didn't like the way the guy looked. I kept talking constantly about this, that and everything else, until he decided to pull off some time the next day and have a bit of a rest. He took some more whites, and then lay down to wait for them to take effect. It took about three hours. Then he got up, and he was atomic once again. I was starting to get a bit haggard, not just because I wasn't used to keeping such hours, but because of sitting inactive for so long and having to keep up the constant stream of conversation. It was still great, though, to see the American countryside flying by outside and to know that every mile was bringing me closer to my folks. As we were getting near Chicago, where he was going to let me off, he asked me if I would be willing to continue on up to Madison, Wisconsin. He said: "A lot of the time you get shitbirds working on the loading docks, and they're either real low people or out and out thieves." I told him that he'd helped me out and I'd do the same for him, so we continued on down the road together for another few hundred miles. When we got to Madison, I helped unload his cargo. He was hauling big 300lb bags of spices, and it took both of us to lift a bag. The truck was crammed full of the bags, and all I could think of was – you'd certainly be able to fill a heck of a lot of spice bottles with all this stuff.

It took us about three and a half hours to unload it all, and once we were done I went with him to pick up a load down at one of the Great Lakes seaports. As it turned out, it was a port off Lake Superior and once we loaded up we were on our way once again. I went with him as far as the Mississippi River, to a location that he told me would be good for hitching another ride. I said goodbye to Rocket Man and wished him well – and silently added: "I hope you never overdose on those truck driver's whites. He roared off down the road, leaving me standing there wondering what would happen next.

It wasn't long before a US Army captain in a car pulled over and offered me a ride. We started chatting about the military, and eventually pulled into one of those wayside greasy spoon cafes. We had a couple of beers and he bought me a sandwich. We continued chatting about the military and my time in Israel. It felt really good to be talking to an American once again. He told me he'd drop me off at a spot near a main highway, which he did. As he pulled away, I realized that I was totally fagged out and decided to camp there for the night, rather than try and hitch another ride right away. I walked off into some bushes, laid my sleeping bag out and lay there listening to my transistor radio. I looked up at the stars and drifted off to sleep (very peacefully, I might add). I must have slept for nearly 10 hours, because when I woke up the sun was already shining brightly. It was a new day, the weather was good and as I packed up my gear, I felt pretty positive about everything.

I caught a ride not long after from a guy who said he'd take me to a truck stop a couple of miles down the road. He figured it would be easier to get a long-distance ride from there. I walked around for a while, looking for trucks that had California license plates, or something written on the doors saying the trucking company's headquarters were located in California. I finally saw one that looked promising. It had Stroud Trucking of El Monte, California, written on the cab doors. I went up and pounded on the driver-side door, but no one opened up. I figured he was just in a deep sleep and I probably better not wake him up if I hoped to get a ride with him. I wandered around some more, looking for other California-bound trucks and then I saw smoke coming out of the smoke stack on the rig from El Monte. I ran over and pounded on his door and shouted: "Hey! If you're heading to California, I'll buy you dinner every night. I'm from West Covina, which is only a few miles from El Monte. I'll even wash your truck for you! I'll do anything you want, just give me a ride. I'll keep you awake!" Evidently I was too much for him at that time of the morning because he told me: "Stop, please stop! Just get in and we'll see what happens. I'm having some trouble with the differential. Maybe you'll be able to help me after all." This was great. I was talking a 1900-mile ride here. It was a hitchhiker's dream ride! I threw my bag into the storage compartment, and off we went. From then on, it was talk, talk, talk all over again. We rolled across state after state, finally stopping in Wyoming to get a shower. It was my first shower in days, and as you can imagine, I was getting pretty high-smelling. "Two Guns" – I remember the driver's call sign was Two Guns – had a very dry sense of humor. Every time I told him a joke, he'd look over at me and say "Judas Priest!" He was quite a character. We stopped again outside Rawlings, Wyoming, where Two Guns said he needed to catch a couple of hours of sleep. I thought I'd knock around the town for a couple of hours, even though I was pretty beat myself. The town itself was a very typical of small western towns, and it actually had quite a history from back in the old Wild West days. I stopped off at a bar, got myself a beer, and listened to the banter of the locals. It was so good to be back in the States where I could finally get Coors, my favorite beer, once again. After I'd finished my bottle, I walked around the town, just having a look round. All I remember thinking was that these people lived very mundane lives, and I could never live in a place like that. I know it wasn't very charitable, but I couldn't help but think that all the people living there must have been brain-dead. This judging from what I heard in the bar.

I made my way back to the truck and lay down for a few hours to get some sleep. About 3:00 a.m., Two Guns woke up when his whites had taken effect, and we were ready to roll once again. From Wyoming, we moved on into Utah and made one fuel stop, then headed into Nevada. It wasn't long before we rolled through Las Vegas and then soon after across the California border. I could feel the excitement rising inside me. I was finally back in my home state! As soon as we crossed the state line, I started noticing California Highway Patrol cars everywhere. I saw more cops in California then I had seen going across the entire United States, Europe and my whole three years in the Middle East!

We continued rolling down the highway, ever closer to home, and the excitement was building even more. By noon, we had reached Victorville, and

Two Guns decided to stop for lunch. From there we went on down over the Cajon Pass and then on to Highway 10, the good old San Bernardino freeway which went right by West Covina. Two Guns pulled off on the Puente off ramp, which was the closest to my folks' house, and we went into Denny's and had a cup of tea. I told him I was willing to go on with him and would wash out his truck as I'd promised originally. He just said, "Don't worry about it. Go home and be with your family." I told him one last parting joke and he didn't let me down. He said, "Judas Priest!" one last time and then he was on his way. He was a great guy, and I really felt like we'd become friends during the time we spent on the road together. I put my bag on my shoulder and started the 15-minute walk home.

I walked along the streets that I'd explored as a kid, first on foot and then on my bicycle. It had been three years since I'd seen the familiar scenes and I realized just how much I'd missed everything. I can honestly say that nothing had changed since I'd left. It looked the same, smelled the same, even the smog was the same. That walk home was very emotional for me, and it felt very symbolic. I'd returned very much a different person than when I had left. When I turned the corner on to Siesta Avenue, our street, it was like I'd never been away. There was Pete Via outside his house, pruning the hedge that served as a fence between my folks' place and his. I continued down the block, past the three remaining houses, to number 1317, went to the door and knocked. My mother answered the door and she couldn't believe her eyes. There I was! Tears of joy immediately began rolling down both of our faces. My dad was coming home from work, and pulled into the driveway at that moment – and then he was there, joining in all the hugging. It was a wonderful reunion and a very special moment.

We had the rest of the afternoon together, talking about everything that had happened since we had last seen each other. That night, lying in my own bed, I though about all that I'd experienced in the last three years. I thought about all of the different places I'd seen, the military training I'd been through and all the people I'd met. I realized then the enormity of what I had done. To go to the other side of the world, not knowing the language or anyone there, and then to get into a foreign army and do well, really was an achievement to be proud of. The only thing that I regretted when I looked back on my time overseas was that I had never actually fought in any major battles. I had not taken the supreme test. When I'd signed up to go into the marines, it was specifically to go to Vietnam and fight in the war. I guess I was expecting to do the same in Israel. In my mind, a soldier without a war is like a doctor without a patient. Not the best analogy for sure, but it makes the point, I think. I know that there are many military people who would disagree with me on that point. All in all, though, that last three years had been a very enriching experience, and I wouldn't have traded it for the world.

I woke up the next morning and made the final entry in my diary. It was really a big thing for me to write in it one last time and I guess it brought home that my time in Israel – of this great adventure – was over. I signed off the entry the same way I had signed off every diary I'd kept while I was away, "David Scott Barr; soldier, adventurer and idealist." I guess I had some pretty wild thoughts about myself at the time, but it's what I really felt. I can look back on it now and laugh, but at the time, I truly meant it every word.

I was to spend roughly the next year and a half back in the States, but I have to say that it was not a very happy time. The first constructive thing I did when I got back was to pull my Harley-Davidson out. It was stored, having been broken down and bundled up before I left three years before. The frame, the engine, and the transmission were still together. The front end, the wheels and everything else were all over the garage. I unwrapped all of the parts and started sorting it out. My dad took it down to where he was working and we steam-cleaned it. Over the next few days, we got it back together and then took it over to the local Harley shop to do the wiring. They gave me a call not long after and told me that it was ready to pick up. I went down to Pomona, where the shop was located, and started my Harley up for the first time in three years. I can't really describe how good that first ride felt. It was fantastic to get the old knees out in the breeze again. I remember cruising down the highway, feeling like the king of the road while my machine pounded away underneath me. I was on top of the world. I got home, cleaned up the motorcycle a bit and continued working on it in the garage. I stood back and looked at it and then thought to myself, "Well, I've come full circle. What am I going to do now?"

A friend of mine, Manny Gonzales, got hold of me after he heard that I got back. He suggested that I work as a private investigator and put me on to a firm that hired people for that kind of work. So I tried my luck at it, but I can't say that I was crazy about it. I did one undercover job and it went quite well, but my paperwork left something to be desired. Reports had to be written up every day, and at the best of times my handwriting had never been good. Everyone got very concerned because although I'd done a good job, they couldn't read a word of what I'd written in the report. After that, they suggested that I might be better suited to security work. I did that for about a month and then said, "No more!"

My next job was at a Harley-Davidson shop. I worked for a fellow named Dan Parush for about eight months. I didn't make much money as a salesman, only $125.00 a week, but I liked the atmosphere at the shop. I rode my motorcycle to work, sold motorcycles. It was the perfect job for me.

It wasn't long before my mind was casting about for the next cause; being here and living this way was not for me. Soon it would be time to move on again, and as we know, when one journey ends another one begins. Stand by!

The End.

